The Leader of the Future 2

Other Publications from the Leader to Leader Institute

The Leader of the Future 2

Visions, Strategies, and Practices for the New Era

Frances Hesselbein

Marshall Goldsmith

Editors

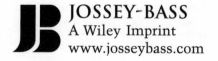

JOSSEY-BASS
A Wiley Imprint
www.josseybass.com

Published by Jossey-Bass
A Wiley Imprint
989 Market Street, San Francisco, CA 94103-1741   www.josseybass.com

Jossey-Bass books and products are available through most bookstores. To contact Jossey-Bass directly call our Customer Care Department within the U.S. at 800-956-7739, outside the U.S. at 317-572-3986, or fax 317-572-4002.

Jossey-Bass also publishes its books in a variety of electronic formats. Some content that appears in print may not be available in electronic books.

Library of Congress Cataloging-in-Publication Data
The leader of the future 2: visions, strategies, and practices for the new era/Frances Hesselbein, Marshall Goldsmith, editors.
    p. cm.
  Includes bibliographical references and index.
  ISBN-13: 978-0-7879-8667-4 (cloth)
  ISBN-10: 0-7879-8667-4 (cloth)
  1. Leadership. 2. Strategic planning. I. Hesselbein, Frances. II. Goldsmith, Marshall.
III. Leader to Leader Institute. IV. Title: Leader of the future 2.
  HD57.7.L418 2006
  658.4'092—dc22

                                       2006023715

Printed in the United States of America
FIRST EDITION
HB Printing   10 9 8 7 6 5 4 3 2 1

leader to leader
INSTITUTE

Established in 1990 as the Peter F. Drucker Foundation for Nonprofit Management, the Leader to Leader Institute furthers its mission—to strengthen the leadership of the social sector—by providing social sector leaders with the wisdom, inspiration, and resources essential for leading for innovation and for building vibrant social sector organizations. It is the social sector, in collaboration with its partners in the private and public sectors, that is key in changing lives and building a society of healthy children, strong families, decent housing, good schools, and work that dignifies a diverse, inclusive, cohesive community that cares about all of its members.

The Leader to Leader Institute provides innovative and relevant training materials and resources that enable leaders of the future to address emerging opportunities and challenges. With the goal of leading social sector organizations toward excellence in performance, the Institute has brought together more than four hundred thought leaders to publish over twenty books available in twenty-eight languages and the award-winning quarterly journal, *Leader to Leader*.

The Leader to Leader Institute engages social sector leaders in partnerships across the sectors that provide new and significant opportunities for learning and growth. It coordinates unique, high-level summits for leaders from all three sectors and collaborates with local sponsors on workshops and conferences for social sector leaders on strategic planning, leadership, and cross-sector partnerships.

Building on a legacy of innovation, the Leader to Leader Institute explores new approaches to strengthen the leadership of the social sector. With sources of talent and inspiration that range from the local community development corporation to the U.S. Army to the corporate boardroom, the Institute helps social sector organizations identify new leaders and new ways of operating that embrace change and abandon the practices of yesterday that no longer achieve results today.

Leader to Leader Institute
(formerly the Drucker Foundation)

320 Park Ave 3rd Fl   E-mail: info@leadertoleader.org
New York, NY 10022 USA   Web: leadertoleader.org
Tel: +1 212-224-1174   Fax: +1 212-224-2508

Contents

Part Three: Leading in a Time of Crisis and Complexity

Part Four: Leading Organizations of the Future

Preface

Ten years ago we had a very simple yet powerful idea—call many of the greatest thinkers in the world, ask them each to write a chapter sharing their vision for the future of leadership, and put together an edited book titled *The Leader of the Future*, with the proceeds supporting the Peter F. Drucker Foundation for Nonprofit Management, to help develop leadership in the social sector.

What happened next were three of the most pleasant surprises we have ever experienced!

To begin with, we were moved by the generosity of the thought leaders we asked to contribute. Even though the authors we contacted were very busy people, over 90 percent enthusiastically replied, "Sign me up!" Even the ones who were not able to make a contribution were incredibly encouraging. Because no one was paid for their efforts, our authors clearly were people who wanted to make a significant contribution to their field and to the social sector. With Peter Drucker leading this group of distinguished authors, every chapter was a generous gift to our small foundation—one that is small in staff and budget, but has enormous vision, a clear mission, and plenty of determination.

Second, we were amazed at the support we received from our publisher, Jossey-Bass. *The Leader of the Future* was a labor of love for them as well as for us. Everyone at Jossey-Bass went above and beyond the call of duty to make our effort a success.

Third, we were—and still are—shocked at the positive reaction we received from our readers. Edited books normally don't make the best-seller list. *The Leader of the Future* not only made the *Business Week* top fifteen best-seller list, it has become probably the greatest-selling edited book in the history of our field. Hundreds of thousands of copies of *The Leader of the Future* are moving around the world, in twenty-eight languages! The Drucker Foundation—now the Leader to Leader Institute—has since published twenty books. Although we are proud of all of our titles, *The Leader of the Future* is still our most successful in reaching our global colleagues for an adventure in learning.

Ten years later, post–September 11, we live in a different world with a new context. The leaders of the next decade face new and distinctive challenges. As Abraham Lincoln put it so eloquently in a different time of testing, "The dogmas of the quiet past are inadequate to the stormy present. The occasion is piled high with difficulty, and we must rise to the occasion. As our case is new, so we must think and act anew." Our times too call for new thought and action, yet the basic principles, basic values, and basic fundamentals of leadership have not changed. *Leadership is still a matter of how to be, not how to do.*

A lot has happened in the past ten years. Because the world has changed, we have decided that it was time for us to look back upon the past—with eyes to the future. Ten years later we are again moved by the generosity of the thought leaders we asked to make a contribution. The authors in *The Leader of the Future 2* are an amazing collection of thinkers who have extensive experience in all sectors—the private sector, the social sector, government, education, and the military. How do these great thought leaders and great writers, in the turbulence of a world at war, find the language, the message that can inspire, guide, and sustain leaders in an uncertain future? You will find out in the passages of this book! In its pages we hear Peter's voice saying, "I never predict. I simply look out the window and see what is visible but not yet seen."

The ideas that you will encounter in this book flow exactly from this kind of prescience, discernment, wisdom, and observation. Indeed, we could say that our authors are the thought leaders of the future. For they have not been content to plow the old furrows; instead they stake out new fields of opportunity, challenge, and transformation—new messages for a new day. This book delivers a "battle cry" that will mobilize the leaders of the future to build viable, relevant organizations that will sustain us in the times ahead.

Many of us can remember the days when organizations, with seeming certainty, developed highly structured ten- and twenty-year plans. Planning in the past was rigid, inflexible, and hierarchical, but planning for the future will require leaders to be fluid and flexible, and to move easily across their organizations. *The Leader of the Future 2* is indeed part of a new blueprint for planning in a dynamic new world. We hope that it will be an indispensable partner in your leadership journey!

Although our Institute has experienced many moments of joy in the past ten years, we have also experienced moments of sorrow and grief. One of the three coeditors of our first book, Richard Beckhard, is no longer with us. Dick Beckhard was our friend and supporter, and a legend in the field of leadership and organizational development. He will be missed but not forgotten.

It is with the deepest gratitude that we dedicate this book to the inspiration of our Founding Honorary Chairman, Peter F. Drucker. Peter's life continues to illuminate our lives and our times. This is the Institute's twenty-first book, but our first since the loss of Peter Drucker. We hope that, in some small way, it builds upon his legacy. We believe that Peter's writings—and his inspiration to those who are still writing—will continue to have a positive impact on the leaders of the future. We can do no less.

As a reader, you should feel free to follow your instincts on where to begin your journey through this work. You may wish to begin with a favorite author, or you may wish to start with an intriguing or provocative title. There is no need to follow our chapter sequence, although we did attempt to organize them by the types of leadership issues they address. Begin with what is most important to you—and be open to learning from people that you may not have heard of or considered as teachers. For example, Peter Drucker noted on several occasions that leaders in the for-profit sector had a lot to learn from leaders in the social sector!

The Leader of the Future 2 is divided into five parts. In Part One, our book begins where it should, with Peter Drucker's vision of leadership. We both had the opportunity to visit with Peter near the end of his life. We were amazed at the sparkle in his eyes, and the wisdom in his words, as he discussed his views for the world ahead. Even as Peter faced death, he maintained his love of learning, growing, and teaching. Joseph Maciariello, a professor in the Claremont Graduate University's Drucker and Ito Graduate School of Management, has years of experience in collaborating with Peter. In "Peter Drucker on Executive Leadership and Effectiveness," Joe has done a masterful job recording some of Peter's final thoughts and his insights for the future. Peter's thoughts on creating organizations that have a spirit of performance built upon the "theory of the business," creating a positive social impact and demonstrating consistent effectiveness, challenge the reader to both embrace change and become a change leader.

Part Two, "Leading in a Diverse World," begins with the recognized world authority on building a learning organization. "Systems Citizenship" presents MIT's Peter Senge at his best, as he challenges us to understand systems, implement systems intelligence, and build partnerships that are a mandate for the new millennium. America's acknowledged thought leader on diversity, Roosevelt Thomas, draws from his vast experience to give future leaders a way to move from "diversity as representation" to "diversity as complexity." Jan Masaoka's chapter is not based upon theory, but rather is derived from her real-life experience—lessons learned from working with executive directors who are women of color and who share their unique perspectives on leadership challenges and the role of race in leadership. Harvard business professor Rosabeth Moss Kanter takes leaders from where they are today—wherever they are in the world—and describes how they can draw upon universal human values to convert global challenges into opportunities for positive change.

Part Three, "Leading in a Time of Crisis and Complexity," begins with Ron Heifetz of Harvard's Kennedy School. Ron describes new approaches to solving leadership dilemmas as he challenges leaders in "Anchoring Leadership in the Work of Adaptive Progress." As president of the Center for Creative Leadership, John Alexander oversees the research and teaching of leadership development professionals around the world. He discusses the increasing complexity that will be faced by leaders in the future and how they can effectively grapple with new and complex challenges. Tom Tierney has moved from being the CEO of one of the world's most successful consulting firms, Bain & Company, to a career that is dedicated to helping nonprofit organizations in the social sector at The Bridgespan Group. In "Understanding the Nonprofit Sector's Leadership Deficit," he describes the challenges that lie ahead for this sector and presents ideas to meet these challenges. John Mroz has had the opportunity to work with leaders around the world and to help these leaders build bridges that have turned potential adversaries into allies. In "Leadership Over Fear" he describes how fear is a part of the daily life of many leaders and shows how taking action, taking risks, and overcoming prejudice and isolation can help demonstrate the courage required to be a future leader. Ponchitta Pierce is a journalist, TV host, producer, writer, and community activist. Her views on the qualities of the leader of the future incorporate interesting, diverse, and varied perspectives in "Leading in a Constantly Changing World." We have had the opportunity to meet many wonderful leaders in our journeys through life. A hero to both of us is General Eric Shinseki. Former chief of staff of the U.S. Army, General Shinseki is admired by leaders around the world. He provides a very different view of leadership development in "Leaders of the Future: Growing One-Eyed Kings."

Part Four, "Leading Organizations of the Future," shows how changing context has an impact leadership needs, demanding changes in leadership styles. Charles Handy is one of the great social philosophers of our time. Who better than Charles to discuss "philosopher leaders?" These future leaders will address philosophical questions—questions concerning mission, the relationship of the individual to the organization, issues of justice and fairness—in their efforts to define the issues clearly and precisely. Michigan's Dave Ulrich and his partner Norm Smallwood, authors of "Leadership as a Brand," are two of the world's leaders in discussions of that topic. Dave and Norm challenge leaders and organizations to consider leadership development as a part of their larger brand and identity. They show how to make investments that can turn leadership into a competitive advantage for the organization. Ken Blanchard is one of the world's best-selling nonfiction authors and authorities on leadership development. He and Dennis Carey, a partner at Spencer Stuart, deliver a leadership imperative in "Regaining Public Trust: A Leadership Challenge." Their vision of leaders focused on the customer—those who serve the customer as well as each member of the organization helping others succeed—is a model for ethical, principled leaders at every level. In "Leading New Age Professionals," Marshall Goldsmith describes how many organizations of the future—organizations that rely on knowledge workers—are becoming like professional services firms. He shows how the types of leadership that produce effective results with professionals are going to become the norm in many organizations of the future. Srikumar Rao teaches one of the most popular, impactful, and insightful courses at Columbia Business School. In "Tomorrow's Leaders," Srikumar looks at fulfillment for leaders as going well beyond the standard "bottom line" toward becoming connected to a compelling mission and serving our larger society. Sally Helgesen is a world authority in the area of inclusion. Her chapter, "Challenges for Leaders in the Years Ahead," addresses issues of fostering inclusion while achieving sustainability, redefining diversity, and focusing on values.

Michigan's Noel Tichy and Chris DeRose, in "Leadership Judgment at the Front Line," talk about how the new organizational environment will produce the need for skilled decision makers at all levels. Part Four concludes with Jim Kouzes and Barry Posner, best-selling authors, speakers on leadership, and developers of leadership profiles, whose work has had an impact on over a million leaders. Their chapter, "It's Not Just the Leader's Vision," moves leaders toward a shared vision of a future that is owned by the members of an organization.

Part Five, "The Quality and Character of the Leader of the Future," begins with one of the most influential thought leaders in history, Stephen Covey. In "Leading in the Knowledge Worker Age," Stephen builds on one of Peter Drucker's key concepts, showing that leadership is really an "enabling art." He discusses the importance of leaders who "find their own voice" and lead in a way that both models and inspires authenticity. Stanford's Jeff Pfeffer follows Stephen by asking, Are the best leaders like professors? He shows how the same skills possessed by great teachers—asking provocative questions, making evidence-based decisions, and helping others learn—are going to become key attributes of the leader of the future. Usman Ghani helps organizations from all sectors with integration and transformation. In "The Leader Integrator," he challenges us to see integration in its many forms—integration of roles responding to changing circumstances; integration of people, processes, and problems—as a key competency for creating the organization of the future. MIT's Edgar Schein is one of the thought leaders that other thought leaders most admire. In "Leadership Competencies: A Provocative New Look," Ed defines new skills needed by the leader of the future. He challenges leaders to learn to "think like an anthropologist," "have the skills of a family therapist," and "cultivate and trust artistic inclinations." Lynn Barendsen and Howard Gardner, of the GoodWork Project and Harvard Graduate School of Education, define in powerful terms the "three elements of good leadership"—technical excellence, ethical orientation, and full engagement. With these key strengths, the leaders of the future can address the challenges caused by globalization, market pressures, and the scarcity of positive examples. In "Distinctive Characteristics of Leaders of Voluntary Organizations: Past, Present, and Future," Brian O'Connell of Tufts University, cofounder of INDEPENDENT SECTOR with John Gardner, uses his lifetime of experience to make the connection between the characteristics of leadership that have always mattered—such as commitment to service, tolerance, maturity, and hard work—and the application of these characteristics by leaders of the future. Darlyne Bailey, former dean of Columbia Teachers College, finishes our book with a chapter titled "Leading from the Spirit." She describes how managers can draw upon deeper beliefs such as authenticity, humility, compassion, faith, patience, and love in their desire to be great role models as servant leaders for the people whose lives they touch.

The Leader of the Future 2 has emerged from great inspiration—the wisdom of Peter Drucker and the ideas of wonderful teachers and leaders who have inspired us over the years. We hope to build upon this treasured legacy with this new collection of wisdom and insights. The best will develop inspired, principled leaders who will transform our organizations and create the future we all desire.

We at the Leader to Leader Institute, successor to the Peter F. Drucker Foundation, are deeply grateful to our authors, thought leaders who with incredible generosity share with us in this book their intellectual capital, philosophies, experience, and faith in a bright future for the leaders of tomorrow. Every chapter in The Leader of the Future 2: Visions, Strategies, and Practices for the New Era is a gift. And we are deeply grateful to you, our readers, fellow travelers on a journey to significance, service, and transformation.

July 2006

Frances Hesselbein
New York, New York

Marshall Goldsmith
Rancho Sante Fe, California

Part I

A Vision of Leadership

Peter F. Drucker on Executive Leadership and Effectiveness

Joseph A. Maciariello

Joseph A. Maciariello is Horton Professor of Management at the Peter F. Drucker and Masatoshi Ito Graduate School of Management at Claremont Graduate University. He has collaborated with Peter Drucker to publish The Daily Drucker *(HarperCollins, 2004),* The Effective Executive in Action *(HarperCollins, 2005), three Internet executive development modules titled* Leading Change *(Corpedia Education, 2003, 2004), and two articles on management in the social sector. In addition he has written three articles providing a systematic, integrated description of some of the major works of Peter Drucker—"Peter F. Drucker on a Functioning Society" (Leader to Leader, Summer 2005), "Mastering Peter Drucker's* The Effective Executive*" (Leader to Leader, Summer 2006), and this current article. He teaches the course "Drucker on Management" for M.B.A. and Executive M.B.A. students and is working on* The Peter F. Drucker Curriculum Project *for use at the Drucker-Ito School and at universities throughout the world.*

Peter Drucker's writings on management and executive leadership are extensive and varied. Yet through all of his work a definite vision of what executive leadership and management is and how leaders and managers should operate does emerge. These intertwined and overlapping subjects can be distinguished, at least in theory, by separating the principles of governance of organizations, which Drucker refers to as the *practice of management*, from the principles of the conduct of leaders in these organizations, which he refers to as the *effective executive*.[1]

A simplified systems representation is presented in Figure 1.1. This figure integrates Drucker's views on executive leadership and management into a framework that leaders can apply in their own organizations. The elements of the figure interweave leadership skills and management practices, both of which are required to attain performance.

This chapter describes these interrelated elements as a system. Please use Figure 1.1 as a reference point as each element is described in an iterative manner. Seek to understand the system of leadership

Figure 1.1. Systems View: Executive Leadership and Effectiveness.

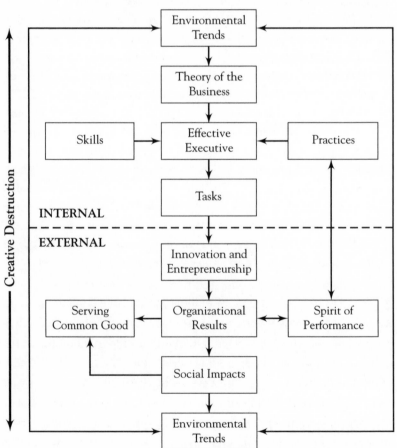

and effectiveness as an organic whole and not merely as a set of isolated elements.

Because Drucker's primary focus is on organizational performance and integrity of leadership, we start our discussion of the elements in Figure 1.1 with what he calls "the Spirit of Performance." This element is located in the lower right-hand portion of the figure.

Executive Leadership and Effectiveness

Executive leadership is concerned with creating organizations that have a high *spirit of performance*. To attain such a spirit of performance, leaders must

- Exhibit high levels of integrity in their moral and ethical conduct

- Focus on results

- Build on strengths—one's own and others'

- Lead beyond borders to meet at least minimum requirements of all stakeholders, including customers, shareholders, and the public, thereby serving the common good

An organization high in spirit of performance is one that is led by executives who are committed to *doing the right thing* and to *getting the right things done*. These executives possess integrity of character; have a vision for the purpose of their organization; focus on opportunities; are change leaders; and follow essential tasks, responsibilities, and practices of management.

Executive skills, practices of effective executives, and executive tasks are acquired through knowledge and experience. Although there may be "born leaders," leadership principles and practices must be learned and can be learned. Executive leadership principles are required, first, to formulate purpose (the "theory of the business") and to pursue performance objectives (for organizational results). These principles focus organizational resources on innovation and entrepreneurship, which must be learned, exploited, and integrated into an organization's activities. Innovation is necessary to remain ahead of those changes imposed on an organization by an ever-changing environment.

Innovation is focused primarily outwardly, on opportunities, on the customer, on technology, on competitors, and so on. Results, such as customer satisfaction, revenue, and profitability, are always on the outside.

The elements in Figure 1.1 are not independent of one another; they interact and exert their own gravitational pull. The primary focus of executive leadership is formulating and implementing an organization's "theory of the business." This requires that executives be competent in performing certain "practices of effective executives." Effectiveness also requires that executives perform certain tasks—specifically, "executive tasks." To perform these practices and tasks, executives must learn and use a set of "executive skills."

Implementing an organization's theory of the business inevitably leads to "social impacts," foreseeable consequences such as employment and purchasing practices, and consumption of natural resources that have an impact on the environment and create demands for public services. An organization is responsible for making certain that these and other impacts are directed in support of the common good.

The Spirit of Performance: True Test of an Organization

As noted earlier, the true test of an organization is the presence of a spirit of performance. An organization that is high in spirit builds on and develops the strength of each person, and this results in common people doing extraordinary things. To guard against weaknesses created by an emphasis on strengths, a highly spirited organization will cover members' weaknesses by overlapping the strengths of others upon these weaknesses like shingles on a roof.

A demand for performance characterizes a high-spirited organization. Executives here will focus members' activities primarily on opportunities and results. Careful attention is placed on people decisions; these decisions signal to employees what is really valued and desired. People decisions—selection, rewards, and promotion—are the true control of an organization. People decisions direct behavior because they indicate the actual values in action of the organization. These decisions reveal what is truly rewarded and punished, and therefore they direct human behavior.

Executive integrity is crucial to creating an organization with a high spirit of performance because the character of an organization's management serves as an example for subordinates. Actions of executives are highly visible. Consequently, the actions of executives must be based on strict principles of conduct regarding responsibility, performance standards, and respect for individuals. These principles serve as examples for the entire management group and organization. "For the spirit of an organization is created from the top. If an organization is great in spirit, it is because the spirit of its top people is great."[2]

An executive who establishes the spirit of performance in daily practice is a *leader* of his or her organization, for leadership involves

> the lifting of a person's vision to higher sights, the raising of a person's performance to a higher standard, and the building of a person's personality beyond its normal limitations.[3]

And there is no better way to create the conditions for the emergence of such leaders than to create an organization that is great in spirit.

The Theory of the Business

Drucker's ideas about leading organizations all start with the organization's "theory of the business." A theory of the business is the way an organization intends to create value for its customers and is therefore applicable to all organizations, not just business organizations. It requires answers to the following questions:

- What is our mission?

- What are our core competencies?

- Who are our customers and noncustomers?

- What do we consider results for the enterprise?

- What should our theory be? (Which in turn focuses executives to look for opportunities for innovation.)

The theory of a business is often not obvious, nor can it be formulated without controversy. Formulating a theory of business requires executives first to look beyond the walls of the organization to the external environment. The environment is not limited to where the enterprise is currently operating, but also includes other "environments," such as those where noncustomers are being served and where future customers are likely to be served. This means that formulating a theory of the business must be a forward-looking exercise—creating a mission that compels it to systematically evaluate emerging trends, future changes in its environments, and current or emerging social problems that may be turned into business opportunities.

In determining core competencies, an organization must ask, What are we really good at? and What should we be doing?

Assumptions about mission, core competencies, and customers not only must fit reality, but also must be consistent with each other. It is for this reason that a company's theory must be constantly checked and updated, since, for example, one doesn't want to be selling only mainframe computers, as IBM once did, when one's customers are shifting their preferences to personal computers.

If the theory of the business is different from an organization's current business, then the concepts of *abandonment* and of *innovation* and *change* become obvious. Leaders must be able to recognize when to give up products, processes, and customers and reallocate resources toward more promising opportunities. In summary, the theory of the business sets direction; it should be used to communicate to the organization's members where the business is going, provide the rationale for why it is going down a given path, and align the activities of its members.

The Environment and Social Impacts

The ethical rule that managers should live by when pursuing their organizations' missions is *primum non-nocere*—"first do no harm." Organizations are public institutions, and their actions have impacts on society. Their codes of professional ethics must be to *not knowingly do harm*. Legal and ethical violations should be met with stiff penalties for those who break the law and who otherwise knowingly do harm.

Drucker describes two different types of social impacts:

- Those negative ones that an organization creates

- Social ills that are turned into business opportunities

Both impacts are important and must be managed since the first deals with what an organization does to *harm* society, and the second with what an organization can do to *help* society.

An organization's social impact is properly defined as activities, or results of activities, that are achieved in an organization's pursuit of its purpose. Each institution must be dedicated to a purpose—for example, a hospital should heal the sick; a business should satisfy economic wants; and a church, synagogue, or mosque should nourish people spiritually. Detrimental impacts to society created in this process must be minimized because they are harmful to the common good and are also outside the proper mission of any organization.

There is also a balance between cleaning up after one's negative impacts and, in doing so, incurring costs that create a competitive disadvantage for an organization within its industry. In the latter case, it is in the interest of executives in an industry (for example, the accounting profession) to agree upon appropriate regulation (that is, to avoid auditing scandals such as those involving Enron, WorldCom, and so on) that minimizes negative impacts and simultaneously eliminates undue disadvantages among competitors.

Organizations must focus on their missions, minimize negative social impacts, and take a proactive interest in the common good. Institutions are organs of society. As such they are significantly dependent upon the welfare of society for their own welfare. To this end, management must work to obtain appropriate regulations so as to level the competitive playing field within its industry when executive insiders know that substantial negative social impacts are present.

The difficulty and expense executives are now incurring complying with the requirements of the Sarbanes-Oxley Act of 2002, enacted as a result of the public outcry over numerous accounting scandals of the 1990s, were preventable. All that was needed was self-regulation by members of the accounting profession as represented by the American Institute of Certified Public Accountants and the Financial Accounting Standards Board. Such self-regulation would have led to far more effective legislation for preventing accounting abuses, because it would have been developed by the professional groups best informed to propose the regulation to Congress and later to enforce the regulation on their members.

The second type of social impact, *social ills* or *dysfunctions*, should be thought of as challenges and treated as potential business opportunities. Organizations should aggressively pursue activities that turn the elimination of social dysfunctions into business opportunities (for example, Branch Rickey, general manager of the Brooklyn Dodgers, breaking the color line by bringing Jackie Robinson into Major League Baseball).

Finally, management must also support the common good by helping community organizations financially—personally, in the form of corporate donations and by encouraging employees to donate money and volunteer their time supporting the work of community, and professionally, by lending their executive expertise to help these community groups address major social problems (in one example, the revitalization of downtown Cleveland, Ohio, was aided by the executive expertise of local CEOs). Executives should remember that "an organ [a business] cannot prosper in a dying body [society]." Yet, in the process of seeking to promote the common good, executives should never lose sight of their principal mission, for if they lose sight of their principal mission, they will be of little use to society.

Executive Practices, Skills, and Tasks

Executive leadership and effectiveness consist of three interconnected areas, as shown in Figure 1.1.

- Personal attributes and practices that make an executive leader effective

- Specific skills executives must acquire to be effective as leaders

- Particular tasks that executives must perform to lead their organization to be effective

Practices of Executive Effectiveness

The five individual practices of an effective executive for getting the right things done are those contained in Drucker's *The Effective Executive* and the new companion journal *The Effective Executive in Action.*[4] The five practices are summarized in this section.

Executive practices begin with the need to perform *time management*. Time is our most limiting resource; once used it is irreplaceable. We can acquire more of every other resource. The way we use our time may seem obvious at first. But how many executives think they spend most of their time on strategic planning and decision making only to find out, upon careful study of their actual time use, that they are mostly occupied with the repetitive and unproductive demands of others?

Drucker suggests that executives

- Record the actual use of time and prune time-wasters in order to free enough time to accomplish high priority tasks that require major blocks of time to do right

- Focus most upon activities that produce results in three major performance areas: direct results, developing people, and nurturing values

Consistent with effective management of an executive's time is the requirement to set priorities so as to concentrate time on opportunities, on those tasks that show promise of producing results rather than on those tasks that constantly demand the executive's attention but are less important than result-producing activities.

Setting priorities—doing the most important things first, one at a time—gives the executive the best opportunity to achieve superior performance. Superior performance is achieved by focusing effort on the performance areas.

People decisions are among the most important decisions executives make—one of the three key performance areas. These decisions should attempt to match the strengths of a person with the specific assignments of a position. These decisions have their own rules, including understanding the specific assignment, considering a number of qualified candidates, examining the performance records of candidates, and making certain the selected candidate understands the new assignment. An effective executive builds on the strengths of employees, overlapping responsibilities and thereby covering weaknesses. In this way each member of an organization can be made productive.

Concentration on superior performance also requires that executives abandon unproductive activities. They should ask themselves, If we were not doing a particular activity, making a particular product, or participating in a particular process already, would we do it now? And if they would not, then they should ask, What should we do about it now? Should we attempt to make it more effective, abandon it, or, in the case of a product line, sell it?

The final practice of the effective executive is *making effective decisions*. Making effective decisions is both a skill—following the right steps in the right order—and the specific practice of the executive. Only executives make decisions that affect the result areas. Decision making thus distinguishes the work of the executive leaders from all others in the organization.

Decision making is in this way the link between individual executive practices and executive skills.

Executive Skills

Executives must acquire skills in five areas in order to be effective:

- Decision making

- Communications

- Budgeting

- Measurement and control

- The management sciences

Effective executives make effective decisions. There are six steps of effective decision making and five characteristics of effective decisions, which may require certain questions to be asked. Briefly, regarding the steps, effective decision makers start by *defining* and *classifying* the problem. These are almost simultaneous steps in the decision-making process.

Defining the problem requires making sure that all observed symptoms of the problem are taken into account in the definition. It is much easier to fix the wrong solution to a problem if the problem has been defined correctly than it is to fix a correct solution to a problem that has been defined incorrectly! If a problem has been defined incorrectly, no proposed solution to that problem can be found. Conversely, if a problem is defined correctly, then an incorrect solution will provide useful feedback information, leading the executive closer to the right solution.

After defining the problem, executives classify it by asking, "Is this problem generic *or* unique?" Decisions that are generic to the organization or to the industry ought to be solved by finding and applying a rule that has been used to solve the problem by someone else.

If a decision is classified as unique, the decision maker next *determines the boundary conditions* that have to be satisfied for the decision to be effective. Establishing boundary conditions requires an answer to the question, What does the decision have to accomplish to be effective in solving the problem?

Once these boundary conditions are defined, the decision maker then asks *what is the right solution* given these conditions? Next—and this is where a great many decisions fail—the decision maker must *convert the decision into action* by assigning responsibilities for carrying out the decision and by eliminating any barriers faced by those who must act. Finally, the effective decision maker follows up on the decision and *obtains feedback* on what actually happened as a result of the decision and compares this with intended or desired results.

When it comes to characteristics of an effective decision, decision makers first ask, *"Is a decision necessary at all?"* If it is, they explore alternatives by soliciting opinions from those closest to the problem. Next, they ask proponents of decisions to test their "hypothesis" against the facts to determine if the facts support their opinions (in other words, what would the facts have to be for a specific opinion to be correct?).

Effective decision makers *encourage dissent* on alternatives and then *act on the chosen alternative* if the potential benefits of doing so outweigh costs and risks. Dissent, properly carried out, taps the imagination of the parties involved to find an appropriate decision and leads to a more complete understanding of what the problem is all about. And if a decision should fail to meet the boundary conditions after vigorous debate, the decision maker will have a better understanding of the possible causes of failure having considered other alternatives.

Finally, *effective decision making takes courage*, since, as with many effective medicines, effective decisions can sometimes have side effects or unintended outcomes.

Next we turn to a discussion of the remaining skills that executives must acquire to carry out their tasks. First, executives must be *good communicators*. Effective executives must engage in upward communication, in which communication is initiated as well as received by the recipient. This helps ensure that the recipient understands what is being communicated, because unless the recipient "hears," communication has not taken place. Information and communication are different. Communication does not take place unless the emitter is sure that the receiver understands what action is to be taken as a result of, say, a conversation or a memo. The most effective way to ensure that real communication has taken place is to ask the receiver to describe what he or she has heard from the conversation, including the demands for action required, and to make sure it is what the emitter implied.

Budgeting is the most widely used tool of management. Budgets are revenue and expenditure plans developed for each unit to help management decide where to apply the financial and human resources of an organization. In estimating revenues and expenses, executives are able to establish communications with each part of the organization and integrate the objectives, plans, and expenditures of each part with the whole of the organization. Budgets, correctly used, are thus major tools for integrating the plans and performance of the organization—upward, downward, and sideways. By holding each unit responsible for the plans and expenditures in the budget, the budgeting process provides a framework for achieving accountability for performance for each unit and person in the organization. Budgeting is thus crucial to the process of achieving "control" in an organization.

Operating and capital budgets are established to maintain current operations. For these budgets, the appropriate question is, What is the *minimum amount* of resources necessary to keep existing operations going? Administered budgets, however, are discretionary, opportunity-focused budgets, used for new programs, products, research, and other activities such as management development. Opportunity budgets often integrate resource expenditures following from strategic decisions.

Here executives must ask a different question: "What is the largest sum these activities can use effectively to accomplish future objectives?" Activities in opportunity budgets often extend beyond the period of operating budgets. They should be estimated over the life cycle of the opportunity in order to guarantee funding and achieve desired outcomes.

The budget process provides a forum for evaluating existing markets, products, processes, and programs for continuation. Activities that would no longer be initiated if not already in place are prime candidates for abandonment. So as not to cause chaos each period, a periodic review (sometimes called a *zero-based review*) of the activities for each unit should be established well in advance. This helps to institutionalize a systematic process of abandonment within the organization.

Creating appropriate measurements and maintaining control are other skills that effective executives must acquire. An organization's choice of controls indicates to people what is valued and what is desired. Controls are therefore not neutral. They reflect the values of the organization and they direct behavior. Consequently, controls must focus on results. They should be easy to understand and be considered a resource for the person who is responsible for the work that is being controlled. Controls must also be timely and congruent with goals.

Qualitative assessments that the executive also must receive and evaluate are in many cases much more appropriate indicators of performance than are quantitative measurements (for example, is one person a better fit for an open position than another?), and therefore qualitative assessments must supplement quantitative assessments.

The *management sciences* concern themselves with evaluating the assumptions of management through the use of quantitative tools such as statistics, system simulation, project management techniques, and information for decisions extracted from the accounting system. These tools help executives develop factual information for analyzing decisions. Management science tools, such as Six Sigma quality and lean methodologies, are extensively employed for improving the operational processes.

Executives can use the management sciences to help create a true whole that is greater than the sum of its parts (that is, to prevent suboptimization of parts of the organization) and to balance the requirements of the present with those of the future. Executives must understand that "[t]he whole of a system is not necessarily improved if one particular function or part is improved or made more efficient. In fact, the system may well be damaged thereby, or even destroyed. In some cases the best way to strengthen the system may be to weaken a part to make it less precise or efficient."[5]

Executive Tasks

The five tasks of the executive are aimed at fulfilling these system requirements.

1. The theory of the business (THOB) is the starting point for *setting objectives*. Management by objectives (MBO) is a well-defined method of setting objectives to achieve the mission of the organization as defined in the THOB. MBO involves setting goals and objectives to balance short-range and long-range objectives. These objectives become the basis for organizing the human and capital resources of the firm and for making work assignments.

The MBO process brings together aspects of executive leadership and management. For example, to determine mission and objectives, an executive must determine an organization's theory of the business. And to make sure that an organization is properly implementing its THOB, managers must engage in a communication process, make decisions, and use measurements and the management sciences. But management by objectives is not only a technique that executives should learn; it is a genuine philosophy of executive leadership.

MBO embodies a process that supports and facilitates teamwork. Communication—upward, downward, and sideways—is essential to setting and accomplishing objectives. Upward communication must be used to ensure that each executive has a clear picture of where the organization is going and how his or her objectives fit into the whole. Most important, when properly employed, MBO relies on a process of self-control and seeks to achieve alignment between individual needs and the goals of the organization. MBO thus seeks to meld individual freedom and responsibility with organizational performance and results. It rests on a high concept of human motivation and behavior. It is the underpinning for a highly spirited organization.[6]

2. An executive's responsibility to *organize* would appear simple on its surface; however, organizing requires analytical skill in order

to understand the activities, decisions, and relationships required in the organization's structure if the organization is to achieve its mission. Organizing requires that managers classify activities and place them in the organization's structure according to their contribution to objectives. Organizing should result in minimizing the number of relationships required for each position to achieve performance.

The organization's structure should allow decisions to be made at the lowest level possible, consistent with minimizing the number of people that must be consulted to make decisions. Executives should seek clarity, simplicity, and economy in their structures, and they should keep to a minimum the number of levels required, because each layer is a communication link that adds complexity and noise to the decision process.

3. A manager must also *motivate* and *communicate*. This requires social skills, trust, a focus on results, and other conditions for a highly spirited organization. It includes providing equitable rewards that balance the merits of the individual with the needs and stability of the group. Motivation comes from people decisions, job design, high expectations for performance, and sound decisions on compensation and rewards.

4. To ensure that efforts in the organization are directed toward objectives, a manager must establish *yardsticks of performance*. Performance in each position is measured in relationship to the objectives of the person and those of the organization. Establishing controls and appropriate reporting mechanisms facilitates the process of self-control as well as the processes of developing oneself and others.

5. *Managing oneself and one's career* and *developing others* is becoming more important with the advent of knowledge work, the knowledge economy, and competition brought about by the forces of globalization. Managing oneself requires the individual to establish a process for determining what one is good at (in other words, one's strengths) and for determining where one's efforts in

their work will be the most fruitful (that is, will make the greatest contribution).

If one were to take a poll, it is likely that few people would identify themselves as having ever considered topics such as, Am I a listener or reader? How do I learn most effectively? Is my job aligned with my values? But these are important issues to settle in order to set the direction of one's career. One must determine where one belongs—in a large or small organization; as a freelancer; in a corporation, government, or social sector institution; or perhaps as an executive or a technologist.

Not only do workers have to understand how they work, they must also understand how the people around them work so they can help these people maximize their contributions. Managing these relationships is crucial to effectiveness.

Executives also must take responsibility for developing the abilities of subordinates and coworkers around them. This is a key result area for the executive. This process is crucial for cultivating future leaders of an enterprise and for helping employees acquire skills that will prepare them for the future. Development is, however, a double-edged process. One cannot develop oneself unless one is actively engaged in the development of others.

To summarize our discussion of Figure 1.1, executive skills, executive tasks, and executive practices must be combined into principles of effectiveness in order to implement an enterprise's theory of the business. Executive principles must be directed toward developing and maintaining a high spirit of performance, achieving organizational results, and managing social impact to derive the common good.

But this is not all effective executives must do. The Internet provides everyone with equal access to information. It results in eliminating distance in the world economy. Globalization and outsourcing have intensified competition in labor, product, and capital markets. The rate of change is becoming torrid and one can react to it, adapt to it, or become proactive and lead it—thus influencing future environmental trends. A highly spirited organization consists of executives who are proactive in leading change by discerning the "future that has already happened."

By taking advantage of these trends, these executives embrace the ongoing process of creative destruction[7] that is characteristic of free and global markets, and by doing so these executives become change leaders. They recognize that an organization that seeks to maintain the status quo is already in decline.

Change leaders formulate entrepreneurial strategies and look for windows of opportunity to apply these strategies. They also create an internal culture and set of management systems that encourage and reward innovation and entrepreneurship. In the pages that remain, let's examine discernable environmental trends in the early twenty-first century and the windows of opportunity they create.

Identifying the Future That Has Already Happened: Seizing Opportunities Created by the Process of Creative Destruction to Become a Change Leader

Peter Drucker's article "The Next Society: A Survey of the Near Future"[8] and the current and soon to be upon us trends it describes do not change the theory of the business, executive practices, skills and tasks, and social impacts model, but they do shift the opportunity set based on known and projected changes that are fast taking place in the environment.

Executives will have to focus much more on making knowledge work productive and the knowledge workers achieving members of their organizations, given the growing importance of both in the developed and the developing economies. This requires attention to building on strengths and to increasing the productivity of knowledge workers, but also to integrating specialists into the performing whole.

Demographic changes in the developed world include a population that is getting older, accompanied by a birthrate in many of these countries that is below the level required to maintain stability in the population. Consequently the traditional workforce is shrinking. Such demographic changes mean that marketing strategies and the theory of the business of an enterprise may have to change. Split markets in which both the younger and older generations make up the population dictate very different value propositions and marketing strategies. "What is value?" to customers will have to be viewed through two different generational value systems (for example, the values of the millennium generation versus those of the baby-boom generation).

Another important area bearing on corporations is managing environmental and social impacts. The size of our global population already exerts a negative impact on the environment. Organizations are likely to face stricter regulations in the future. They will have to find new and cleaner sources of energy, because the world's demand for fossil fuels, especially in rapidly developing economies such as China and India, is likely to continue to drive up prices of these sources and to increase environmental pollution.

These environmental issues will raise the importance of creating accurate measures of emissions and of outcomes associated with reduction efforts of business units. These issues will create business opportunities, as well as social responsibility objectives and measures.

For example, the recent emphasis by General Electric on "17 clean-technology businesses" and the expectations that the new emphasis will expand sales of products supported by these "green" technologies "from $10 billion in sales in 2004 to $20 billion by 2010, with more ambitious targets thereafter"[9] is indicative of the potential opportunities created by the global increase in greenhouse gases (GHG). In addition, the company has established different targets for each business unit for reducing emissions of carbon dioxide and overall GHG.

The corporation of tomorrow will be far more complex than previous corporations, or those of today, since it will constitute a web of partnerships, joint ventures, alliances, outsourcing contractors, and various other kinds of associates or affiliates that are unprecedented in the current breadth and intricacy. Each aspect of the corporation may have its own management, but the relationships among entities will certainly have to be more coordinated and made to perform.

People and communication skills are going to be increasingly important for the executives of the future as they navigate and negotiate their way through their organizations' complex, system, network, and cellular structures.[10]

Organizations increasingly must rely on technology to support and guide their business (for example, the idea of a performance dashboard for each position is not uncommon at present). The blizzard of data will have to be converted into information that is pertinent for each knowledge worker and executive. Broadly, technology is enabling continual increases in productivity for service and knowledge work in the twenty-first century as it had for manufacturing and agricultural work in the twentieth century. This is enhancing the ability of executives to expand output per hour for both service and knowledge workers.

To prosper, networked organizations must rely on communications technology such as the Internet, mobile electronic devices, and videoconferencing to enhance their ability to collaborate amongst their parts and to coordinate the whole. Creating data networks and knowledge management systems also will be important in order to link databases and create simple access to relevant information across global supply chains.

The increased use of technology will have an impact on executives and will require that the list of management science skills be expanded to include the ability to take advantage of information technology.

The changes in our society will open up numerous opportunities for and sources of innovation. Consider the following:

- The shift in demographics will create an opportunity for organizations to bring new value to different customer market segments.

- The growth in the number of single parents will have to be thought through in terms of customer needs and customer values.

- Changes in industry structures, such as in health care, education, and financial services, will allow organizations in these industries to reformulate the way they deliver value, while also creating new sub-businesses to provide goods and services to niche markets.

- Managing an organization's human resources will become significantly more important since these resources are rapidly becoming the most important assets and means for gaining competitive advantage. In addition, major parts of the human resource function, the routine and not-so-routine parts, are and will be outsourced (for example, note the emergence of professional employment organizations and business processing organizations).

- Performance objectives of organizations will have to reflect the requirements of knowledge workers who supply "human capital" to organizations as well as those of outside investors who supply "financial capital."[11]

- Organizations are going to have to be closely connected to what their employees need, especially training, health, and retirement benefits. These are among key motivators for employees and must be carefully managed, especially if employees are wanting to work until they are seventy and beyond.

- The answer *in part* to the reduction in the available workforce in the United States is immigration, but if everyone's birthrate in developed countries is declining, then we are still left with a zero-sum outcome as to the supply of knowledge workers, meaning that many developed countries will have to manage a smaller workforce or to continually educate a larger portion of their populations.

The most effective way to seize opportunities to manage "the future that has already happened" is to be proactive, take advantage of emerging trends, embrace change, and become a change leader. Executive leadership and management practices must change to fit these new realities of the global, knowledge-based, information society and at the same time they must strive to achieve a high spirit of performance.

Conclusion

Figure 1.1 presents a systems view of Peter Drucker on leadership and effectiveness. In this chapter, I have described each of the elements in Figure 1.1, and attempted—however imperfectly—to systematically capture Drucker's monumental achievements in both codifying management as a discipline and describing the practices of an effective leader. These elements, in whole or in part, have been used to advantage by leaders in business, government, and the social sector, in the United States and around the world, and they will continue to do so for the forseeable future.

Endnotes

1. The literature on leadership and management is inconsistent in classifying activities as clearly "leadership" or "management," but there is a fair consensus that providing vision, values, competence, standards, encouragement, optimism, and a sustaining spirit are leadership activities. The remaining five tasks—objective setting, organizing, motivating, assessing progress, and developing people— are almost always classified as management activities. Nevertheless, these activitites are not as separable as implied by such a classification scheme. Those who engage primarily in leadership activities also manage, and those who are primarily engaged in day-to-day

management do also carry out leadership activities. As a result, I believe the term *executive* is now more appropriate than either the term *leader* or *manager*. *Executive* is applied to individuals in an organization—leaders, managers, and knowledge workers—who make decisions that have significant influence on one or more of the three key performance areas—direct results, values, and people decisions. I believe this is consistent with Drucker's view that effective executives "get the right things done" and that leadership is not rank or privileges, "[i]t is responsibility" for performance!

2. P. Drucker, *Management: Tasks, Responsibilities, Practices* (New York: Harper & Row, 1974) p. 462. Drucker has consistently emphasized the importance of character and integrity for executive and leadership responsibilities. In a revealing interview with Rich Karlgaard conducted in late October 2004, he ends the interview with a discussion of "character development." He notes, "We have talked a lot about executive development. We have been mostly talking about people's strength and giving them experiences. Character is not developed that way. That is developed inside and not outside. I think churches and synagogues and the 12-step recovery programs are the main development agents of character today" (Rich Karlgaard, "Peter Drucker on Leadership," Forbes.com, November 19, 2004).

3. P. Drucker, *Management: Tasks, Responsibilities, Practices*, p. 463.

4. The five practices are fully described in Drucker's management classic, *The Effective Executive* (HarperCollins, 1966). These practices must be worked out by each individual executive or knowledge worker. A comprehensive guide for working out these practices is contained in *The Effective Executive in Action* by Drucker and Maciariello (HarperCollins, 2006).

5. P. Drucker, *Management: Tasks, Responsibilities, Practices*, p. 508.

6. MBO embodies Drucker's notion of responsibility and freedom. "Responsibility . . . is both external and internal. Externally it implies accountability to some person or body and accountability for specific performance. Internally it implies commitment. The responsible worker is a worker who not only is accountable for specific results but also has authority to do whatever is necessary to pro-

duce these results and finally, is committed to these results as personal achievement" (P. Drucker and J. Maciariello, *The Daily Drucker*, New York: HarperCollins, 2004, p. 104).

7. The process of "creative destruction" was described fully by the great Austrian economist, Joseph A. Schumpeter. The most accessible explanation of the process by Shumpeter is in Chapter Seven of his *Capitalism, Socialism and Democracy* (New York: Harper & Row Publishers, 1942, pp. 81–110). For example, "The opening up of new markets, foreign or domestic, and the organizational development from craft shop and factory floor to such concerns as U.S. Steel, illustrate the same process of industrial mutation . . . that incessantly revolutionalizes the economic structure from *within*, incessantly destroying the old one, incessantly creating a new one. This process of Creative Destruction is the essential fact about capitalism. It is what capitalism consists in and what every capitalist concern has got to live with" (p. 83). And, "competition of the kind we have in mind acts not only when in being but also when it is an ever present threat. It disciplines before it attacks" (p. 85).

8. P. Drucker, "The Next Society: A Survey of the Near Future," *The Economist*, Nov. 3, 2001, reprint, pp. 3–20.

9. "Special Report: The Greening of General Electric," *The Economist*, December 10, 2005, pp. 77–78.

10. See M. Gladwell, "The Cellular Church," by Malcolm Gladwell, *The New Yorker*, Sept. 12, 2005, pp. 60–67. Gladwell is the author of *The Tipping Point* and *Blink*.

11. Southwest Airlines, with its focus on attracting, managing, and retaining the right human resource talent, is surely an example of the recognition of the importance of human capital (in both knowledge and services). Given the turbulence in the airline industry, Southwest has proved the competitive advantage of a focus on human resources. Southwest is now one of the leading airlines in the country, and it has achieved these results without cutting its workforce.

Part II

Leading in a Diverse World

2

Systems Citizenship
The Leadership Mandate for This Millennium

Peter Senge

Peter Senge is a senior lecturer at the Massachusetts Institute of Technology and founding chair of Society for Organizational Learning Council (SoL). He is the author of The Fifth Discipline: The Art and Practice of the Learning Organization, *coauthor of the three related fieldbooks, and most recently coauthor of* Presence: An Inquiry into Profound Change. *Peter works with organizations throughout the world on decentralizing the role of leadership to enhance the capacity of all people to work toward healthier human systems.*

"The only enduring source of competitive advantage is an organization's relative ability to learn faster than its competition," wrote Arie de Geus in the *Harvard Business Review* in 1988.[1] With these words the organizational learning movement was born. Although many understood the idea only superficially, seeing *learning* as a more fashionable word for *training*, for de Geus, learning was "the process whereby an organization evolved to remain in harmony with a changing environment," and it was the key to whether organizations survived and prospered.[2]

By de Geus's definition, today's organizations face unprecedented learning challenges, which we are only starting to perceive. These challenges go beyond adapting to the Internet and other new technologies or dealing with global competition. They go to the very DNA of the Industrial Age business model, a model that shapes modern societies as well.

For all of human history, societies that endured appreciated that their economies could be no healthier than the larger natural and societal systems upon which they depended. Historian Jared Diamond has shown how many one-time flourishing cultures that forgot this truism passed into oblivion, often with surprising speed.[3] But there is one big difference today. The society whose future is in question is increasingly a global society. Speaking at the fiftieth anniversary of Japan entering the post–World War II "Bretton Woods" monetary accords, World Bank Vice President for South East Asia Mieko Nishimizu pointed out that our interdependence now reaches well beyond the monetary dimension:

> "The future appears *alien* to us. It differs from the past most notably in that the Earth itself is the relevant unit with which to frame and measure that future. Discriminating issues that shape the future are all fundamentally global. We belong to one inescapable network of mutuality: mutuality of ecosystems; mutuality of freer movement of information, ideas, people, capital, goods and services; and mutuality of peace and security. We are tied, indeed, in a single fabric of destiny on Planet Earth. Policies and actions that attempt to tear a nation from this cloth will inevitably fail."[4]

As individuals and organizations, we have never had to be concerned about how our day-to-day decisions, like the products we buy and the energy we use, affect people and larger living systems who live thousands of miles away, even on the other side of the planet. While Arie de Geus's learning imperative was directed initially to individual organizations, especially businesses, the challenge of evolving to remain in harmony with our environment today applies also to larger supply networks, entire industries, and whole societies. This is the real message of "globalization," and it is, indeed, an *alien* one for all of us. We've never been here before—and the future is watching.

Societies Waking Up

Societies and their governments around the world are waking up to the fact that industrial growth as we have known it is now encountering severe social and environmental limits, the costs of which are getting harder and harder to ignore.

For example, the amount of carbon dioxide (CO_2) in the atmosphere is 30 percent greater than at any time in the past four hundred thousand years, and the rate of CO_2 emissions, which itself is rapidly rising, is somewhere between three and five times the rate at which CO_2 is being removed from the atmosphere through carbon sequestration.[5] Scientists have been warning about possible CO_2 effects on global climate for a long time, but now the human and economic costs are starting to become hard to ignore for governments and insurance companies faced with the consequences of weather instability and spreading tropical diseases.

Consider also the simple fact that, in order to support the average American's lifestyle, we cause over one ton of waste to be generated, per person *per day*. Closely related to the volume of waste is the chemical footprint of manufacturing industries and the related toxicity of everyday products and the processes that produce them.[6] Like the CO_2 effects, human costs are starting to show up in public health consequences such as cancers in middle-age people that were unheard of two decades ago. Rather than search for a "cure" for cancer, we need to look for its source in our way of living.

As these costs become recognized and their sources understood, they need to be allocated back to the businesses and industries from which they originate. For example, starting in February 2003 the European Union (EU) began to require that makers of automobiles take them back for recycle or remanufacture at the end of their lifetime. Similar EU regulations are now in effect for many consumer electronics products. The EU has also begun a systematic phasing out of diverse sources of toxicity in products, starting with heavy metals such as mercury, cadmium, and hexavalent chromium. These regulations are part of historic steps in the direction of making "extended producer responsibility" the norm for industry.[7] Today in China, for example, both the president and premier talk frequently about an idea that takes extended producer responsibility to its logical conclusion: the "circular economy," an economy that works like natural systems, in which there is no "waste" and all materials move in continuing cycles of reuse. The implications would be profound for the linear "take-make-waste" industrial model of extractive industrialization, as Paul Hawken called it over a decade ago.[8]

In short, whether it is weather instability; waste disposal; health effects of rising toxicity levels; or depletion of water aquifers, fisheries, and agricultural topsoil, former "externalized" costs for businesses are starting to show up on the profit statements of insurers, health care providers, and producers of diverse products and services. The era of "privatizing" profit and "socializing" many social and environmental costs is passing. These costs are growing, and they can no longer be regarded as somebody else's problems at some indefinite time in the future. The future is now.

Consumers and Investors Taking a Stand

Social and environmental imbalances are likewise becoming salient to more and more consumers. "Fair trade" coffee, once assumed to be a small-niche product for well-off consumers, is the fastest growing segment of the coffee business in the United States and Europe. Nestlé, one of the four major coffee sellers in the world, recently announced its intent to get into the fair-trade business. This seems to reflect a growing number of consumers who are realizing that the terms of global trade often unfairly favor the rich. For example, Oxfam's report on global trade's "rigged rules and double standards" has catalyzed a growing "make trade fair" consumer movement in Europe, which more and more businesses are watching closely as an indicator of shifting consumer values.[9]

Even investors, the presumed last bastion of business-as-usual growth at any cost, are starting to be a force for change. Over 10 percent of equity capital in the United States goes through some sort of social and environmental "screen." Although many are fairly minimal, this represents a major change from less than 1 percent ten years ago. Plus, a small but increasingly influential group of investors are making sustainability the cornerstone of their thinking. Four years ago, I heard the president of one of the world's largest pension funds share, in a private meeting, his core criteria for managing his investment portfolio: ten aspects of social and environmental responsibility that he regarded as the best indicators of "good management and long-term financial return."

Frank Dixon, research director for a major investment advisory firm, claims that "sustainability will be THE competitive advantage strategy of the twenty-first century."[10] Dixon and his colleagues have developed a framework that includes over one hundred risk factors stemming from questionable social and environmental practices, which they now apply to "sustainability analyses" of over two thousand firms. While the "corporate social responsibility (CSR) movement has driven initial improvements in environmental and social performance," Dixon sees it as just a first step. The current "economic and political systems essentially force firms to be irresponsible and unsustainable by not holding them fully accountable for negative impacts on society."[11]

Businesses Discovering That They Cannot Go It Alone

A small but growing group of global firms see these historic changes in their environment as being truly strategic. In the fall of 2005, Wal-Mart CEO Lee Scott committed the company to long-term goals of zero waste, 100 percent renewable energy, and selling sustainable products—a speech Dixon called "probably the most important business speech ever given."[12] Six months earlier, GE's CEO declared the firm's intent to invest in a broad range of more sustainable products.

By these actions, GE and Wal-Mart joined a small group of industry leaders who have been pursuing strategic opportunities relating to sustainability for many years. For almost a decade, Unilever, one of the largest consumer goods companies in the world, has had three strategic imperatives: sustainable agriculture, sustainable fishing, and water. In the late 1990s the company began working toward a global certification process for sustainable fisheries, now established as the independent Marine Stewardship Council.[13] BP and its CEO John Browne have spurred the oil industry to take global climate change seriously, starting with Browne's historic speech at Stanford in 1997, the first ever by an oil company CEO on the subject.[14]

But what even the most powerful firms can achieve in isolation is limited. As Dixon notes, the goals of these companies "cannot be achieved without large-scale change in areas including supply chain, regulatory and consumer awareness." All businesses sit within much larger commercial systems, and it is these systems that must change, not just individual company policies and practices. In a real way, the most important role of leading organizations like GE, Wal-Mart, Unilever, and BP is to catalyze development of larger learning communities and to, as Dixon says, "proactively work with others to achieve system changes."[15] And the partners in these larger communities will be not only other companies *but NGOs and governmental organizations as well.* There is very little historical precedent for such learning partnerships. But then, there is very little precedent for learning challenges of the scope we now face.

For example, in 2002, Unilever, Oxfam, and the Kellogg Foundation began conversations about the challenges of shifting global agriculture systems. Despite little public recognition in rich north-

ern countries, the global food system is arguably the greatest gener-
ator of poverty, and consequently social and political instability, in
the world today. Prices for agricultural commodities have fallen 30
to 90 percent over the past fifty years, making cheap food readily
accessible for the rich northern societies and simultaneously making
living incomes increasingly inaccessible in poorer food-producing
countries. A 2002 Oxfam report showed how falling prices for coffee have created a "crisis for 25 million coffee producers around the
world," many of whom "now sell their coffee beans for much less
than they cost to produce."[16]

The coffee growers' plight exemplifies the harsh realities of
global food markets for more than a billion people in agriculture
worldwide. These global markets are dominated by large multinational food companies whose basic business model is driven by
investing in technology to boost productivity—resulting in continually declining prices and continually increasing production.
Unfortunately, this business model, though it takes little heed of
social and ecological realities, goes unquestioned. According to the
economic theory of commodity industries, rising production and
falling prices continue until profits are so low that investment capital moves elsewhere. However, poor farmers do not have this
option. In fact, poor farmers typically keep trying to expand production even when costs exceed prices in desperate attempts to
maintain their incomes and stay on their land. In so doing, they
often deplete the long-term fertility of the soil, leading to still more
desperate attempts to expand (overproduction worldwide in the past
fifty years has caused loss of topsoil equal to an area that exceeds the
size of India and China combined).[17] The result, in the words of an
industry expert, is that "When incomes are up production rises;
when incomes are down production rises."

Only by getting enough of the key players in this system working together is there any chance of reversing the tragic "race to the
bottom." Today, one example of this is the Sustainable Food Laboratory, a group that involves more than fifty major businesses,

NGOs, and governmental organizations working together to "bring sustainable food practices into the economic mainstream." While there is a long way to go, an extraordinary network of committed and diverse actors has developed, and a host of initiatives demonstrating alternatives have been launched. For example, a "business coalition for sustainable agriculture" has formed that includes many of the largest food businesses and is seeking to establish clear and agreed upon standards for sustainability that could guide all.[18] The Food Lab also includes on-the-ground projects focused on specific supply chains, for example, one striving to make the distribution of profit among all key actors throughout visible to all those key actors—including consumers. Imagine going to the grocery store and seeing two bins of green beans: one is the cheapest and one 30 percent more expensive. Atop each is a picture showing where the money goes in each supply chain, along with an assessment (verified by an independent body) of the extent to which each provides a "living income" to all the players, including the farmers. Which would you purchase?

What Does All This Mean for Leadership?

When Frances Hesselbein asked me to write this article, she asked the sort of simple but penetrating question that those of us who know her recognize as her leadership gift. "Are the basic fundamentals for sound leadership the same and we are just responding to a different world, or are the fundamentals shifting?" After some thought, my response is an unequivocal, "Yes."

For me the fundamentals start with a set of deep capacities with which few in leadership positions today could claim to be adept: systems intelligence;[19] building partnership across boundaries; and openness on three levels: head, heart, and will. To develop such capacities requires a lifelong commitment to grow as a human being in ways not well understood in contemporary culture. Yet in other ways, these are the foundations for leadership that have been understood for a very long time. Unfortunately, this ancient knowledge has been largely lost in the modern era.

Systems Intelligence

Problems like those created by our global food systems are largely invisible because people do not know how to see such systems. "The inability of leaders to see the systems and patterns of interdependency within and surrounding our organizations threatens our future," says Ford's CIO and head of strategy, Marv Adams. "Many big problems that could be solved are sitting there unsolved because of this failure."[20]

Two particular systems thinking skills are vital: *seeing patterns of interdependency* and *seeing into the future*. It is one thing to say that "we are interdependent," and it is another to actually understand what this means, especially for problems created by the present systems that no one knows how to solve. Before the members of the Food Lab could work effectively together, they needed to share understanding of the forces driving the "race to the bottom" and how they were all part of these forces: as companies pursuing "business-as-usual" business models with little regard for the effects on farming families and communities or on environmental systems, as farmers unable to moderate pressures for continual production growth, and all of us as consumers whenever we buy food at the cheapest price with little thought as to where the food comes from.

Once people start to see systemic patterns and understand the forces driving a system, they also start to see where the system is headed *if* nothing changes. The power of the "race to the bottom" metaphor for the Food Lab participants is that it helps everyone think about what "the bottom" means to them, and to realize why this is not a future in which they want to live.

"Seeing into the future" is not a prediction in the statistical sense; it is simply seeing how a system is functioning and where it is headed. For example, today the world is in desperate need of seeing into the future regarding CO_2 emissions and climate change because of the inability of leaders to sift through confusing scientific data from a systems perspective. Given the rate of CO_2 emissions as described earlier, stabilizing carbon dioxide in the atmosphere will require a global reduction in emissions of *more than 70 percent*. This is far beyond any targets embedded in existing multilateral agreements, such as the Kyoto protocols.[21] If enough people could grasp this simple fact, the sense of public urgency for accelerating the transition to a post-fossil-fuel energy system would shift significantly. But unfortunately, few leaders in business or government yet understand this. This is a massive failure of leadership foresight.

Building Partnerships Across Boundaries

In some ways the most challenging aspect of the Food Lab has been simply getting such diverse actors to actually be willing to work together. "Doing something about sustainable agriculture will require bringing parties together that normally do not cooperate," says Andre van Heemstra, recently retired member of the Unilever management board.[22] This not only means diverse businesses collaborating across complex supply chains, it means leaders from NGOs and government, who normally would never work with business counterparts.

Transforming larger systems will not arise from the traditional transactional relationships that characterize interactions among business, government, and NGO. "The relationships among leaders across normal boundaries might be the most crucial ingredient to major change," says Hal Hamilton, director of the Sustainable Food Lab.[23] Building genuine partnerships takes time and real commitment. It is not just that those who might form potential partnerships have never worked together. It is that they have mostly fought each other, often seeing the other as a primary obstacle to progress as they defined it. When they have interacted, it has been almost entirely to negotiate with one another to achieve their individual aims. It took many months of close work in a process that fostered deep reflection and candor before participants in the Food

Lab found themselves developing real connections, trust, and respect for each other, gradually recognizing that their strength as a team came from their differences.

This same challenge of working with those who are very different from us arises within organizations as well. "Organizations are coercive systems," as Edgar Schein says.[24] They tend to enforce a "party line," even when they do not do this overtly but subtly. Listening to the "periphery," those who do not share the views of the management mainstream, is a skill that more and more leaders will need because, increasingly, the management mainstream will have only limited understanding at best of the forces shaping change.

Partnering with those different from us is also becoming more important as organizations become increasingly networked. Reflecting on her experiences as a black woman in a major global corporation, Ilean Galloway of Intel sees that the "diversity challenge" for the future involves more than just hiring and promotion practices, though these remain important. "One of the big changes I've seen is the need to work with people who are very different from you." Traditionally, people tended to work "in small homogeneous circles, but now the circles are getting much bigger. If I am uncomfortable working with my Chinese colleague, or he with me, the networks that form will preclude good solutions to our problems."[25]

Openness

Leaders who can build partnerships for seeing larger systems must also be open to not having all the answers. There is no "right model" for a complex system. For all intents and purposes, the global food system is infinitely complex. Good system models like those used in the Food Lab are by their nature incomplete and flawed. The criteria by which they must be judged is usefulness, not absolute accuracy.

This means that effective leaders must cultivate open mindedness, in order to continually challenge their own favored views and to learn how to embrace multiple points of view in the service of building shared understanding and commitment. This is easy to say but extraordinarily difficult to do. The Sustainable Food Lab was designed so that its members have to continually face their very different ways of seeing. For example, after a visit with a small farmers cooperative, a list of observations from the team included "hard working," "very political," "not sustainable," "very sustainable," "needs to be modernized," "needs time to mature," and "an excellent model." One lab team member commented, "I am so amazed that this number of people can look at the same thing and see something so different. . . . There is so much I don't understand about others' perspectives."

But open minds ultimately also require open hearts, becoming vulnerable to seeing how we are all part of the problem. If people do not see how they are part of the problem, they will remain in a "blaming" mode and never tap the deeper forces for change. Their attitude will always be that "they need to change," an especially disempowering signal when it comes from leaders at the top of the organization. For example, Unilever and Oxfam recently formed a historic joint project to assess the success of Unilever's efforts to reduce poverty in Indonesia. The team from the two organizations worked together for over a year, including an intense half-year period to jointly author a summary report.[26] During this time they also learned a lot about their own defenses that limited learning. "We gradually discovered," according to one member of the Oxfam team, "that whenever there was a breakdown in communication, the Unilever people would go into 'corporate speak,' talking about all the wonderful things they were doing, and we [Oxfam] would assume the 'moral high ground.' After a while, we would all just laugh at ourselves and go back to work."

The third opening, of the will, involves discovering that our deepest commitments arise almost despite ourselves. It involves letting go of the last remnants of what Otto Sharmer calls "our small 's' self" and letting come "the future that comes into being through us and with what we are here to do."[27] This opening has been described by countless poets and mystics—indeed it is one of the oldest and most universal aspects of diverse spiritual traditions. It is what George Bernard Shaw called "the true joy in life, the being used for a purpose you regard as a mighty one."[28] Or as one of the Food Lab team members said, "We had come to a profound place of connection, with one another and with what we are here to do."

Speaking in ways like this may seem romantic for today's times, but the subtle developmental processes behind these three openings have been understood for a very long while, and the loss of them may be a major reason we now struggle. In the famous "The Great Learning," Confucius described "seven meditative spaces" through which those seeking to become leaders must pass in letting go of old ideas and identities and coming to a place of stillness and peace where the mind no longer imposes itself on reality.[29] He summarized by saying that to become a leader, "One must first become a human being." The meaning of this simple assertion remains hidden so long as we think we understand humanness. However, if we regard the human as a great mystery, if we understand humanness as being connected to the universe in ways that we can barely imagine, if we believe that the journey to discover and actualize who we are *is* the journey of our lifetimes, then there may be some chance that the leadership required for this new millennium will come forward.

Endnotes

1. A. P. de Geus, "Planning as Learning," *Harvard Business Review*, March-April 1988, 74–78.

2. A Shell study directed by de Geus in the mid-1980s found that the majority of highly successful Fortune 500–size companies around the world failed to survive beyond a few generations of management. Despite enormous resources and talent, "signals that their world was changing failed to penetrate the internal management worldview." This finding was popularized a decade later by Jack Welch as, "when the rate of change inside an institution becomes slower than the rate of change outside, the end is in sight (GE 2000 Annual Report).

3. J. Diamond, *Collapse: How Societies Choose to Fail or Succeed* (New York: Viking Books, 2005).

4. Mieko Nishimizu, "Looking Back, Leaping Forward," keynote address, The 50th Anniversary of Japan's Bretton Woods Membership symposium, Tokyo, September 10, 2002.

5. See J. R. Petit et. al, "Climate and Atmospheric History from the last 420,000 years from the Vostok Ice Core by an Inverse Method," *Nature*, 1999, 399, 429–436. The UN Global Climate Change Commission estimated total carbon sequestration at roughly half global emissions in 2001 ("Climate Change 2001: The Scientific Basis. Summary for Policymakers." A report of Working Group I of the Intergovernmental Panel on Climate Change, available at www.grida.no/climate/ipcc_tar/wg1/005.htm.), but many scientists claim this is too high due to saturation of many of the "carbon sinks" combined with continued deforestation. *Scientific American* (September 2005) estimates placed long-term carbon sequestration rate at only about 20 percent of global emissions in 2004.

6. See W. McDonough and M. Braungart, *Cradle to Cradle: Remaking the Way We Make Things* (New York: North Point Press, 2002); and W. McDonough, M. Braungart, P. T. Anastas, and J. B. Zimmerman, "Applying the Principles of Green Engineering to Cradle-to-Cradle Design," *Environmental Science and Technology*, 2003, 37(23), 434A–441A.

7. Surprisingly, many of the EU mandates have quickly become de facto global standards, because of the global integration of business. Automakers who design and manufacture cars from "common platforms" around the world find that if they remove mercury from switches for Europe, they do likewise for cars sold elsewhere—because it is uneconomic to do otherwise. This raises the prospect that large trading blocks may have impact far beyond their legal borders.

8. P. Hawken, *The Ecology of Commerce* (New York: HarperCollins, 1993).

9. *Rigged Rules and Double Standards: Trade, Globalisation and the Fight Against Poverty* (Oxford: Oxfam, April 2002).

10. F. Dixon, "Wal-Mart: Making Sustainability Mainstream," December 5, 2005 (working paper: available from fdixon@innovestgroup.com).

11. F. Dixon, "Total Corporate Responsibility: Achieving Sustainability and Real Prosperity," *Ethical Corporation Magazine*, December 2003, www.ethicalcorp.com.

12. Dixon, "Wal-Mart."

13. See marinestewardshipcouncil.org.

14. In the speech, Browne stated that the time "to consider the policy dimensions of climate change is when the possibility cannot be discounted and is taken seriously by the society of which we are a part . . .", adding, "We in BP have reached that point." Today BP is a leader in the use of solar power as well as a variety of technologies to reduce emissions from oil production and use. (See also J. Browne, "The Carbon Challenge," *Foreign Affairs*, July-August 2004.)

15. Dixon, "Total Corporate Responsibility."

16. "Mugged: Poverty in Your Coffee Cup," Oxfam International, September 2002, available from advocacy@oxfaminternational.org or www.maketradefair.org.

17. Overproduction and depressed prices are further exacerbated by $500 billion dollars worth of agricultural subsidies in the rich northern countries, keeping more excess production on the market.

18. One of the problems with which they are wrestling is the proliferation of "sustainability": standards that are inconsistent with one another.

19. This is a term I have borrowed from colleagues Raimo Hamalainen and Esa Saarinen. See "Systems Intelligence: Discovering a Hidden Competence in Human Action and Organizational Life," available at www.sal.hut.fi/Publications/r-index.html.

20. P. Senge, *The Fifth Discipline*, rev. ed. (New York: Doubleday, 2006).

21. If all countries agreed to the Kyoto protocols, CO_2 emissions would plateau at roughly their 1990 levels, roughly 90 percent of present global emissions. This would mean that CO_2 concentration in the atmosphere would grow forever!

22. Senge, *The Fifth Discipline*, 353.

23. Senge, *The Fifth Discipline*, 357.

24. D. L. Coutu, "The Anxiety of Learning," *Harvard Business Review*, March 2002, 80(3), 100–106.

25. Senge, *The Fifth Discipline*.

26. "Exploring the Links Between International Business and Poverty Reduction: A Case Study of Unilever in Indonesia," an Oxfam GB, Novib, Unilever, and Unilever Indonesia joint research project (Information Press, Eynsham, UK, 2005). Available from the Oxfam UK Website: www.oxfam.uk.org.

27. See for example, P. Senge, O. Scharmer, J. Jaworski, and B. Flowers, *Presence* (New York: Doubleday, 2005).

28. George Bernard Shaw, quoted in Senge, *The Fifth Discipline*, 137.

29. See Senge, Scharmer, Jaworski, and Flowers, *Presence*, or O. Scharmer, "The Seven Meditative Spaces of Leadership Cultivation: Interview with Master Nan Huai Chin," available at dialoguesonleadership.net.

3

Diversity Management
An Essential Craft for Future Leaders

R. Roosevelt Thomas Jr.

Over the past twenty years, Dr. R. Roosevelt Thomas Jr. has been at the forefront of developing strategies for maximizing organizational and individual potential through diversity management. He currently serves as CEO of Roosevelt Thomas Consulting & Training, Inc., and as president of The American Institute for Managing Diversity (AIMD). Dr. Thomas is the author of five published books; his most recent is Building on the Promise of Diversity: How We Can Move to the Next Level in Our Workplace, Our Communities, and Our Society *(October 2005). Dr. Thomas has been recognized by the* Wall Street Journal *as one of the top ten consultants in the country, and cited by* Human Resource Executive *as one of HR's "Most Influential People."*

The idea of diversity in business has undergone rapid change over the past several decades. Although in the early 1960s use of the term in the business world was virtually nonexistent, diversity has rapidly made the transition from a necessary evil to a competitive advantage for the businesses that manage it effectively—an advantage that no successful leader today can ignore.

For twenty years I have been involved as a diversity consultant, researcher, and author. Now, as never before, I see the need to broaden and redefine our ideas about and behaviors around diversity. Indeed, what happens in the next decade will be crucial in determining whether America's organizations and its leaders move forward in their efforts to create cohesive, effective, and globally competitive entities, or simply "muddle through." Diversity management is a key business skill for leaders of the future, and it will have an enormous impact on their success—and on the success of their organizations.

Rethinking Diversity

Putting diversity to work effectively requires a complete rethinking of the complex concepts behind this simple word. But why now? Aren't current definitions of diversity doing the job?

Actually, they aren't. Business leaders and diversity professionals alike are increasingly concerned that the field is stuck on ideas of "representation" and "relationships"—constructs that have been with us since the mid-1960s. All are asking, "Isn't there more to diversity than 'counting' and 'getting along?'"

The evidence is that there must be. But truth be told, the current reality shows that there is much room for improvement. Cynicism has crept into many organizational diversity efforts and, as a result, some observers place little faith in the true motivation driving their implementation. They often believe that such efforts are being made only to protect the organization from legal or public relations embarrassments, not to bring about needed change.

I do not believe that America's leaders will remain content with paradigms and programs that foster cynicism and discontent. They have consistently risen to important challenges, and I am convinced that they will rise to this one as well.

Ten Expectations for the Future

I have identified ten expectations for what diversity practices might look like in the future. While I cannot precisely predict the rate of evolution, I am confident that these expectations will become reality for tomorrow's organizations—and for their leaders.

1. Future leaders will differentiate between representation and diversity. *Representation* will refer to the presence of multiple races and both genders in the workplace, while *diversity* will refer to the

differences, similarities, and tensions that can and do exist between the elements of these different mixtures of people.

This approach will be quite different from current practice, which focuses discussions about diversity on representation. The emphasis on representation is evident in most diversity best-practices lists, in which the selection criteria are centered on representation ("the numbers") and relationships ("awareness and sensitivity").

In the future, leaders will be forced to make this differentiation. Leaders in the 1960s and 1970s accepted race and gender representation but assumed that nontraditional entrants to the workforce would conform their behavior to existing norms. But as we have seen, increased representation has been accompanied by increased *behavioral* diversity, as well.

Leaders who fail to address these differences and similarities (in areas such as personal style, thought processes, personality, and the like) will lose their representation gains as behaviorally diverse employees seek out employers that offer a more welcoming environment. Leaders who recognize, however, that they must manage representation *and* diversity will gain a competitive edge by fully accessing the potential of *all* of their associates.

2. Future leaders will not think in terms of "diversity," nor will they see it as an extension of the Civil Rights Movement. Instead, they will think in terms of diversity *management* and view it as a craft—one that can complement traditional civil rights initiatives that focus efforts solely on issues of race and gender. And they will see this new craft of diversity management as one that is applicable to *any* diverse mixture of people in any workplace.

While some see this as a radical change to the status quo, it actually is not. In fact, this change will be more congruent with the historic reality that the origins of the modern concept of diversity can be traced back to applications preceding the relatively recent emphasis on civil rights. My own introduction to the topic, for example, was as a doctoral student studying functional diversity in corporate settings. The key question then was, How can you have functions appropriately differentiated to match their different task environments, yet also effectively integrate them into a cohesive, purpose-driven whole?

The way researchers attempted to answer this question was by focusing their efforts on finding ways to achieve cohesiveness in the midst of differences, similarities, and tensions. These challenges, of course, parallel the traditional ones facing the Civil Rights Movement with respect to race and gender, for which the key question has been, How do we foster the mainstreaming of African Americans and women, while simultaneously achieving and maintaining a cohesive, patriotic whole?

3. Future leaders will define *diversity management* as "making quality decisions in the midst of differences, similarities, and related tensions." As such, they cannot help but become aware of this craft's ability to help them understand and unravel complex situations, and they will count on it when approaching situations in which diverse perceptions, purposes, and people come into play. And this will be true not only when the issue is race and gender complexity, but also for the complexity created by other diverse mixtures of people such as customers, acquisitions and mergers, functions, products, and geographic business locations.

4. Future leaders will not automatically assume that all racially inappropriate behavior is caused by racism. They will recognize that people can have difficulty making the right decisions in the midst of differences, similarities, and tensions for reasons other than bias.

For example, the white male senior executive who prefers his white male friends when selecting direct reports may do so because of comfort and trust considerations, and not because of racism or sexism. However, the fact that his consistent avoidance of minorities and women is not driven by bias does not make his behavior any more acceptable.

5. In contrast to today, future leaders will be more willing to admit to having difficulty making decisions in highly diverse organizations. They will also be more comfortable discussing specific

ways in which they are challenged by particular types of diversity. As a result, difficulty with diversity will less likely be seen as a moral offense and more likely be seen as managerial uncertainty or ineffectiveness—particularly in those instances in which the "isms" are not the undergirding factors.

6. As noted, future leaders will come to recognize diversity management as a craft. As a craft, they will be motivated to master it and its key components. Diversity management concepts and fundamental dynamics, while unfamiliar to many, are not that difficult to learn. More difficult are the tasks of achieving diversity maturity and acquiring and practicing the requisite skills.

The relationship between diversity management skills and diversity maturity parallels the relationship between driving skills and driving maturity. As a youth of twelve, I had driving skills (the abilities to see over the hood, reach the pedals, and hold the car in the road), but I did not possess driving maturity (wisdom, judgment, and experience required for effective use of my driving skills) until my early twenties. I gained the maturity by practicing driving and observing the automobile experiences of youthful colleagues.

Neither diversity skills nor diversity maturity can be achieved without practice. In accepting the need for such practice, future leaders will depart from current thinking. They will not expect that a single training session ranging from two to eight hours in length can provide the necessary capability. Simply, it cannot.

7. Future leaders, experienced in the diversity management craft, will become more comfortable with tension and complexity. This will make a remarkable difference in their organizations and with their employees. We all have witnessed the ineffectiveness of individuals who are uncomfortable with diversity and with the complexity of human dynamics that results. But tension and complexity are a natural part of life and often cannot (and should not) be avoided. Indeed, avoiding complexity may appear to reduce tensions, but it does so at the risk of distortion of reality and ineffectiveness. Keeping it simple is okay if it *is* simple, but often it's not.

The craft of diversity management provides a methodology for making quality decisions in the presence of organizational tension and complexity. While diversity management will not necessarily increase leaders' comfort level with tension and complexity, it will help them become more comfortable with being uncomfortable. For them, manifestations of tension and complexity will not mean that progress toward mission and vision is impossible or impeded.

8. As leaders around the world begin to face their own diversity issues, future leaders will make diversity management a global craft as opposed to one confined just to the United States or the countries in which they live. Leaders will use the craft both within and across borders as globalization becomes ever more the norm.

Today, leaders outside of the United States often see diversity management as a phenomenon related to this country's unique struggle with race and slavery. As a result, they believe it is irrelevant to their own national circumstances. However, as recent clashes resulting from increasing immigrant frictions within many European countries and other places has shown, diversity management is not solely the concern of American leaders. Decoupling diversity from the Civil Rights Movement's agenda will help to generate clarity about the true nature of diversity and diversity management.

9. Future leaders will be more strategic in their approach to diversity and diversity management. Decisions as to where to focus attention and how to respond to diversity issues will depend on an organization's mission, vision, and strategy. Accordingly, what will be appropriate in one setting may not be in another if differences exist with respect to mission, vision, and strategy. Strategic context will be defining.

10. As future leaders master the application of the craft of diversity management in their workplaces, they will inevitably turn their attention to diversity issues within their communities and within their countries. In the United States, for example, this will mean addressing the various divides we experience along at least the following lines: race, class, ethnicity, gender, politics, geography, and religion.

An understanding of the diversity management craft will provide an approach that leaders and the rank-and-file citizenry can use to work through diversity challenges. Use of the craft won't eliminate the divides, but it will provide the capability for addressing them when and wherever they threaten the ability to achieve local or national goals.

This capability will enhance the likelihood of achieving a natural cohesive, purpose-driven unity in spite of our divisions. For the United States and indeed all countries, such a contribution would be enormous.

Evidence of Change

What makes me think that our approach to diversity and its management will change? The fact that it is changing now. The future is surfacing as I write.

Diversity professionals who historically have relied primarily on benchmarking to determine what to do next are backing away from this practice. Instead, they are less likely to assume that the answers exist, waiting to be discovered. They are more inclined to rethink the basic assumptions that have guided their efforts in the past in hopes that doing so will lead to different and more effective alternatives. Stated differently, they are more willing to pioneer and less inclined to play follow-the-leader.

Still another example of change is evident as shown in one global corporation's approach to global diversity training. When discussing an upcoming training session for managers from a variety of countries, company leaders asked that my colleagues and I not use the word *diversity*. They felt that it did not work for individuals outside the United States.

We agreed to the company's request, offering *complexity* as an alternative. They agreed to the change, and we then went through our materials and systematically replaced every appearance of the word *diversity* with *complexity*. The result was a rich experience—with learnings and understandings far beyond what we typically encounter—that highlighted the depth of the notion of "diversity," even more so than if we had used the word.

Summary

While we have made significant progress in our journey over the past several decades, we have not yet reached our ultimate destination. Clearly, much needs to be done if my expectations of the future of diversity management are to be realized. And there will be opposition, particularly in the willingness to uncouple diversity management from the Civil Rights Movement and social justice agenda.

Yet, I believe that this uncoupling should occur, and that it will occur. It is time for the diversity focus to shift from a concept centered on race and gender, the Civil Rights Movement, and social justice, to a craft that leaders can use to make quality decisions in the midst of organizational differences, similarities, tensions, and complexities.

The more quickly leaders can differentiate between diversity management and the social justice agenda, the more rapid will be the speed of the shift. This differentiation will be expedited once civil rights advocates recognize that the mastery and application of the diversity management craft can facilitate minimization of social injustices. I therefore anticipate that diversity management will become a valued complement to traditional civil rights initiatives as opposed to compromising or replacing them.

4

Ten Things I Learned About Leadership from Women Executive Directors of Color

Jan Masaoka

Jan Masaoka is executive director of CompassPoint Nonprofit Services, a nonprofit consulting firm working with community-based and community-led organizations, especially those serving vulnerable populations and in communities of color. CompassPoint consults, trains, researches, convenes, and publishes in the areas of community and nonprofit leadership, nonprofit boards, executive transition, and sustainability. Jan Masaoka also writes the Board Café, *an electronic newsletter for nonprofit boards with forty-four-thousand subscribers. More information on the Women Executive Directors of Color Network and about CompassPoint can be found at www.compasspoint.org.*

What's different about being a woman nonprofit leader who is also an executive director and a woman of color? We are asked, What are the special challenges? In that very question lies the assumption that being a woman executive of color is about facing more "special" challenges. In fact, women of color may have faced more challenges in the sector than white women (and different challenges than men of color), but such backgrounds also grow powerful skills and attributes to bring to the executive director job.

The women leaders of color that I know are acutely conscious of the moment-to-moment impact on others of their gender, race,

Michelle Gislason assisted with this article.

nationality, age, and personal styles. They pay attention both to working within common perceptions and making use of the ability to bend those perceptions. Nearly all of the research and literature in the nonprofit sector on leadership either assumes a largely white population (which is true), or tries to be color-blind and "transcend" race issues. When I was asked to submit a chapter for this book, it seemed appropriate to look at and speak to a small but rapidly growing company of women executive directors of color.

Women Executive Directors of Color is a loose network in the San Francisco Bay Area, convened by CompassPoint Nonprofit Services, where I work. As the executive director of CompassPoint and a Japanese American woman, I enjoy being part of this network and have come to think that being a "WEDOC" is also a state of mind.

Not all women executive directors of color will agree with all of the following points. They are what *I* have learned from listening, observing, and laughing with these comrades over these years.

1. *Note to funders: Give us (unrestricted) money.* Give us the chance to experiment, to make mistakes, to sleep at night, and to take the time to nurture leaders within our organizations. I remember one meeting of about thirty women executive directors of color at which we talked about what we might ask for as a group. Should we ask a foundation for a special speaker? For a weekend at a retreat center? For a facilitator? For tuitions to expensive leadership development programs? After a long pause, one woman spoke up: "Give us money."

One of the biggest challenges that leaders face is responding to various constituencies, and nonprofit leaders work hard to manage funding to do so. Working with restricted grants and government contracts is like having fifteen part-time jobs—with each employer designating which type of your expenses your salary can be used to pay for. It's not just the disproportionate expense in accounting that makes this practice harmful to leaders and to organizations; it's the constant contortionism, wheedling, spinning, and fitting mismatched and incomplete pieces into an organization that will change the world.

To support leaders you believe in, invest in their organizations. The tool we lack for *exercising* our leadership skills is so often *money*—to give raises, to hire a COO or a development director, to spend time in community leadership roles, to investigate opportunities, to write, to meet with government officials—in short, to lead.

2. *The strongest leaders have worked in the fields and have hard as well as soft skills.* Women leaders frequently share a generosity of spirit and soft skills such as facilitation and active listening. But in those I admire most, that generosity and those soft skills are informed by hard-won technical skills and by first-hand experience at the street level. They have handled kids who are out of control, then turned around and advocated for them. They have fired people for using drugs in a drug counseling center. They practiced law before working in a housing organization. Hard-won skills show, whether in social work, finance, science, community organizing, or nursing.

"Try not to be a success," said Albert Einstein; "try to be of value." A lesson for young people who want to be leaders: start in the fields.

3. *Leadership lingo is tolerated by real leaders, but less frequently embraced.* Theories, models, and programs on leadership abound, but are often academic, corporate, pseudo-religious, or infused with pop psychology, or even cross the line into psychotherapy. Many days it seems like the language of yet another world to be navigated. One long-time woman executive director of color went to a leadership development conference and commented, "They were almost all young and white and I had no idea what they were talking about." Women executives of color respond best when leadership language is direct, practical, applicable, and relevant—their personal journeys are toward getting the work done well.

4. *Being a woman of color is both an asset and an obstacle to success, and leaders focus on the positive.* A study of women executive directors of color showed that women executive directors do face obstacles related to gender and race, but that there are advantages as well.[1] For organizations that serve people of color, an executive director from that same community is clearly an asset. Such executives

quickly gain trust from staff and constituents, and they are well-positioned to represent their organizations to the broader community. Especially for women of color leading mainstream organizations, rarity can be turned to advantage. "I work in the environmental field," said one. "I tend to stand out."

For me, the lesson is that race, gender, and age (like any attribute, for that matter) bring with them advantages and disadvantages. "Something offensive to me as an African American hits me every time I walk into the school district building," commented one leader. But rather than focus on negatives, successful leaders figure out how to make every attribute work for them. This same leader comments, "Being African American, I know how to deal with them and get what I need for my families."

5. *When we observe leaders, there's a lot we don't know.* At a meeting with a foundation, I remember another nonprofit executive—a white man with an M.B.A.—bringing useful insights into the discussion that he had gained from his dinner the night before with his wife and her coworkers at a think tank. At the end of the meeting, a woman executive director of color I chatted with as we were leaving told me she was struggling to take care of her nephew, whom she had recently taken in because her sister was on drugs. The juxtaposition reminded me of two realities: that we never know what personal lives lie behind the professionals we know, and that people from low-income families often bear responsibilities invisible to their professional colleagues.

We want to value both the theoretical insights and the life experience—each more easily accessed by some people than others. How do we bring both into our work?

6. *Over-hiring is a danger both to organizations and to leaders.* But it's not always easy to tell when over-hiring is happening.

In any group of managers, you're likely to find some who have been hired into jobs beyond their capabilities. This is also true among women executive directors of color. Perhaps the board members, in a hurry to hire, have let wishful thinking about a young, inexperienced candidate cloud their judgment. Not only do such over-hired executives often disappoint their organizations, their careers and achievements can be hurt. One foundation executive— herself a woman of color—commented about a young woman of color who was looking for a job, "She was in over her head on her last job, but now she's been spoiled into thinking she can move up from there."

7. *Underestimating young talent is also a danger.* At a very early get-together of women executive directors of color, one of the participants was a nineteen-year-old woman named Lateefah Simon, who was three weeks into a job as executive director of San Francisco's Center for Young Women's Development. "You could be getting set up to fail," we older executives told her. One even suggested she quit right now. Seven years later, still on the job, she was awarded a MacArthur Foundation "genius" award for her work.

On the Rise, the CompassPoint study of women executive directors of color, showed that a remarkable 43 percent were hired from within the organization—compared to 36 percent of executive directors in general.[2] One possible reason for this: when board members have had time to become comfortable with a woman of color, they are more likely to hire her than they would be to consider someone of comparable experience they don't know.

8. *Listen to all the advice, and keep your own counsel.* Leaders get a lot of advice—from everybody. One of the benefits of working in a nonprofit organization is "continuous access to free (and unsolicited) advice from management experts in business and government."[3]

We might add: "And from people in foundations, government, and leadership development programs." And a lot of this advice is so abstract it is inadvertently patronizing. "Be bold." "Take risks." "Focus on outcomes." "Trust yourself." One exec commented, "Back when I was a journalist and sitting on boards I used to give advice to the executive director. Then I became one, and people started giving *me* advice like, 'Keep your eyes on the prize.' I realized how obnoxious I had been before."

Learning from my colleagues, I try to accept every piece of advice into my heart as a message, no matter how trite and no matter who it comes from, as a truth for the moment.

9. *Fire drills are a fact of life.* Just as our Women Executive Directors of Color conference was about to begin at the Levi Strauss Corporation, there was a fire drill and the building was evacuated. It interrupted the conference and confused the opening, but it was all fine, and fire drills are a good thing. No one in the group got agitated, and we all got acquainted standing on the sidewalk. In other words, stuff happens. It's how you respond to it that defines you as a leader.

10. *Leaders—and everyone—appreciate articles that are brief.*

Endnotes

1. *On the Rise: A Profile of Women of Color in Leadership.* San Francisco: CompassPoint Nonprofit Services, 2002.

2. *On the Rise.*

3. Phil Anthrop, "Why Save $100 Billion When You Can Save $500 Billion?" *Nonprofit Quarterly,* Summer 2003.

5

How Cosmopolitan Leaders Inspire Confidence
A Profile of the Future

Rosabeth Moss Kanter

Rosabeth Moss Kanter holds the Ernest L. Arbuckle Chaired Professorship at Harvard Business School, where she specializes in strategy, innovation, and leadership for change. Her strategic and practical insights have guided leaders of large and small organizations worldwide for over twenty-five years, through teaching, writing, and direct consultation to major corporations and governments. The former editor of Harvard Business Review (1989–1992), Professor Kanter is the author of sixteen books, which have been translated into seventeen languages. Her most recent bestseller is Confidence: How Winning Streaks and Losing Streaks Begin and End. *Other best-selling books include* The Change Masters, *named by the* Financial Times *as one of the hundred most influential management books of the twentieth century,* When Giants Learn to Dance, World Class, *and* Evolve. *She has received twenty-two honorary doctoral degrees and the Academy of Management's highest award.*

L eaders of the future will be progressively more cosmopolitan, innovative, diverse, and values-oriented. They increasingly will come from countries with enormous growth potential outside of North America and Europe, such as the BRIC nations (Brazil, Russia,

India, and China), places where leaders also must address daunting obstacles such as poverty or environmental degradation, regardless of the sector or the focus of their enterprise.

In short, these leaders will resemble Fabio Barbosa.

Senhor Barbosa, together with Maria Luiza Pinto and the rest of the leadership team in which he places his confidence, has led a come-from-behind Brazilian bank into a "winning streak"—a success cycle that fuels both internal and external confidence in the bank's ability to create value. The team at ABN Amro Real is applying enduring skills to complex new challenges, leading their bank to address social and environmental problems with non-governmental organization (NGO) partners, and thereby creating a model for the future of global capitalism.

Before exploring the nature of these enduring skills, let's see how Fabio and colleagues fit the profile of the leader of the future.

The New Face of Leadership

Born in Brazil, Fabio Colletti Barbosa earned his M.B.A. degree from IMD in Switzerland. He began his career in finance with Nestlé in Switzerland, the United States, and Brazil; joined Citicorp; and rose through the ranks before becoming president of a Brazilian bank and, in 1995, joining the Brazilian unit of ABN Amro, a Dutch multinational. He became president a year later, shepherding the acquisition of a large domestic bank in 1998 to form ABN Amro Real, the company he has headed as CEO ever since.

His colleagues are equally cosmopolitan, and they work as a team. COO Jose Luiz Majolo had experience at five multinational banks (three American, one British, and one Dutch) before joining Barbosa at ABN Amro Real in 1998. Also Brazilian born and bred, Maria Luiza de Oliveira Pinto studied at the University of Michigan in the United States and worked at the Japanese company Sharp before bringing her HR skills to banking. She worked in the Netherlands at ABN Amro's Dutch headquarters as well as in Brazil. Eventually she became head of the Education and Sustainable Development Directorate, a new position at the top of the Brazilian bank.

This group of bankers has built the confidence to convert societal challenges into opportunities for business innovation. In a large, emerging, but troubled nation, with over a quarter of the population living on less than $2 a day and high rates of illiteracy, they have taken an unusual step, certainly for Brazil but also for companies anywhere. They chose to emphasize corporate, social, and environmental responsibility as a central part of the bank's brand, attempting to differentiate the bank in the marketplace not only by close customer relationships but also by the values reflected in their products and services. This led to actions and services such as socioenvironmental screening for credit analysis, environmentally focused products (such as a loan for converting cars to emit less greenhouse gas), micro-finance for poor entrepreneurs in the *favelas* (shantytowns) of major cities, an "ethical" mutual fund, socioenvironmental tests for suppliers, internal reduction of waste and recycling, and a major commitment to workforce diversity and diversity training.

Fabio Barbosa made clear from the beginning that he was not establishing a "green bank." Traditional measures of financial performance were important, and the bank has met those high standards. Net profit doubled from 2000 to 2004, and return on equity was at least 15 percent each year. By 2004, ABN Amro Real had become the fourth largest nongovernment bank in Brazil, the third major market for its Dutch parent (after the Netherlands and the United States), and fifteenth on the list of Brazil's most-admired companies (up from number 153 in 2003). In a national survey, 21 percent of customers said that Real would be their bank of choice if they were switching, second only to a much larger, well-known bank; and commercial customers that did switch often indicated they were attracted to the bank's values.

To support the efforts to combine value and values, ABN Amro Real partners with numerous NGOs, such as Friends of the Earth,

Greenpeace, Ethos Institute, and the World Bank, asking them to assess progress or provide training for bank staff. ABN Amro Real was chosen by the World Bank to administer a large loan pool for development projects, a first for Brazil. Taking partnership a step further, Maria Luiza and her colleagues convened suppliers to meet with NGOs and consider joint projects. The supplier mobilization committee, working with Maria Luiza's team, first invited fifteen very diverse companies, ranging from IBM to small local service suppliers, to join with ABN Amro Real in embracing corporate social responsibility. Among the projects that resulted, a coalition of companies created two training centers to teach computer skills to young people from economically disadvantaged communities.

The openness of dialogue Fabio fosters is unusual in a region that is still shaking off the legacy of an authoritarian past, where it is said that hierarchical privilege still reigns. The social responsibility theme, Banco de Valor (Bank of Value), was adopted after open brainstorming by the executive team, sharpened by a self-assessment based on NGO guidelines, and refined through educational sessions for nearly two thousand managers and employees. The bank went public with its commitments, and Fabio acted as a role model for transparency. When he received a letter from a disgruntled customer who questioned the bank's talk of making capitalism more humane and inclusive in light of high interest rates, he invited her to their headquarters. A partial transcript of their conversation was published in a bank report, *Human and Economic Values, Together*. Fabio calls dissent a source of hope for improvement.

Employee participation, creativity, and development are encouraged. In 2003 alone, nearly eighty thousand e-learning sessions took place. Communication is abundant, and employee ideas are solicited. Not surprisingly, employee satisfaction is high. Surveys in 2003 showed that 95 percent of the staff said they are proud of working for the bank, and 93 percent said that they trust in the communication they receive from the company. The bank is routinely high on lists of the best places to work in Brazil and the best companies for women.

The bank's leadership is a model for the country and the world. As vice president of the Brazilian banking federation, Fabio Barbosa has influenced other banks to adopt similar practices. ABN Amro is using the Brazilian success as a model for its growing operations in India. It was widely rumored that Fabio Barbosa, respected as a public figure, had been the Brazilian president's first choice to serve as economic minister (with Fabio declining in order to stay with the bank). ABN Amro Real has not only succeeded itself, it has helped improve the image of banks and the free market system in a region that often tilts toward socialism.

Fabio, Jose Luiz, and Maria Luiza are cosmopolitan, entrepreneurial, collaborative, values-driven, and performance-oriented bankers accountable to shareholders as well as other stakeholders. They lead beyond the boundaries of their organization to improve the community around them and to engage partners in improving the entire ecosystem, social as well as environmental. They care about people, and they provide abundant opportunities for others to lead.

How Cosmopolitan Leaders Deliver Confidence

Top leaders in many countries will soon be more cosmopolitan—international, diverse in culture and gender, and values-oriented. But like Fabio's team, they still will carry out their essential, enduring task: building confidence to master challenges and turn threats or problems into positive results. Values and vision are a starting point, but leaders must develop the vehicles for high performance.

Leaders must deliver confidence at every level: self-confidence, confidence in each other, confidence in the system, and the confidence of external investors and the public so that their support is warranted. Leaders create organizations and cultures that develop confidence in advance of victory, in order to attract the investments that make victory possible—money, talent, support, loyalty, attention, effort, or people's best thinking.

I have seen this kind of leadership not only in American and European companies such as Gillette, Continental Airlines, and the

British Broadcasting Corporation that I worked with for my book *Confidence: How Winning Streaks and Losing Streaks Begin and End*, but also in a range of economic situations throughout the world, in prosperous South Korea as well as Turkey, India, South Africa, or the economically struggling Caribbean. For example, William Clarke, CEO of Scotiabank in Jamaica, resembles Fabio Barbosa in creating a high-performance culture of confidence, based on strong internal professionalism and values of service to Jamaica's poor communities. Clarke, like Barbosa, has his pick of the country's best talent, because they want to work under his leadership.

Leadership is not about the leader, it is about how he or she builds the confidence of everyone else. Leaders certainly need self-confidence. ("Often wrong, never uncertain," Gillette CEO Jim Kilts cheerfully described himself.) Self-confidence helps leaders persist through problems and triumph over troubles. But self-confidence is not the secret of leadership. Leadership involves motivating others to their finest efforts and channeling those efforts in a coherent direction. Leaders must believe that they can count on other people to come through—like a high school principal's faith that inner city children can learn and that her teachers can teach them. If the people in charge rely only on themselves as heroes who can rescue any situation, while focusing on other people's inadequacies, they undermine confidence and reinforce losing streaks. In contrast, when leaders believe in other people, confidence grows, and success becomes more attainable.

Leadership is plural. Mastering the most difficult business or societal challenges is associated with not just one but many leaders— and often, as in the case of ABN Amro Real, leaders operating in collaboration with a range of external partners. Leaders of organizations in success cycles are a little like rabbits, constantly reproducing, just as the team of Fabio, Jose Luiz, and Maria Luiza stimulated leadership throughout the bank. Winning teams and successful organizations become increasingly less dependent on the person called the commander-in-chief—even though, ironically, it is also more likely that the same top managers stay in place during winning streaks, as many people at many levels take on leadership roles.

Cosmopolitan leaders who guide their teams toward success espouse the values of accountability, collaboration, and initiative in their messages to others, model them in their own behavior, and create formal programs and structural mechanisms to embed them in institutions. Consider the following three "ME"s of leadership:

Messages Leaders Espouse. Cosmopolitan leaders articulate standards, values, and visions. They give pep talks. Their messages can incite action when that is appropriate, or they can calm and soothe people to prevent them from panicking. Their messages should provide practical information, inspiration, and a feeling of inclusion, as everyone knows that everyone else heard the same message.

Models Leaders Exemplify. Cosmopolitan leaders serve as role models, leading through the power of personal example. "I don't believe as a leader you can ever expect anybody to do things you are not willing to do yourself," one said. They provide examples of the kinds of accountable, collaborative behavior they seek in others, as Fabio Barbosa did when holding an open dialogue with a critic. Certainly the personal example of truth and reconciliation, inclusion, and empowerment set by Nelson Mandela, South Africa's first democratically elected president, reflected one of the most remarkable and admirable personal journeys of the twentieth century. Turkish CEO Akin Ongor of Garanti Bank was an inspiring business role model with courage, and compassion—offering to resign when he discovered that the bank had lost $14 million due to a junior manager's mistake that control systems had not caught because he said he "shared the mistake," or mobilizing the bank's employees to help in the aftermath of an earthquake in Turkey.

Mechanisms Leaders Establish. Cosmopolitan leaders develop processes, routines, and structures, like the tools, trainings, and ventures at ABN Amro Real. They embed confidence in the culture not just through person-to-person and generation-to-generation transfers of norms but also through the formal mechanisms that embed positive behavior in team and organizational routines. Nelson Mandela's leadership in South Africa was manifested not just through his inspiring message and model but through the structure of a new government, legislation, formal events such as town meetings on a new constitution, and hearings by the Truth and Reconciliation Commission.

Cosmopolitan leaders influence public confidence by their messages and models, which shape an emotional climate and help determine whether expectations are positive or negative, and by their actions—whether they increase or decrease accountability, collaboration, and initiative. In boom times, just as in winning streaks, confidence is carried by the momentum of success. But times of distress are the true test of whether leaders meet the challenge of shaping a culture of confidence.

Nelson Mandela's leadership actions are classic examples of how to convert challenges into opportunities, as he turned around a country that had spiraled into decline because of the racial oppression of apartheid. He and his colleagues made positive choices that set a new model and led people down a new path. Despite having been imprisoned for twenty-seven years under the previous regime, he let go of anger and blame. He rejected victimhood. He promoted accountability, collaboration, and initiative, and this produced renewed confidence on the part of many, inside and outside of the country. The hope he delivered set a climate of positive expectations that changed not only social and political institutions but also the mood and behavior of the population. And those changes encouraged white expatriates to return and restored international investment.

Cosmopolitan leaders define a culture of success or failure by choosing whether to

- Make decisions in secret behind closed doors or use transparent processes involving open debate and dialogue

- Restrict the flow of information or expose facts and communicate them

- Blame problems on external forces or seek solutions by taking actions under one's own control

- Act unilaterally or seek allies and collaborators

- Fuel partisan divides or stress collective goals that unite people

- Underscore suspicion and mistrust of groups that are "different" or promote mutual respect and relationships

- Allow excuses for inaction or encourage initiatives for improvement, however small

- Concentrate resources at the center in the hands of elites or invest in numerous small wins in many places by many people

- Use fear to justify decisions or emphasize sources of hope

Which end of the scale a leader chooses sets the standards for negative or positive behavior, restricts or opens opportunities for action, depresses energy or raises spirits, and influences how much people are willing to invest. Secrecy, blame, revenge, unilateral action, partisan divides, and motivation by fear are, of course, the stuff of losing streaks. Sending messages (explicitly or implicitly) that those phenomena are acceptable, and exemplifying them in policy and practice, tilts the odds toward slipping into decline and losers' habits. This limits the capacity to solve problems and erodes confidence at all levels, from self to system, internally and externally.

Cosmopolitan leaders who guide winning streaks make a different set of choices, toward positive, inclusive, empowering actions that build confidence, as we have seen in the ABN Amro Real example. By believing in other people, such leaders make it possible for others to believe in them. Working together, they increase the likelihood of success, and of continuing to succeed.

These leadership lessons are suitable for any century, in any nation on earth. That we can find them used in so many places, stemming from seemingly diverse cultures yet drawing on universal human values, gives me hope that leaders of the future will be able to convert global challenges into opportunities for positive change.

Part III

Leading in a Time of Crisis and Complexity

6

Anchoring Leadership in the Work of Adaptive Progress

Ronald A. Heifetz

Ronald A. Heifetz, cofounder of the Center for Public Leadership and King Hussein bin Talal Lecturer in Public Leadership at Harvard University's John F. Kennedy School of Government, is known worldwide for his seminal work on the practice and teaching of leadership. His research at Harvard focuses on how to build adaptive capacity in societies, businesses, and nonprofits. For more than two decades, Heifetz's courses on leadership have been among the most highly valued at the university, and his first book, Leadership Without Easy Answers, *currently in its thirteenth printing, has been translated into many languages. Heifetz speaks extensively in the United States and abroad and consults widely with presidents and senior executives in government, business, and nonprofit organizations.*

Our language fails us in many aspects of our lives, entrapping us in a set of cultural assumptions like cattle herded by fences into a corral. Gender pronouns, for example, corral us into teaching children that God is a he, distancing girls and women every day from the experience of the divine in themselves, and distancing men from the traditionally feminine virtues in themselves.

Adapted from the article "Adaptive Learning" in the four-volume *Encyclopedia of Leadership*, edited by George R. Goethals, Georgia J. Sorenson, and James MacGregor Burns, copyright 2004 Berkshire Publishing Group, Great Barrington, Massachusetts. Reprinted by permission of Sage Publications.

Our language fails us, too, when we discuss, analyze, and practice leadership. We commonly talk about "leaders" in organizations or politics when we actually mean people in positions of managerial or political authority. Although we have confounded leadership with authority in nearly every journalistic and scholarly article written on "leadership" during the past one hundred years, we know intuitively that these two phenomena are distinct when we complain frequently in politics and business that "the leadership isn't exercising any leadership." This is a contradiction in terms, resolved by distinguishing leadership from authority and realizing that we actually mean to say, "People in authority aren't exercising any leadership." Whether people with formal, charismatic, or otherwise informal authority actually practice *leadership* on any given issue at any moment in time ought to remain a separate question answered with wholly different criteria than those used to define merely that relationship of formal powers or informal influence. As we know, all too many people are skilled at gaining formal and informal kinds of authority, and thus a following, but do not then lead.

Moreover, we assume a logical connection between the words *leader* and *follower*, as if this dyad were an absolute and inherently logical structure. It is not. The most interesting leadership operates without anyone experiencing anything remotely similar to the experience of "following." Indeed, most leadership mobilizes those who are opposed or who sit on the fence, in addition to allies and friends. Allies and friends come relatively cheap; it's the people in opposition who have the most to lose in any significant process of change. When mobilized, allies and friends become not followers but activated participants—employees or citizens who themselves often lead in turn by taking responsibility for tackling tough challenges within their reach, often beyond expectations and often beyond their authority. They become partners. And when mobilized, the opposition and fence-sitters become engaged with the issues, provoked to work through the problems of loss, loyalty, and competence embedded in the change they are challenged to make. Indeed, they may continue to fight, providing an ongoing source of diverse views necessary for the adaptive success of the business or community. Far from becoming "aligned" and far from any experience of "following," they are mobilized by leadership to wrestle with new complexities that demand tough trade-offs in their ways of working or living. Such is the work of progress. Of course, in time they may begin to trust, admire, and appreciate the person or group that is leading, and thereby confer informal authority on them, but they would not generally experience the emergence of that appreciation or trust by the phrase "I've become a follower." I doubt Alabama's Governor George Wallace would have seen himself after his conversion on civil rights as a "follower" of the Reverend Martin Luther King Jr. It is far more likely, and appropriate, for Wallace to have seen himself as a political adversary and colleague of King's in the struggles of American populist politics. And even among King's more natural allies, I doubt that Bernard Lafayette saw himself as King's follower when he went wandering with a bloody shirt through the streets of early 1965 Selma to mobilize middle-class black people to risk their hard-earned security by joining in the demonstrations for the right to vote. I imagine he knew himself as another leader and collaborator in the movement.

If leadership is different from the capacity to gain formal or informal authority, and therefore more than the ability to gain a "following"—attracting influence and accruing power—what can anchor our understanding of it?

Leadership takes place in the context of problems and challenges. Indeed, it makes little sense to describe leadership when everything and everyone in an organization is humming along fine, even when processes of influence and authority will be ubiquitous in coordinating routine activity. Moreover, it's not just any kind of problem for which leadership becomes needed and relevant as a practice. Leadership becomes necessary to businesses and communities when people have tough challenges to tackle, when they have to change their ways in order to thrive or survive, when continuing to operate according to current structures, procedures, and processes no longer will suffice. We call these adaptive challenges. Beyond technical problems, for which authoritative and managerial expertise will suffice, adaptive challenges demand leadership that engages people in facing challenging realities and then changing those priorities, attitudes, and behaviors necessary to thrive in a changing world.

Mobilizing people to meet adaptive challenges, then, is at the heart of leadership practice. In the short term, leadership is an activity that mobilizes people to meet an immediate challenge. In the medium and long term, leadership generates new cultural norms that enable people to meet an ongoing stream of adaptive challenges, realities, and pressures likely to come. Thus, with a longer view, leadership develops an organization or community's adaptive capacity, or adaptability.

The subject of cultural adaptability and the practice of leadership that generates it is a big frontier. In this short article, I suggest eight properties of adaptive work. Leadership anchored in the adaptive growth and development of an organization or community begins with an understanding of these properties.

1. *An adaptive challenge is a gap between aspirations and reality that demands a response outside the current repertoire.* Whereas technical problems are largely amenable to current expertise, adaptive challenges significantly are not. Of course, every problem can be understood as a gap between aspirations and reality. What distinguishes technical problems from adaptive challenges is whether that gap can be closed through applying existing know-how. For example, a patient comes to his doctor with an infection, and the doctor uses her knowledge to diagnose the illness and prescribe a cure; that's a technical problem.

In contrast, an adaptive challenge is created by a gap between a desired state and reality that cannot be closed using existing approaches alone. Progress in the situation requires more than the application of current expertise, authoritative decision making, standard operating procedures, or culturally informed behaviors. For example, a patient with heart disease may need to change his way of life: diet, exercise, smoking, and the imbalances that cause unhealthy stress. To make those changes, the patient will have to take responsibility for his health and learn his way to a new set of priorities and habits. Philip Selznick described this distinction between "routine" and "critical" challenges in his seminal 1957 monograph, *Leadership in Administration*.[1]

This distinction is summarized in Figure 6.1.

2. *Adaptive challenges demand learning.* An adaptive challenge exists when progress requires a retooling, in a sense, of people's own ways of thinking and operating. The gap between aspirations and reality closes when they learn new ways. Thus, a consulting firm may offer a brilliant diagnostic analysis and set of recommendations, but nothing will be solved until that analysis and those recommendations are lived in the new way that people operate. Until then, the consultant has no solutions, only proposals.

3. *With adaptive challenges, the people with the problem are the problem, and they are the solution.* Adaptive challenges require a shift in responsibility from the shoulders of the authority figures and the

Figure 6.1. Technical and Adaptive Work.

Kind of Work	Problem Definition	Solutions and Implementation	Primary Locus of Responsibility for the Work
Technical	Clear	Clear	Authority
Technical and adaptive	Clear	Requires learning	Authority and stakeholder
Adaptive	Requires learning	Requires learning	Stakeholder > authority

Source: Ronald A. Heifetz, *Leadership Without Easy Answers* (Cambridge: Harvard University Press, 1994), p. 76.

authority structure to the stakeholders themselves. In contrast to expert problem solving, adaptive work requires a different form of deliberation and a different kind of responsibility-taking. When adaptive work is being done, responsibility needs to be felt in a widespread fashion. At best, an organization would have its members know that there are many technical problems for which looking to authority for answers is appropriate and efficient, but that for the adaptive set of challenges, looking to authority for answers becomes self-defeating. When people make the classic error of treating adaptive challenges as if they were technical, they wait for the person in authority to know what to do.[2] He or she then makes a best guess—probably just a guess—while the many sit back and wait to see whether the guess pans out. And frequently enough, when it does not, people get rid of that executive and go find another one, all the while operating under the illusion that "if only we had the right 'leader,' our problems would be solved." Progress is impeded by inappropriate dependency; therefore, a major task of leadership is the development of responsibility-taking by the people with a stake in the problem.

4. *An adaptive challenge requires people to distinguish what's precious and essential from what's expendable within their culture.* In cultural adaptation, the job is threefold: to take the best from history, to leave behind that which is no longer serviceable, and through innovation to learn ways to thrive in the new environment.

Therefore, adaptive leadership is inherently conservative as well as progressive. The point of innovation is to conserve what is best from history as the community moves into the future. As in biology, a successful adaptation takes the best from its past set of competencies and discards the "DNA" that is no longer useful. Thus, unlike many current conceptions of culturally "transforming" processes, many of which are ahistorical—as if one begins all anew—adaptive work, profound as it may be in terms of change, honors ancestry and history at the same time that it challenges them. Apparently, neither God nor evolution do zero-based budgeting.

Adaptive work generates resistance in people because adaptation requires us to let go of certain elements of our past ways of working or living, which means to experience loss—loss of competence, loss of reporting relationships, loss of jobs, loss of traditions, or loss of loyalty to the people who taught us the lessons of our heritage. An adaptive challenge generates a situation that forces us to make tough trade-offs. The source of resistance that people have to change isn't resistance to change per se; it is resistance to loss. People love change when they know it's beneficial. Nobody gives the lottery ticket back when they win. Leadership must contend, then, with the various forms of feared and real losses that accompany adaptive work.[3]

Anchored to the tasks of mobilizing people to thrive in new and challenging contexts, leadership is not simply about change; more profoundly, leadership is about identifying that which is worth conserving. It is the conserving of the precious dimensions of our past that make the pains of change worth sustaining.

5. *Adaptive work demands experimentation.* In biology, the adaptability of a species depends on the multiplicity of experiments that are being run constantly within its gene pool, increasing the odds that in that distributed intelligence some diverse member of the species will have the means to succeed in a new context. Similarly, in cultural adaptation, an organization or community needs to be running multiple experiments, and learning fast from these experiments in order to see "which horses to ride into the future."

Technical problem solving appropriately and efficiently depends on authoritative experts for knowledge and decisive action. In contrast, dealing with adaptive challenges requires a comfort with not knowing where to go or how to move next. In mobilizing adaptive work from an authority position, leadership takes the form of protecting elements of deviance and creativity in the organization in spite of the inefficiencies associated with those elements. If creative or outspoken people generate conflict, then so be it. Conflict becomes an engine of innovation, rather than solely a source of

dangerous inefficiency. Managing the dynamic tension between creativity and efficiency becomes an ongoing part of leadership practice for which there exists no equilibrium point at which this
tension disappears. Leadership becomes an improvisation, however
frustrating it may be not to know the answers.

6. *The time frame for adaptive work is markedly different from that
for technical work.* It takes time for people to learn new ways—to
sift through what's precious from what's expendable and to innovate in ways that enable them to carry forward into the future that
which they continue to hold precious from the past. Moses took
forty years to bring the children of Israel to the Promised Land, not
because it was such a long walk from Egypt, but because it took that
much time for the people to leave behind the dependent mentality
of slavery and generate the capacity for self-government guided by
faith in something ineffable. Figure 6.2 helps depict this difference
in time frame.

7. *Adaptive challenges generate avoidance.* Because it is so difficult for people to sustain prolonged periods of disturbance and
uncertainty, human beings naturally engage in a variety of efforts

Figure 6.2. Technical Problem or Adaptive Challenge?

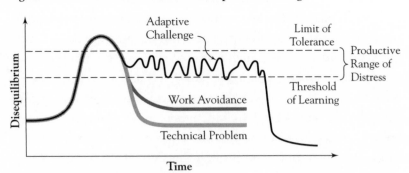

Source: Ronald A. Heifetz and Donald C. Laurie, "Mobilizing Adaptive Work:
Beyond Visionary Leadership," in Conger, Spreitzer, and Lawler (eds.), *The Leader's
Change Handbook: An Essential Guide to Setting Direction and Taking Action* (New
York: John Wiley & Sons, 1988).

to restore equilibrium as quickly as possible, even if it means avoiding adaptive work by begging off the tough issues. Most forms of failure when addressing adaptive challenges are a product of our difficulty in containing prolonged periods of experimentation, and the difficult, conflictive conversations that accompany them.

Work avoidance is simply the natural effort to restore a more familiar order, to restore social, political, or psychological equilibrium. Although many different forms of work avoidance operate across cultures and peoples, it appears that there are two common types: the displacement of responsibility and the diversion of attention. Both methods function terribly well in the short term for avoiding adaptive work, even if they leave people more exposed and vulnerable in the medium and long term. Some common forms of displacing responsibility include scapegoating, blaming the persistence of problems on authority, externalizing the enemy, or killing the messenger. Diverting attention can take the form of fake remedies, like the Golden Calf; an effort to define problems to fit one's competence; repeated structural adjustments; the faulty use of consultants, committees, and task forces; sterile conflicts and proxy fights ("Let's watch the gladiator fight!"); or outright denial.

8. I suggest that *adaptive work is a normative concept*. The concept of adaptation arises from scientific efforts to understand biological evolution.[4] Applied to the change of cultures and societies, the concept becomes a useful, if inexact, metaphor.[5] For example, species evolve whereas cultures learn. Evolution is generally understood by scientists as a matter of chance, whereas societies will often consciously deliberate, plan, and intentionally experiment. Close to our normative concern, biological evolution conforms to laws of survival. Societies, however, generate purposes beyond survival. The concept of adaptation applied to culture raises the questions, Adapt to what, for what purpose? What does it mean to "thrive"? What should we mean by progress, as a business or community?

In biology, the "objective function" of adaptive work is straightforward: to thrive in new environments. Survival of the self and one's gene-carrying kin defines the direction in which animals adapt. A situation becomes an adaptive challenge because it threatens the capacity of a species to pass on its genetic heritage. Thus, when a species is fruitful by multiplying and protecting its own kind and succeeds in passing on its genes, it is said to be "thriving" in its environment.

Thriving is more than coping. There is nothing trivial in biology about adaptation. Some adaptive leaps transform the capacity of a species by sparking an ongoing and profound process of adaptive developments that lead to a vastly expanded range of living. Still, thriving in biological systems is defined by progeny.

In human societies, "thriving" takes on a host of values not restricted to survival of one's own kind. Human beings will even sacrifice their own lives for values such as liberty, justice, and faith. Thus, adaptive work in cultures involves both the clarification of values and the assessment of realities that challenge the realization of those values.

Because most organizations and communities honor a mix of values, the competition within this mix largely explains why adaptive work so often involves conflict. People with competing values engage one another as they confront a shared situation from their own points of view. At its extreme, and in the absence of better methods of social change, the conflict over values can be violent. The Civil War changed the meaning of union and individual freedom. In 1857, ensuring domestic tranquility meant returning escaped slaves to their owners; in 1957, it meant using federal troops to integrate Central High School in Little Rock.

Some realities threaten not only a set of values beyond survival but also the very existence of a society if these realities are not discovered and met early on by the value-clarifying and reality-testing functions of that society. In the view of many environmentalists, for example, our focus on the production of wealth rather than coexistence with nature has led us to neglect fragile factors in our ecosystem. These factors may become relevant to us when finally they begin to challenge our central values of health and survival, but by then, we may have paid a high price in damage already done, and the costs of and odds against adaptive adjustment may have increased enormously.[6]

Adaptive work, then, requires us to deliberate on the values by which we seek to thrive, and demands diagnostic inquiry into the realities we face that threaten the realization of those values. Beyond legitimizing a convenient set of assumptions about reality, beyond denying or avoiding the internal contradictions in some of the values we hold precious, and beyond coping, the work of adaptive progress involves proactively seeking to clarify aspirations or develop new ones, and then involves the very hard work of innovation, experimentation, and cultural development to realize a closer approximation of those aspirations by which we would define "thriving."

In other words, the normative tests of adaptive work involve an appraisal both of the processes by which orienting values are clarified in an organization or community and of the quality of reality testing by which a more accurate rather than convenient diagnosis is achieved. By these tests, for example, serving up fake remedies for our collective troubles by scapegoating and externalizing the enemy, as was done in extreme form in Nazi Germany, might generate throngs of misled supporters who readily grant to charlatans extraordinary authority in the short run, but this would not constitute adaptive work. Nor would political efforts to gain influence and authority by pandering to people's longing for easy answers constitute leadership. Indeed, misleading people over time may likely produce adaptive failure.

Endnotes

1. Philip Selznick, *Leadership in Administration* (Berkeley, CA: University of California Press, 1957, 1984).

2. Ronald A. Heifetz and Donald Laurie, "The Work of Leadership," *Harvard Business Review*, January 1997, republished December 2001.

3. Ronald A. Heifetz and Marty Linsky, *Leadership on the Line: Staying Alive Through the Dangers of Leading* (Boston: Harvard Business School Press, 2002), Chapter One.

4. See Ernst Mayr, *Toward a New Philosophy of Biology: Observations of an Evolutionist* (Cambridge, MA: Belknap/Harvard University Press, 1988); Marc W. Kirschner and John G. Gerhart, *The Plausibility of Life: Resolving Darwin's Dilemma* (New Haven: Yale University Press, 2005).

5. See Roger D. Masters, *The Nature of Politics* (New Haven: Yale University Press, 1989).

6. Ronald A. Heifetz, *Leadership Without Easy Answers* (Cambridge, MA: Belknap/Harvard University Press, 1994), pp. 30–32.

7

The Challenge of Complexity

John Alexander

John Alexander is president of the Center for Creative Leadership. CCL's highlights during his tenure include being ranked by the Financial Times *among the world's top providers of leadership education, expansion of the Center's operations in Europe and Asia, and increased research and publication activities.*

At the Center for Creative Leadership (CCL), we continually remind our clients that leadership development is never an event—it's an ongoing and arduous process. The art of leadership itself, we tell them, is exceedingly difficult to master. A recent CCL study reinforces why, and raises critical questions about the future of leadership for individuals and organizations.

A team headed by CCL researcher André Martin asked practicing managers if the definition of effective leadership has changed in the past five years. An astounding 84 percent agreed that it has. This same group, surveyed by Martin and his team for the CCL research report "The Changing Nature of Leadership," said that the nature of outstanding leadership will shift even further over the next five years, with the "soft skills" of building relationships, collaboration, and change management becoming more crucial.

Why is the very definition of leadership changing? At CCL, we believe this phenomenon is connected to the rise of complex challenges, those for which no preexisting solutions or expertise exist. Such challenges test the limits of an organization's current strategies. They reveal the shortcomings of leadership as it is commonly practiced. They create the demand for a new kind of leadership, whether one is working in the private, public, or social sectors.

The Complexity of Crises

In August 2005 America's Gulf Coast was devastated by Hurricane Katrina, one of the most destructive storms ever to hit the United States. Subsequent flooding killed hundreds of people and left residents and businesses in the region reeling. Within weeks, the region was blasted by another major storm, Hurricane Rita. If ever a problem could be defined as a "complex challenge," the crisis caused by Katrina and complicated by Rita was it. The process of rescuing victims and assisting displaced individuals and ruined communities, while making decisions about recovery and rebuilding efforts, was multidimensional and vast—and initially overwhelming. The painfully slow and uncoordinated reaction of government leaders in the early days of this disaster sparked an extended debate as to who was to blame for the poor preparation and inadequate response to Hurricane Katrina, with general agreement that "leadership" failed at all levels because a more collaborative approach had not been defined in advance or enacted during and after the initial crisis. Part of the complexity of this challenge was that the key players could not agree on whose job it should have been to provide that advance coordination and the emergency response—whether federal, state, or local authorities, or some combination thereof. And further complicating matters was the fact that the role active units of the U.S. military (as opposed to the National Guard) could assume during a domestic crisis of this nature was limited by certain legal constraints.

Another large-scale crisis in the United States—the terrorist attacks of September 11, 2001—turned the spotlight on the need for more interdependent responses on the part of leadership throughout government. Once the initial response of rescue and recovery subsided, debate raged in Washington, D.C., over the lack of communication and cooperation between the CIA and the FBI in investigating and countering terrorist activities before September 11. The complexity of the terrorist challenge and threat was not adequately addressed, owing to a messy combination of poor leadership, siloed organizational cultures, and a lack of cooperative spirit throughout the structures and systems that surround government and politics. Complex challenges initiated by crises, of course, are as prevalent and as varied internationally as they are in the United States. The massive relief effort in response to the tsunami that struck Southeast Asia in December 2004 offers one example of such a complex challenge for international leaders.

When existing strategies and tools fail—as occurred with 9/11, the 2005 hurricanes, and the South Asian tsunami—something new is needed. Today's leaders are being called upon by necessity to develop responses to complex challenges brought on by unexpected or unimagined events or situations. We don't know exactly what their answers will be, but we do know this: the best leaders of the future will embrace complexity and the skills needed to harness it.

The Rise of Complex Challenges

Beyond the extraordinary challenges posed by crises, including natural disasters and terrorists, change and uncertainty in the business, political, and social environments of the United States and the rest of the world are a fact of life now. Globalization, technology, and the relentless pace of change challenge the strategic and tactical skills of executives and managers each day. The world has become increasingly complex, and so have the challenges of operating effectively in it as a leader. The complex challenges that leaders face are multidimensional; they defy existing solutions, resources, and approaches; they erode fundamental assumptions and mental models; and they demand new learning and creativity. Complex challenges often seem to demand quick and decisive action. Yet, because individuals and organizations frequently have no previous reference point for responding to them, there is also a need to slow down, reflect, and collaborate before taking action.

Understanding Complex Challenges

If we are to respond effectively to complex challenges, it is first essential to understand their particular nature. To begin, complex challenges can be thought of in terms of three categories: *technical, adaptive,* and *critical*. A problem or complex challenge may involve just one of these categories, or the challenge may be complex because it features elements of all three.

Technical challenges are those that fall within the range of current problem-solving expertise but stand out as unusual nevertheless. To solve a technical challenge is a matter of applying the right person or tool to the problem to create the right solution. The Atlantic coast of the United States, for example, is hit by hurricanes with some frequency, creating a variety of technical challenges— evacuating residents, cleaning up damage, restoring basic services, and rebuilding where necessary. Officials have developed plans that are often quite effective in addressing the initial emergency response and the recovery afterward, provided the storms are of a certain size and behave in predictable ways. With regard to terrorists, law-enforcement officials have clear strategies for responding to certain types of challenges, such as hostage situations. In business, established procedures exist for undertaking a merger or acquisition— again, on the assumption that the deal is of a certain size and familiarity.

Significantly, though, only 43 percent of the challenges managers face at work are viewed as technical, according to initial CCL research. This means that only 43 percent of problems that arise can be fixed by applying existing skills, resources, and processes. The rest of our work demands different approaches altogether.

Adaptive challenges require new perspectives, expertise, and solutions. With an adaptive challenge it is difficult even to name or to diagnose what the challenge is, let alone identify the right tool to solve it. An adaptive challenge calls into question fundamental assumptions and beliefs, sprawls across organizational boundaries, and surfaces divergent and opposing points of view. CCL findings show that 37 percent of the challenges managers described were adaptive and thus required new ways of working.

Critical challenges, too, require new ways of working, but often these challenges are less controlled or predictable. Unexpected events, crises, and circumstances that have an impact on health and safety are clearly critical challenges. Significant economic, social, or political change may provoke critical challenges. Typically, the intensity of the situation demands immediate action. Paradoxically, the impulse to respond quickly when facing critical challenges might, in fact, undermine the recovery, so a balance is needed. Slowing down initially helps everyone involved see clearly and assemble collective resources so that action can be focused, fast, and efficient. About 10 percent of challenges fall into this category.

Hurricanes Katrina and Rita saddled the Gulf Coast with dramatic critical challenges, such as unprecedented flooding, that compounded one upon another, as well as difficult-to-define adaptive challenges. The shortcomings in the emergency response to Katrina's damage, particularly in the city of New Orleans, have been well-documented, with many of the problems apparently rooted in isolated organizational cultures, poor communication, and self-serving political agendas and systems. Individual mistakes and misjudgments on the part of key state and federal leaders have also been well-documented. Virtually the same judgments have been made about U.S. intelligence and law-enforcement agencies in the aftermath of the September 11 attacks. Considering the multiplicity and complexity of the challenges posed by Katrina and groups of terrorists, it's certainly not surprising that there were failures in leadership. And plenty of examples can be found in business. Here the issues may not rise to the level of life-and-death urgency of these crises. But events such as global recession, changing market conditions, rapidly rising oil prices, and the ascendency of India and China as global competitors have caused CEOs to rewrite their playbooks overnight and, in some cases, these events have caused organizations to suffer extreme turbulence. The question now becomes, How can leadership be transformed so that the complex challenges of the future, whether they are rooted in natural disasters or organizational turmoil—technical, adaptive, or critical—are addressed in innovative ways?

The Changing Nature of Leadership

As the complex nature of challenges becomes clearer, leaders are thinking more deeply about how to address them through collaborative and interdependent work. The Center for Creative Leadership has found in particular that individual leaders are becoming more aware of the necessity of developing the soft skills needed to thrive interpersonally in the workplace. The new leadership skill set emphasizes participative management, building and mending relationships, and change management. Resourcefulness, decisiveness, and doing whatever it takes, which had dominated the list of critical leadership skills in recent years, remain important but not pivotal. In our research we have found that managers are articulating the need to develop and to improve in areas such as teamwork, long-term objectives, and innovation. Rather than judging their success merely by the standard of their own individual performance, future leaders also will need to assess if they are creating an environment in which others can help them succeed.

The direction individual leadership appears to be taking is reinforced by our data showing that organizational approaches to leadership have also changed in recent years and will continue to do so. Many organizations are moving from more traditional, individual leadership approaches to more innovative, collaborative approaches. When the Center asked managers to tell us specifically how complex challenges are affecting their organizations, half of the sample agreed or strongly agreed that because of these types of challenges, people in their organizations increasingly were working across functions and more collaboratively. When looking to a future in which complex challenges will be more common, respondents believed that organizations will tend to view leadership as a process that happens throughout the organization and involves interdependent decision making.

As the understanding of effective leadership shifts from an emphasis on the individual leader acting alone to a more collaborative model, the extent to which organizational approaches to leadership are changing is far more striking in the global data than in the U.S.-based numbers. The international population made a more significant jump from individual to collective approaches over the past five years. Further, these respondents expected to see additional changes in the future. They saw greater shifts toward viewing leadership as a process, a boundaryless orientation that occurs throughout the organization.

New Perspectives on Leadership

Clearly, we need a new way of thinking about leadership to account for the new complexity that leaders and organizations face. The traditional understanding of leadership focuses on individuals in positions of authority in a hierarchical structure. Even when the view of leadership was expanded, it was rooted in individual skills, behavior, and influence. Although these factors remain important and relevant, CCL's emerging definition looks at leadership more inclusively, across functions and organizations and from the middle out. We view leadership as the collective activities of organizational members to accomplish three tasks: setting direction, building commitment, and creating alignment.

Setting direction is the articulation of mission, vision, values, and purpose. Key questions include Where are we going? What are we going to do? Why are we doing it? If a CEO articulates a compelling mission—*setting direction*—then that is an example of leadership.

Building commitment involves the creation of mutual trust and accountability, including addressing questions such as, How can we stay together? How can we work better as a group? What steps might improve cooperation? If organizational members come together to confront a critical challenge and develop greater trust and respect, *building commitment* through their interactions, then that is an example of leadership that can tackle complexity.

Creating alignment involves finding common ground and areas of interrelated responsibility. People need to ask, How can we develop a shared understanding of our situation? How can our actions be better coordinated? If a cross-functional group reaches across organizational boundaries to align IT systems—*creating alignment*—then that is an example of leadership.

From this perspective, leadership is the potential outcome of interactions between groups of people, rather than specific traits or skills of a single person. If these interactions lead to the accomplishment of the tasks of direction, commitment, and alignment, then leadership capacity exists.

By this definition, organizations are underperforming and will need to adjust to face complex challenges. We asked managers to tell us how well their organizations are doing in achieving the three key tasks of leadership as we define them. Only 50 percent said they agreed or strongly agreed with the statement, "In my organization, leaders set direction effectively." Just 46 percent of respondents said leaders in their organization build commitment effectively. And a mere 40 percent agreed that their organizations are capable of creating alignment. These findings are troubling but not all that surprising. When leaders are challenged by complexity, naturally it becomes considerably more difficult to set direction, create alignment, and build commitment. But individual leaders and those throughout their organizations can respond with greater effectiveness—by learning to identify the particular nature of the challenges they face and developing their skills in collaborative leadership. Indeed, they may have little choice.

The Future of Leadership

CCL's research shows, then, that the very definition of effective leadership has changed in the past five years. It will continue to shift over the next five years and the years to come as more complex challenges arise, demanding innovative responses. To successfully engage leadership in the future, individuals and organizations will need to expand and revise their understanding of leadership and how they practice it. Strong individual leaders will remain important to the success of organizations, particularly as advocates of leadership as a collective effort and by developing the skills in themselves and in others that foster a more inclusive approach to leadership. At the same time, organizations will need to become more adept at drawing on their collective resources to identify their challenges, understand their implications, and work in more interdependent ways to address them.

To return to examples discussed earlier in this chapter, even without the perspective hindsight will offer us, it is fair to say that the "right" answers for leading recovery and rebuilding efforts in the wake of Hurricanes Katrina and Rita will continue to be elusive and complicated. The same might be said of the U.S. government's ongoing efforts to defend against future terrorist attacks. Leaders who understand the importance of working across organizational and administrative boundaries to address such complex challenges will be a critical factor in undoing the knots of technical, adaptive, and critical challenges and beginning to weave together viable and promising solutions.

Complex challenges, in their technical, adaptive, and critical varieties, are here to stay. No single leader in any organization is likely to know how to respond to all or even any of them. Thus, a new set of leadership skills emphasizing participative management,

relationship building, and change management becomes more imperative. Leaders who embrace and develop these skills are finding
that many times effective solutions to pressing challenges exist,
embedded deep within the collective knowledge and experience of
any given member of an organization. The ability to draw this wisdom to the surface through the practice of collaborative leadership
and to put it into action will shape the definition of effective leadership in the future.

8

Understanding the Nonprofit Sector's Leadership Deficit

Thomas J. Tierney

Thomas J. Tierney is the chairman and cofounder of The Bridgespan Group, a nonprofit organization established in 1999 to provide management consulting services to the nonprofit sector. Most recently, he led the development of Bridgestar, a Bridgespan initiative dedicated to talent-matching for the sector. Tierney was the chief executive of Bain & Company from 1992 to 2000. He has contributed to many publications, including the Harvard Business Review, *and is the coauthor of* Aligning the Stars *(Harvard Business School Press, 2002). Tierney is a director of eBay, Incorporated, and serves on numerous nonprofit boards and advisory groups.*

America's nonprofit sector, already expansive, is expanding. Most of us both contribute to the sector and benefit from it: we strengthen our communities when we give time and money to nonprofit organizations. Yet few of us are aware that those organizations face an insidious crisis that could undermine all their good works—a shortage of nonprofit leaders. Our collective response to the accelerating leadership deficit will have an impact on society for decades to come.

Nonprofits face unyielding pressure to make every dollar go a long way. But money is not the only resource in short supply. Many nonprofits are struggling to attract and retain the talented senior executives they need to continue converting society's dollars into social impact. This leadership challenge will only become more acute in the coming years.

Bridgespan recently carried out an extensive study of the leadership requirements of U.S. nonprofits with revenues greater than $250,000.[1] The study found that in 2006, those organizations need to add more than 56,000 new senior managers to their existing ranks. Cumulatively, over the decade from 2007 to 2016, they will need to attract and develop some 640,000 new senior leaders—or the equivalent of 2.4 *times* the number currently employed. To put this challenge in context, filling the gap would require recruiting more than 50 percent of every M.B.A. graduating class, at every university across the country, every year for the next decade.[2]

Whether—and how well—these leadership needs are met will have an enormous impact on individual nonprofits. But that's only one aspect of the challenge. Over the next decades, charitable bequests conservatively estimated at $6 trillion will flow to the nonprofit sector, as wealth is transferred from the baby-boom generation to its heirs.[3] If the nonprofit sector does not address its looming leadership deficit, many of those well-intentioned charitable dollars will be wasted, to the detriment of society as a whole.

Constrained Supply, Booming Demand

A growing body of research and experience defines the challenges that nonprofits face to fill leadership positions.[4] To understand the problem, and why it will intensify in coming years, we must examine the structural dynamics shaping the market for nonprofit leaders.

The supply side of the story revolves around the aging baby-boom generation. As the first wave of this cohort, nearly eighty million strong, exits the workforce or shifts to part-time employment, the reverberations will be felt throughout the economy. Their departure will create a vacuum: from 2000 to 2020, the number of men and women ages thirty-four to fifty-four will grow by only three million.[5]

Nonprofits confront a corresponding demographic reality—the sector's annual executive retirement rate could climb by 15 percent or more before the end of the decade.[6] The supply of potential leaders will shrink even further as some senior managers burn out and others seek more attractive opportunities. Writing in *The Nonprofit Quarterly* in 2002, two seasoned executives estimated that at any given time, 10 to 12 percent of the country's nonprofit organizations undergo leadership transitions. The authors cited surveys indicating that 15 to 35 percent of nonprofit executives plan to leave their current positions within two years and 61 to 78 percent plan to leave within five years.[7] Whatever the precise timing of those transitions, there is little question that there will be significant sector leadership turnover in the next decade.

The demand-side dynamics are also in flux. The total number of nonprofit organizations has tripled in twenty years. The number of organizations with revenues exceeding $250,000 has increased from 62,800 to 104,700 in the nine years from 1995 to 2004—an annual growth rate of almost 6 percent.

Numerous trends contributed to this expansion. Charitable giving equaled or exceeded the organizational growth rate during most of that nine-year period. The roster of philanthropic foundations swelled by an average of 2,900 new entrants annually in the decade ending in 2002.[8] Young people have taken a growing interest in social entrepreneurship. Many corporations have made social responsibility a greater priority. And government has turned steadily to nonprofits to deliver public services.

Some observers label the growth "proliferation" and suggest that sector consolidation is in order. Others applaud the growth as evidence of our civil society in action. By any measure, though, the nonprofit space is steadily enlarging in both the economy and our communities.

As nonprofits pay more attention to strengthening their capabilities and performance, they will both ask more of their senior management teams and require additional, specialized functional skills. Influential board members may insist that a nonprofit be run "more like a business" and urge the hiring of a chief operating officer. Stepped-up reporting standards create an urgent need for skilled finance and accounting professionals. Experienced communications and development executives are in demand as nonprofits reach out more aggressively to potential funding sources. Efforts to recruit and retain frontline staff and screen volunteers require professional expertise.

Understanding the Numbers

Bridgespan has incorporated the trends just described into an analysis of the number of new senior managers that nonprofits would need through 2016. We assumed that the growth in the number of nonprofits in each revenue category would continue at historic 1995 to 2004 rates. We also assumed that retirement rates would remain constant throughout the 1996 to 2016 time period, save for an incremental six-percentage-point demographic boost from 2004 through 2009, attributable to a spike in baby-boomer retirements, and that rates of other forms of transition would be stable.

Using these assumptions, we projected that nonprofits will require 78,000 new senior managers in 2016, up from 56,000 in 2006 and more than a fourfold increase since 1996. The projected increase is attributable to growth in the number of nonprofits (42 percent); leadership transitions, retirement, or other departures (55 percent); and the trend to larger organizations (3 percent). The combined effect of these dynamics is reflected in a base-case estimate that 640,000 new senior managers will be needed over the coming decade.

Now suppose that the growth rate in the number of nonprofit organizations declines dramatically, perhaps because of changes in the flows or magnitude of charitable funding or because of widespread failures of established nonprofits. Future turnover rates might fall below recent projections. *Even with such conservative assumptions, however, the sector will still need some 330,000 new senior executives over the next decade.*

But growth will more likely accelerate, driven by the confluence of the coming wealth transfer and increased societal reliance on nonprofits. Executive burnout and the war for talent might further accelerate turnover. If those more aggressive assumptions prove correct, *the total need for new managers would increase from the base case of 640,000 to 1,250,000.*

Even in the most optimistic scenario, the need for new nonprofit leaders will be acute in the decade ahead. Nonprofit organizations will need an exceptional number of new leaders each and every year. Current practices cannot adequately address this unprecedented deficit.

Understanding the Landscape

The sector's challenge is complicated by the nature of nonprofits. Most nonprofits are too small to provide meaningful career development for next-generation leaders, and few can afford to invest substantially in recruiting and human resources—especially in an environment that tends to view such expenditures as wasteful overhead. Consequently, many nonprofits search outside their own organizations (but within their own networks, as we shall see) for new senior managers. The best available data indicate that nonprofits fill 30 to 40 percent of senior management positions with internal candidates (in contrast, businesses fill 60 to 65 percent of their senior positions from within).[9] The risks notwithstanding, external recruiting is more expensive and time-consuming than internal sourcing. Thus, as the war for talent intensifies, the cost of addressing the sector's leadership deficit will likely escalate.

Nonprofits also face a training and recruiting deficit. Nonprofit management programs are growing, but they are modest compared with traditional business education programs. Nor do nonprofits have a search infrastructure to rival the business world's, in which the executive search industry, job-posting platforms such as Monster.com, and outsourcing service providers such as Hewitt Associates and Convergys are all eager to help. The infrastructure exists because the rewards for serving the business sector are ample.

The nonprofit sector offers no such profit pool, so there is no comparable infrastructure to deliver a robust supply of leadership talent.[10] With notable exceptions, few nonprofits recruit effectively from colleges or graduate schools. The largest search firms devote only a fraction of their resources to the nonprofit sector, and they typically focus on higher-profile, higher-paying positions—an entirely rational approach given their financial incentives. A handful of medium-sized search firms, such as Isaacson Miller, concentrate on nonprofits, yet their business is skewed toward larger institutions. Thousands of outstanding independent recruiters work in the nonprofit sector but are constrained by limited capacity or access to talent. Organizations such as Action Without Borders (Idealist) are emerging to help nonprofits find talent, but their scale is dwarfed by the magnitude of the problem.

Finding the Leaders We Need

The underlying trends of the leadership deficit are beyond anyone's control, but we can control how we react to them. It's not enough to acknowledge and understand the sheer size of the problem; we must make this challenge a top priority in nonprofit governance, planning, and day-to-day decision making. Closing the gap will require action, innovation, experimentation, and leaps of faith at both an organizational and a systemic level.

Within each organization, board members, senior managers, and major donors must commit to building strong and enduring leadership teams. Across the whole sector, foundations, intermediaries, and associations must collaborate to nurture the flow and development of management talent. In short, we must invest in leadership capacity, refine management rewards to retain and attract top talent, and expand recruiting horizons while fostering individual career mobility.

Invest in Leadership Capacity

There's a widespread belief among donors, the media, and even many of the organizations that evaluate and rate nonprofits that overhead is always bad and less overhead is always better.[11] Ergo, recruiting expenses, training costs, compensation, and senior-level positions themselves should be held to a bare minimum. Herein lies one of the major obstacles to remedying the leadership deficit. Donors, board members, and executive directors need to embrace the importance of investing in leadership capacity, despite prevailing pressures to the contrary.

Investment includes both money and time. Many successful business CEOs spend well over half their time on people-related issues, while the executive directors of nonprofits devote the bulk of their time to fundraising.[12] Although entirely rational, this prioritization forces nonprofits to give short shrift to mentoring, training, succession planning, recruiting, and other organization-specific functions. The opportunity costs are substantial.

Refine Management Rewards to
Retain and Attract Top Talent

The greatest rewards of nonprofit careers will always be intangible, but that doesn't mean that compensation doesn't matter. Indeed, as nonprofit managers face increasingly complex challenges and are judged by much more rigorous performance standards, their tougher, riskier jobs will require commensurate rewards. More competitive compensation packages would speed the sector's migration toward more professional management and help nonprofits attract, recruit, and retain talented leaders. By facing the complex realities of executive compensation, nonprofits can better equip themselves to address performance shortfalls, executive burnout, and the need for more sophisticated financial reporting. Of course, they will need the support of funders and donors to do so.

Expand Recruiting Horizons and Foster Individual Career Mobility

Nonprofits typically draw key managers from within their personal and professional networks. This isn't surprising, given the vital importance of fit and a proven affinity for an organization's mission. Candidates not only must possess technical expertise but also must be demonstrably coachable, flexible, and entrepreneurial. Factor in the sector's fragmentation and the strong local roots of most non-profits, and it is clear why organizations prefer to hire friends or friends of friends.

But networking cannot alone ensure that we will place the right leaders in the right jobs during the next decade. Nonprofits must expand their search to several significant pools of new leadership talent.

- *The baby-boom generation.* A recent study by the Metlife Foundation and Civic Ventures indicated that many fifty- to seventy-year-olds want to work during their later years: two-thirds of those surveyed intend to continue working, and fully half hope to work in organizations with social missions.[13]

- *"Repotters."* In addition, more people at the midpoint of their professional lives are thinking about "repotting" themselves. John Gardner wrote eloquently about the value of such career shifts more than forty years ago, as have the late Peter Drucker and, more recently, Bob Buford.[14] The sector would both gain new sources of leadership and provide collegial resources for existing leaders by reaching out to these two pools of talent alone.

- *Young managers in training.* In 1990 there were 17 graduate programs in nonprofit management in the United
  States. Today there are well over 90, and more than
  240 university programs offer nonprofit courses.[15]
  Those figures alone suggest the depth of those students'
  commitment to service.

- *Other pools.* Strong and diverse candidates may also be
  found among civil servants, officers making the transition from military service to civilian life, and women
  reentering the workforce after working at home to raise
  families. Today, many such qualified people are
  excluded from the recruiting process simply because
  they lack the right personal contacts.

The nonprofit sector also needs an infrastructure designed to
ensure that its talent is visible and mobile. Again, promising examples already exist. Community foundations in cities such as
Chicago, San Diego, and New York are expanding programs to build
local leadership capacity. The Annie E. Casey Foundation and others are tracking and attacking issues such as executive director succession. Net Impact is building a global network of M.B.A.s,
graduate students, and young professionals with a mission to grow
and strengthen leaders using the power of business to make a positive net social, environmental, and economic impact. Idealist, a
project of Action Without Borders, offers nonprofits and individuals opportunities to connect via job openings, volunteer opportunities, internships, events, and resources posted by organizations all
over the world. CompassPoint has recently started a division to help
nonprofits prepare for executive transitions, recruit strong pools of
candidates, and support and train executive directors. Bridgestar, an
initiative of the Bridgespan Group, collaborates with universities
and many forms of professional networks to develop pools of management talent, and provides content and recruiting services,

including an online job board, to help match individuals with nonprofits' needs.

It's Up to Us

America relies upon vibrant nonprofit organizations to create substantial social impact. The imperatives surrounding the leadership deficit must be addressed by nonprofit management teams, boards of directors, donors, and volunteers. We cannot wait: nonprofit leaders are retiring, organizations are growing, and society's demands are escalating. Without aggressive support and disciplined investment, our efforts may amount to too little, too late. Nonprofits need the best of tomorrow's leaders—today.

Endnotes

1. We excluded hospitals and institutions of higher learning from our sample, because of their distinctive funding mechanisms, specialized pools of talent, and well-developed infrastructure for developing talent.

2. The National Center for Education Statistics reports that 120,785 M.B.A. degrees were conferred in the 2001–02 school year.

3. Paul G. Schervish and John J. Havens, "New Findings on the Patterns of Wealth and Philanthropy," Social Welfare Research Institute, Boston College, June 2003.

4. CompassPoint, *Help Wanted: Turnover and Vacancy in Nonprofits* (San Francisco: CompassPoint Nonprofit Services, January 2002); TransitionGuides and Management Performance Concepts, *Community Foundation CEO Survey: Transitions and Career Paths* (Silver Spring, MD: TransitionGuides, October, 2003); New England Executive Transitions Partnership, *Executive Director Tenure and Transition in Southern New England* (Boston: New England Executive Transitions Partnership, January 2004); Paige Hull Teegarden, Management Performance Concepts, and TransitionGuides, *Nonprofit Executive Leadership and Transitions Survey 2004: Greater NYC* (Silver Spring, MD: TransitionGuides, November 2004).

5. Committee for Economic Development, *Cracks in the Education Pipeline: A Business Leader's Guide to Higher Education Reform* (Washington, DC: Committee for Economic Development, May 2005).

6. Denice Rothman Hinden and Paige Hull Teegarden, "Executive Leadership Transition: What We Know," *The Nonprofit Quarterly*, Winter 2002.

7. Hinden and Teegarden, "Executive Leadership Transition: What We Know."

8. Foundation Center, *Foundation Yearbook: Facts and Figures on Private and Community Foundations* (New York: Foundation Center, 2004).

9. Ram Charan, "Ending the CEO Succession Crisis," *Harvard Business Review*, February 2005; Russell Reynolds Associates, "The CFO Turnover Study," May 2005; CompassPoint, "Daring to Lead: Nonprofit Executive Directors and their Work Experience," 2001.

10. Orit Gadiesh and James L. Gilbert, "Profit Pools: A Fresh Look at Strategy," *Harvard Business Review*, May-June 1998.

11. Stephanie Lowell, Brian Trelstad, and Bill Meehan, "The Ratings Game," *Stanford Social Innovation Review*, Summer 2005.

12. Lawrence A. Bossidy, "The Job No CEO Should Delegate," *Harvard Business Review*, March 2001; CompassPoint, "Daring to Lead"; David Whelan, "Exploring a New World," *Chronicle of Philanthropy*, January 23, 2003.

13. Metlife Foundation and Civic Ventures, *New Face of Work Survey* (San Francisco: Civic Ventures, June 2005).

14. John W. Gardner, *Self Renewal: The Individual and the Innovative Society* (New York: W.W. Norton, 1995); Peter Drucker, "Managing Oneself," *Harvard Business Review*, January 2005; Bob Buford, *Halftime* (Grand Rapids, Michigan: Zondervan, 1994).

15. Heather Joslyn, "Gaining Success by Degrees" and "Young People Fuel Demand for Nonprofit Study," *Chronicle of Philanthropy*, January 8, 2004.

9

Leadership Over Fear

John Edwin Mroz

John Edwin Mroz is president and founder of the EastWest Institute. EWI, established in 1980, is a fiercely independent nongovernmental organization/network that serves as a global alliance of private-, social-, and public-sector cooperation to prevent conflict and build a more secure world. EWI runs an unusual global leadership program devoted to creating a network of networks aimed at bridging the most dangerous divides of the twenty-first century. Mroz has served as an adviser to more than twenty governments and to many international organizations. His book on the Arab-Israeli conflict, Beyond Security, is considered a landmark publication in its field. He has received numerous international decorations, including Germany's highest award for a noncitizen for his work in that country's reunification. Mroz contributed an article to The Organization of the Future and is a frequent speaker on leadership and international change issues. Visit www.ewi.info.

President Franklin Roosevelt's response to the national despair of the Great Depression was simple and direct: "The only thing we have to fear is fear itself." Today, much of the world lives in fear. Many tens of millions of young people around the world fear they will never secure a job. Increasing numbers of people, including many in the middle class, fear the destruction of their way of life due to global warming, or the powerful and unwelcome influences of globalization. Others fear that the so-called "clash of civilizations" between the Muslim and non-Muslim worlds will become an inevitability. Ever-increasing terrorism around the globe, the spread of weapons of mass destruction, and a renewed fear of global pandemics have added new uncertainties about our safety. Fear breeds a search for simple truths, which in turn contributes to intolerance, alienation, and extremism. This problem is a global phenomenon. A world increasingly devoid of hope and trust is an increasingly dangerous and unpredictable one.

Peter Drucker reminded us a decade ago that the world had entered a prolonged period of profound change every bit as dramatic and turbulent as that ushering in the Industrial Revolution. Since 9/11, we have had to deal with an additional layer of unexpected complexity and uncertainty. Our world is an extremely unpredictable place in which asymmetric threats make it difficult for governments to guarantee the safety of their citizens and the well-being of their economies.

Franklin Roosevelt boldly attacked the hopelessness of his nation in his first inaugural address, when he declared "the only thing we have to fear is fear itself—nameless, unreasoning, unjustified terror which paralyzes needed efforts to convert retreat into advance." FDR convinced the despairing victims of the Great Depression that the only way to gain control of their lives was to overcome fear. He challenged the American people to move beyond their fears and inspired them to take those seemingly impossible first steps forward, thus rekindling the spirit and strength of the nation. In short, he led.

While tens of millions of Americans crowded around their radios, the new president, in one mighty stroke, empowered the populace to take risks and believe again that their lives could and would get better. Millions of self-appointed citizen-leaders rose to FDR's challenge. As that first wave of risk-takers stepped forward, the nation pulled itself out of its deepest abyss since its Civil War some seventy years before. The willingness of one leader to stare down fear worked because he was able to challenge countless would-be leaders across the nation to join him. And those leaders joined their president not only in overcoming the Great Depression but also in fighting and winning the world war that followed.

In today's globalized world, top-down leadership by politicians and governments is simply not sufficient to cope with the challenges of keeping the global ship afloat in such turbulent waters. The public sector must partner with businesses and the social sector in meeting these challenges. A key task is to identify, mobilize, and challenge naturally embedded leaders in our societies to stand up and lead in a world that is increasingly seen by its citizens as being adrift. There are four things we must do: first, natural leaders in a world of fear and change must step up and lead themselves. Second, such women and men must imagine the possibility of change. Third, they must seek out other natural leaders who, like themselves, have had enough of watching and are willing to assert themselves. Fourth, they must set a pace that fits the context.

I am heartened to know that this same pattern of empowering naturally embedded leaders to step forward and take the risks of leadership is alive and well around the world—even in places where fear is the norm and hope a fleeting dream. For example, six years ago in the war-ravaged former Yugoslavia, the EastWest Institute, an independent and privately supported international "think and action tank," recruited a dozen and a half women and men to try to do something that governments and experts said could not be done. Following years of bloody killing based on religious and ethnic lines, families living in these border areas faced their own great depression with no possible hope of life getting better. Moreover, their hatred for families just a town away was intense. They could not forget memories of the wanton killing and destruction inflicted upon one another just a decade previously. Our team of women and men had a single common mission: to mobilize citizens in these war-ravaged regions to work together across borders to build trust and help local communities begin the painful journey of exiting their world of poverty and hopelessness. To accomplish this goal would require our leaders to help build bridges over many years' growth of deep-rooted fears, and to inspire people to themselves become leaders within their communities. What they accomplished during the past six years is well-known to the local populations and to governments all over Europe. It's a story of enormous hope and testimony.

As extraordinary as I think each one of my colleagues is as a human being and a leader, they are "ordinary" women and men. One had no university education; another was a young mother of two small children living in a town where some of the heaviest fighting took place. The first was a Christian, the second a Muslim. Others came from other tough parts of the Balkans, with a few from European countries or the United States. All were driven by a personal commitment to do something larger than themselves. Most of these leaders took on serious personal risks, from the real possibility of becoming alienated from their own communities to endangering their personal safety—all as they worked to build bridges of trust between the two sides. Leaving their war-torn communities was unthinkable. They were men and women who had had enough and were ready to fight fear by taking the risks of going where others feared to go.

I sat with twelve of these brave leaders recently in a remote village hall that billed itself as a restaurant. As the evening progressed, I asked each to explain exactly how they had succeeded in bringing together communities devoid of hope and trust. I told them I thought the key must have been their ability to find others like themselves who shared a common vision for a future of peace. They respectfully begged to differ. They reminded me that for the longest time, no one in any of their communities would speak of peace or a common vision. Everyone believed that more violence was imminent.

Their initial success came in finding individual men and women within their communities who, like themselves, had come to the conclusion that the only way out of the quagmire of poverty and isolation was to try to find somebody—anybody—who also was tired of this hopelessness and wanted change. A tough initial hurdle was persuading communities to trust that the sponsors of this cross-border work were truly committed to impartiality and had no hidden agendas. Would we not take sides when the chips were down? Our leaders in the field and the EastWest Institute itself were tested once again.

The story of how our leaders were able to inspire everyday people to face down their own very real fears and to take leadership roles within their communities is instructive no matter what kind of organization you lead. The smallest incremental steps taken by the local populace became their building blocks to larger initiatives. Because they listened and continued to talk about and probe their most basic common interests, barriers continued to fall. When one previously hostile man proposed that he might let his son play in a sporting event for younger children with boys of a neighboring village of a different religious belief, our team on both sides of that border decided to try to organize a soccer match for younger children. Many months later it happened, although most families escorted their children to the playing field with weapons at their side. Several games later, they came without arms. Eventually they would bring food from home and share a community table after the match.

The initial risks people were willing to take were ones based on plain old self-interest. Could we together find the source of a polluted stream that was tainting drinking water for families on both sides of the border? Could children be given a normal experience of playing sports with other children? Success came by having our staff locally based and of the community; by not rushing; and by being fiercely independent as a sponsoring institution, remaining outside of the politics and focusing solely on the bottom line— improvement of the human condition. In the end, our teams were able to accomplish things no one dreamed possible in three difficult areas of the former Yugoslavia. Their inner drive and sense of purpose at first was tolerated, then came to be respected and even embraced by a growing number in the communities they served.

As I listened to their passionate discourse that evening, I thought about how diverse these leaders and their backgrounds were. In most cases, their success was due not to their particular educational backgrounds or special training, nor to their nationality, religion, family status and upbringing, age, or gender. It seems the only thing that really mattered was that these leaders shared innate leadership strengths springing from a fierce inner drive to face down fear and be part of a force for change that was larger than themselves. This resonated in others who stepped forward, every bit as much leaders as the initiators.

I asked our team of leaders whether their experience had taught them lessons that could be applied elsewhere—perhaps to how we in the West could do better in bridging the growing divide between Muslims and non-Muslims globally. Their enthusiasm then went to an even higher level, and the ideas started spilling forth. At the core was a baseline of shared values, especially a desire for fairness and integrity in others. I wondered what would have happened if we in the Institute had not decided to face our own fears and undertake the seemingly impossible task of cross-border work in the Balkans. In what kind of world would these women and men have found themselves? I thought of how comfortable President Roosevelt would have been at the table that evening some seventy years after he spoke his words that inspired so many.

Leaders willing to take risks to overcome fear are all around us. Therein lies our hope for dealing with the seemingly overwhelming challenges on our planet in this twenty-first century. A key leadership challenge today is how to mobilize sufficient numbers of these naturally embedded leaders across the divides that breed fear and extremism and threaten our future and that of our children. It all starts with our willingness to face up to our own fears, stare them down, and find the emerging natural leader within each of us.

10

Leading in a Constantly Changing World

Ponchitta Pierce

Ponchitta Pierce is a journalist with extensive experience as a television host and producer and as a magazine writer. She began her career in journalism at Ebony magazine, where she rose to become its New York editor and New York bureau chief of the magazine's parent company, Johnson Publishing Company. Ponchitta has worked at CBS News as a special correspondent, and at WNBC-TV in New York, she has served as a contributing editor for Parade and McCall's magazines, and as a roving editor for Reader's Digest.

Long active in community service, Pierce is a member of the board of directors of the Foreign Policy Association; Thirteen/WNET; the Inner-City Scholarship Fund of the Catholic Archdiocese of New York; Housing Enterprise for the Less Privileged (H.E.L.P.); and the Josephson Institute of Ethics in Los Angeles. She is a member of the Columbia Presbyterian Health Sciences Advisory Council, the Council on Foreign Relations, the Economic Club of New York, and the Advisory Board of the University of Southern California Center on Public Diplomacy.

The world of tomorrow will present thorny challenges as we navigate natural disasters, public health crises such as HIV/AIDS, the rising tide of globalization, the constant threat of terrorism and nuclear war, the uncertainty of peace in the Middle East, and the emergence of China as a world power. Technological changes will force us to consider the ethical implications of medical and scientific advances ranging from cloning to stem-cell research. To lead in our constantly changing world, we will need strong, secure men and women with values and a sense of purpose—leaders who are highly disciplined and possess integrity, vision, and the courage of their convictions. World peace, economic progress, and social development will depend on the creativity, the sensitivity, and the compassion of these people.

Hurricane Katrina gave us a perfect example of the leader of tomorrow: Army Lieutenant General Russell Honoré, the three-star general President Bush relied on to bring order to chaos and coordinate the military's response to the havoc wrought by Katrina.

As New Orleans mayor C. Ray Nagin put it, "I give the President some credit on this. He sent one John Wayne dude here. Honoré came off the doggone chopper and started cussing, and people started moving. He's getting some stuff done."

One minute the general could be heard barking at soldiers, "Lower your weapons, goddammit!" At another moment he was seen holding a baby and whispering, "Let's go, Tiger!" as he gently delivered him into waiting arms. With so many other factors spiraling quickly out of control during the aftermath of Katrina, General Honoré oversaw the speedy rescue of thousands of people from the New Orleans Superdome and Convention Center.

I remember the press conference at which the general publicly fretted about the next approaching hurricane, Rita, while reporters continued to obsess over Katrina. "Don't get stuck on Katrina," the general told them. A few minutes later he tartly added, "Don't get stuck on stupid, reporter." You might think the rebuke would have rubbed reporters the wrong way. On the contrary: during a CNN interview an anchor said to him on the air, "You're my hero."

It was clear the press respected a man with backbone, a man who pulled no punches, a man who was confident in his experience, a man who bore the mantle of responsibility with ease. Honoré had been shaped by the military but was imbued with street smarts. Clearly General Honoré was his own man, and that inspired trust, respect, and confidence in others. He could be tough, but he showed sensitivity and compassion when the situation called for it. Honoré's ability to respond instinctively but equitably to events on the ground made people willing to follow his lead.

Why did so many people recognize and welcome the general's gift of leadership? Especially in a time of crisis, people want to know that the man or woman in charge is *decisive:* a straight-shooter, someone who knows what it takes to get the job done, someone who is not afraid to own up to mistakes made. When a city was struggling to survive—when a nation was fighting to reclaim its bearings—General Honoré charted a steady, dependable course to recovery. Our future challenges will demand no less.

The future, of course, will not be defined exclusively by disaster. We are moving in many ways toward a world without boundaries— a world in which the talk is increasingly about "people of color," who constitute the majority of the world's population and who must be reflected in its marketplace.

Witness the emergence of India and China and their rising economic power; consider the fact that, in the not-too-distant future, Hispanics will be a dominant population in America; reflect on the reality that each day America becomes home to a growing number of Muslims and other immigrants from countless other faiths around the world. As a nation whose strength is a function of its diversity, we will require tolerant leaders—leaders who view the world through a wide angle.

That definition fits my first boss, John Johnson, founder and publisher of *Ebony* and *Jet* magazines. When Johnson realized how inadequately the United States was presenting its diverse face to itself and the world, he set out to make a difference. Upon his death last year, the U.S. media focused on his visionary realization, back in the Jim Crow America of the 1940s, of the importance and economic power of expressing America's cultural, ethnic, and racial diversity. Before *Ebony* came along, rarely were African Americans seen in the pages of magazines as lawyers, doctors, or judges—men and women of achievement—even though they populated all those

professions. As a leader, Johnson used his magazines to simultaneously instill racial pride and present a diversified, more accurate picture of America. All this at a time when doing so was neither easy
nor profitable.

Advertisers took a long time to buy into Johnson's vision. "I
couldn't sell ads," he told one interviewer. "I was ready to go out of
business." But Johnson persevered. Eventually he landed Zenith as
his first advertiser; ever so slowly, others followed.

It was clear that Johnson saw America in the grip of a grave
inequality. Emboldened by his grasp of the big picture, he dared to
confront the power structure, pushing advertisers to acknowledge
the economic viability of the black market. Johnson displayed determination, stick-to-it-iveness, creativity, and a positive attitude. He
understood that a knock can be a boost—that it's not where you
came from that matters, but where you are going.

Changing demographics mandate that leaders of the future foster diversity and inclusion in the workplace, especially at the highest levels of corporate America. If they are to expand their market
share, increase shareholder value, and mirror the global marketplace, Fortune 500 companies will have to place more women and
minorities on their boards, in senior management positions, and as
chief executives.

Yet the higher you go in corporate America, the less diversity you
see. It will take real leadership to change this, but it is imperative
that we do so, especially in a world in which diversity is a common-
place of national and international business dealings. Commitment
will be required to stay this course. Willingness will be required to
take a stand when your competitors don't, knowing that you may
have to risk loss in the present to emerge as a winner in the future.
Leaders must be open to new ideas, even when—perhaps especially
when—such notions are out of currency. They must stand in front
of the curve rather than behind it, and they must understand that
what they do is more important than what they say.

Last year Paula Kerger, in her role as executive vice president and COO of Thirteen/WNET and WLIW 21, made the difficult decision to air a children's program on the public broadcast station that included the portrayal of a lesbian family. Negative responses, including those from government and Public Broadcasting Service (PBS) officials, came fast and furious.

Kerger, who in 2006 was selected to head PBS, was convinced that the show reflected American life today—and that it should be seen. "We never wavered, even when times got tough," she told me. "One of the most difficult things was to keep everyone positive and focused on the fact that we must prevail. The role of cheerleader and coach cannot be underestimated, particularly when the staff feels under fire." As we deal with other controversial social realities in the future, Kerger's brand of staunch leadership will be more and more in demand. Like Army Lieutenant General Honoré, she refused to buckle under as the pressure bubbled up. Kerger acted out of her determination to reflect America as it is. It's easy to be a leader when everyone agrees with you. It's harder when you're alone. Kerger's work also brings her in touch with many young people who have grown up on the Internet. "The next generation of leaders need to be encouraged to work with colleagues face-to-face and not hide behind e-mails," she says. "Leadership and social engagement work hand-in-hand."

In the political arena, my ideal leader of the future may well be one from the past: Moon Landrieu, who served as mayor of New Orleans from 1970 to 1978. Landrieu's political legacy includes a daughter, Senator Mary Landrieu (D-La.) and a son, Lieutenant Governor Mitch Landrieu of Louisiana. During field research that I conducted for My Soul Looks Back in Wonder (AARP Books/Sterling, 2004), Mayor Landrieu told me of his resolve to defy the segregationists when he entered politics in the 1960s. Though Landrieu's steadfast support of integration jeopardized his fledgling political career, he chose principles over politics. His personal priorities reflected his trademark independence of thought, vision, and integrity—qualities that any leader in any arena should be prepared to embrace. You wonder, Are people born with these leadership qualities? Or do they learn them in the course of a life well lived? And if these attributes are indeed learned—and learnable—how best can we teach them?

Can lessons be drawn from the way Landrieu and other politicians have served our nation? One clear message can be discerned from their past actions: future political leaders must abandon the petty divisiveness that dominates today's politics. To be truly effective, a leader must focus on consensus, not conflict. He or she must be able to emerge from a tough fight with respect for his or her opponent intact, recognizing what they can agree on and putting the common good before self-interest.

In this Sarbanes-Oxley era of corporate governance, the nonprofit sector will increasingly benefit from developing skills on which corporate and government leaders have always relied. I see this resourcefulness in Barbara Hackman Franklin, who two years ago became the first female chairman of the Economic Club of New York. Secretary of Commerce from 1992 to 1993 and now head of her own consulting firm focusing on international trade, corporate governance, and auditing and financial-reporting practices, Franklin has brought her considerable skills and experience to bear on governing the operations of the nearly one-hundred-year-old club, and the impact has been dramatic.

Franklin and her team created audit and finance committees and rejuvenated the executive committee. She expanded the membership committee and charged it with targeting a new generation of leaders. She has worked closely with the club's new president to make communications, the club's financial structure, and programs more responsive to a twenty-first-century membership.

Although Franklin clearly knows her own strengths as an individual, she is also quick to credit collaboration. "It's important for a leader to give credit to others," she stresses. "It's important to thank people repeatedly for what they are doing, especially in an organization where everyone is a volunteer." Franklin recognized a need for greater efficiency, dared to make the changes that were necessary, and understood that every leader depends on backup to succeed.

Finally, moral leadership will be needed in the future just as much as it has been in the past. I have always found a compass in Pope John Paul II. You did not always have to agree with the pope to admire a leader unafraid to tackle the hard issues. In so doing, Pope John Paul challenged people to think more deeply about those topics, and more carefully. During the pope's 1995 visit to the United States, for example, he spoke often of those in need: "America has a reputation the world over, a reputation of power, prestige, and wealth," he told one audience. "But not everyone here is powerful; not everyone here is rich. In fact, America's sometimes extravagant affluence often conceals much hardship and poverty."

Ten years later, as the aftermath of Hurricane Katrina has ripped aside the curtain concealing America's poor, events have unequivocally shown how right he was.

Poverty, of course, respects no national boundaries, and this was a leader who understood that nearly 1.3 billion of the world's people live on less than $1 a day (as stated at www.worldrevolution.org). Yet with the Internet having collapsed the planet's barriers of time and distance, the have-nots of the world can now see just how much the "haves" possess. Unless leaders of the future tackle this disparity head on, more global unrest and instability will ensue.

When Pope John Paul II died, millions of people around the world mourned his passing, reminding us that here was a leader, indeed, for all times. Like the other leaders described here, he spoke truth. He aspired not to be popular, but to be honest. He also had style, personal warmth, and a quick sense of humor. If he was stern, he was never caustic. And you always knew where he stood.

In ten years, the world has gotten more complicated: information travels faster than jets, pandemics such as avian flu threaten our daily lives, we face the dangers of global warming and much more. In a world that will be increasingly diverse and technologically advanced, the hunger for access and economic equality will only grow sharper. Leaders who are honest but not self-righteous, leaders who understand and respect world cultures, leaders committed to bridging the divide between rich and poor—these are the men and women who will make the difference in how well we manage the next ten years.

11

Leaders of the Future
Growing One-Eyed Kings

General Eric K. Shinseki

General Eric K. Shinseki served in the United States Army for thirty-eight years, most recently as Chief of Staff from June 1999 until June 2003. Prior to that, he held a number of key command positions, including Commander of the U.S. Army, Europe, and Commander of the NATO-led Peace Stabilization Force, Bosnia-Herzegovina. General Shinseki is a graduate of the U.S. Military Academy at West Point, New York, and the recipient of several U.S. and foreign military decorations.

Leaders of the future—2015? 2025? 2030? Do you know who will lead your organization ten years from now, or twenty, or twenty-five years in the future? How about next week? The U.S. Army knows who its leaders will be decades from today, they just don't know their names yet. They're currently on the job, wearing the uniforms of sergeants, lieutenants, captains, majors, and colonels.

Because the Army promotes entirely from within, it knows that it must be a premier learning organization in which leadership development is a daily commitment made by leaders at every echelon throughout a high-performing institution. The Army's future— and, indeed, the future of our nation—depends on it. The next Army Chief of Staff is probably a serving senior general officer today; the chief after next could be a serving division commander but, just as likely, a serving brigadier general today; and that chief's successor will probably be one of our talented brigade commanders, who is, just as probably, on operational deployment somewhere today. The Sergeant Major of the Army in the year 2030 is already in uniform and growing toward an appointment with destiny.

In the military, there is no more important responsibility than growing leaders for the next crisis. And despite all our best hopes and intentions, we know that there will always be another crisis. That is our history. The success of today's missions was ensured years ago, during the Cold War and the turmoil following it, as Army leaders then committed to developing today's leaders for today's missions, long before the current crises arrived. That same commitment to leaders of the future is being repeated in the Army today. Leader development goes well beyond training for today's tasks. The Army must continue investing in the continuous, sequential, and mandatory education of its leaders at every level so that when the next crisis arrives full-blown, it has a competent organization ready to dominate it.

The Certainty of Crisis

Like most organizations, the Army seeks to attract the best and the brightest young people, but makes do with some entirely average ones—men and women whom it grows into competent, confident, and selfless leaders. Those initial decisions about whom to induct into military service take on greater significance when it is understood that the future leaders of the Army, ultimately the few who will serve in uniform at the most senior levels, are being inducted into the force annually.

Learning "follower-ship" early, as well as the importance of positive mentoring, grows young soldiers into leaders, who will guide the Army through the kinds of challenges that have faced the nation for 230 years. Growing leaders is an everyday devotion and, over time, these efforts produce competent organizations, defined by quality leaders, who fill every position throughout the formation—tough, determined, and principled leaders. No single point failures are acceptable—not only are lives at stake, but so is the freedom of our nation.

Although on the surface it might appear that leadership perspectives are quite similar in business and in the military, there are important differences. One notable difference between leadership in business and leadership in the military may stem from our attitudes toward crises. My sense is that business leaders spend much of their day-to-day activity avoiding crises. Military leaders, however, know that there will be crises in their future (history shows us that there will be), and on the day that a threat to the nation is identified, they will be called upon not to avoid that threat but to confront it directly. That is why we have a military, and why each military leader works diligently at being the very best in the profession—self-selected crisis leaders. The military spends enormous time and energy running a series of continuing "what-if" scenarios and assessments that enable it to anticipate any of a series of potential conflicts—anywhere around the world, anytime. As a result, the military is often found posturing for the most likely crises while remaining, at the same time, cognizant of the most dangerous ones. Both dangers are potentially very real, and they compete for attention and scarce resources.

Developing Army leaders who will be capable of dealing with such strategic ambiguity begins early and continues over time in the numerous operations command posts that populate the echelons of command—from battalion level all the way up to Army Headquarters. Command posts are, in reality, leader-development labs. Of these leader labs, the Division's tactical forward command post—commonly known as the "DTAC" for short—is the crucible in which many of the Army's future leaders are forged. Here the range in age and experience among those operating at the DTAC is broad and varied, making it a highly charged learning environment that is equaled in few other places.

The Certainty of Uncertainty

Years ago, I encountered a quotation in a good book that proclaimed, "In the kingdom of the blind, the one-eyed man is king." Some may find this quotation insensitive, but I do not intend any insensitivity by repeating it here. It struck me then, as it does even now, as useful in describing to young officers—who must grow into strategic leaders—what we want them to focus on as we develop their decision-making skills and, equally important, their instincts. I've used the quotation on a variety of occasions, but found it especially useful for helping young leaders working within a DTAC to accept the challenge and responsibility of decision making in the midst of uncertainty, responsibilities that are sure to grow with their demonstrated abilities.

Small, agile, lightly armed, and vulnerable, the DTAC directs the operations of all maneuver formations involved in close combat. During the Cold War, survival of the DTAC meant remaining undiscovered: camouflage, noise and light discipline, and constant displacements—at least every twelve hours by doctrine—were the norm. Hence, little sleep, living by wits and instincts, infrequent showers, cold meals, and nervous tension defined life at the DTAC. The officers and noncommissioned officers assigned there were handpicked functional experts (air and ground maneuver, fire support, air defense, intelligence, engineers, communications, and logistics), who had to be creative and decisive. They numbered just enough to man two twelve-hour shifts—no third shift, no days off, no extra mouths to feed or haul. During the frequent setup and breakdown of the DTAC, everyone pulled a rope, drove a peg, tied a knot—there were no prima donnas.

Life at the DTAC is steeped in uncertainty, yet its mission for its leaders is to make sound decisions consistently and implement them aggressively. Between those two poles lie the art and science of DTAC operations. The DTAC is charged with winning battles decisively. The reference to one-eyed kings encouraged young leaders, who were still growing their professional instincts, to embrace uncertainty and to learn to be decisive. Accept uncertainty as a given, balance risk and opportunity, find ways to generate momentum, master the transitions which always threaten to steal momentum, and retain the freedom to act whenever opportunities present themselves. These are the hallmarks of dominant, decisive operations, and they are the same attributes critical to leaders of the future, whether in the military, in business, or in the social sector.

Under uncertain circumstances, whether on duty at the DTAC or operating at the highest levels of strategic planning in the Army, it is always tempting to defer decisions because situational awareness is not clear enough, or the intelligence picture is not perfect. In fact, the picture will never be perfect, nor clear enough for the timid. It is human nature to hesitate on decisions, hoping for a "better read." That is a luxury most operational commanders in the military do not have. So developing competent, prudent leaders who can adapt to the uncertainties in high-stress and high-risk environments is an institutional priority. The imprudent, the arrogant, the overly emotional, the timid, and the cowardly are liabilities. What are needed are men and women of character who have a deep sense of moral obligation to serve the nation, their organizations, and their soldiers courageously, selflessly, without fanfare, and successfully.

It is understandable why a desire for perfection might creep into the operational thinking of young leaders who are immersed in the uncertainties of the DTAC. The stakes are high. They must learn to make the right decisions in the absence of a complete picture; they must learn to be aggressive without overreaching; they must learn to be confident without the growth of ego; but they must seek to win each and every battle, ten out of ten—nine out of ten will not do.

The Certainty of Change

One consistent lesson that came out of twentieth-century history is that the assumptions of one decade rarely carried over into the next. The strategic environment changed quickly and, for large institutions such as governments and armies, remaining relevant required considerable agility and a culture that willingly embraced change. If you are big and the best at what you do, change, especially fundamental and comprehensive change, is nearly beyond reach.

It will not be any different in the twenty-first century, even with all of its promising technologies, because change is about *people*. Institutions don't change, people do; visionaries don't bring about change, people who embrace their visions do. Those who intend to lead change will have to be visionary and agile, visionary enough to be bold and organizationally agile enough to be decisive. Change is a fact of life. You can either lead change or have it thrust upon you. That is the history of the twentieth century. As I have often observed, "If you don't like change, you're going to like irrelevance even less."

In the Army, growth toward strategic visioning begins early in places such as the DTAC, where young officers and noncommissioned officers are exposed to commander's intent, a tactical statement that envisions how a planned operation will evolve over time. It is an assessment of the knowns, the unknowns, and the givens—terrain, weather, time available—summarized into a commander's simple description of intended outcomes. What begins as tactical visioning in the DTAC develops over time into the strategic visioning skills of senior leaders, who have seen the practical realities of what works and what does not during numerous training exercises and actual operations. The rate of growth varies from officer to officer—the best at it make deep and substantial change in the Army during their tenures.

Visioning is the most demanding task for any institution's senior leadership. Looking into the future is an uncertain task at best, and it requires experienced, creative, and determined risk takers to deliver visions of merit. Visioning is about change and excellence, but it is not without risk. Change confronts all our biases, it undercuts our most closely held beliefs, it challenges our willingness to take risks, and yet it's essential if institutions are to grow and remain relevant. The best institutions know their strengths and are agile enough to leverage their strengths to adjust to changes in the competitive environment. Being more agile than one's competition is powerful in business. In the military profession, there is no alternative to being more agile, more visionary, and bolder than your competition. Simply, it is the difference between victory and defeat.

In the midst of its ongoing operations—fighting wars, defending our nation, launching humanitarian missions both here and abroad—the Army continues to develop its leaders for the unseen and unknown crises that will confront the nation in the future. The Army, after all, must constantly adapt to continuously changing operational environments. Leader-development principles, however, remain unchanged, and the leader labs remain in full production. September 11, 2001—like December 7, 1941—reminds that we will never see our risks clearly enough. That's true both in business and in the military. Organizational competence is about growing leaders who have the skills, knowledge, and attributes to make good, bold decisions in the face of the uncertainties that all organizations face.

The Army seeks to grow one-eyed kings for its future, and there is a tremendously good crop in place. They will continue to serve with loyalty, duty, respect, selfless service, honor, integrity, and personal courage as guiding values. These values provide the foundation on which trust is nurtured—soldier to soldier, leader to led, unit to unit, the Army to the American people. The Army's continuing development of leaders for its future—and our future—remains bright.

Part IV

Leading Organizations of the Future

12

Philosopher Leaders

Charles Handy

Charles Handy is a writer, broadcaster, and lecturer. His books, includ-ing The Age of Unreason, *on the changing shape of work and its effects on our lives and organizations have sold more than one million copies around the world. His latest published work,* Myself and Other More Important Matters, *a series of reflections on his life, was released in May of 2006. In his career, Handy has been an oil executive with Shell, a business economist, a professor at the London Business School, the warden of St. George's House in Windsor Castle (a study center for social and ethical issues), and the chairman of the Royal Society of Arts in London. He is Irish and grew up in Kildare, but now lives and works in London.*

When Plato was designing his ideal state as described in *The Republic*, he gave the top roles to those he called philoso-pher kings. These Guardians, as they were named, would need a special education to fit them for their tasks. Only then would such people, he believed, have the perspective, the understanding, and the discernment to make decisions that would affect all the citizens in their care. The actual doers—the warriors, merchants, and labor-ers—essential though they were, came lower down in the hierarchy. If Plato were around today he might wonder whether the Guardians—a nicer name than CEO, you might think—of our orga-nizations were adequately prepared for the big philosophical issues they had to deal with in these modern times.

What, you may ask, has philosophy to do with the leadership of organizations? Let us take just three issues which leaders have to tangle with today, to demonstrate that, whether they realize it or not, they are already practicing philosophy. The question is, Would they do it better if they were better prepared for it?

Issue One: The Mission Statement

Every organization has a mission statement, even if few read it other than those who composed it. Yet the mission statement deals with one of the great philosophical quandaries—the purpose of our existence. *Quandary*, by the way, is the right word to use in considering every philosophical issue, because philosophy cannot answer the questions, only unravel them and explore the consequences of alternative responses. In the end, any action or response is left with the individual in his or her particular situation. If philosophy does seem to provide an answer, it will always turn out to conceal a further question. Unhelpful? At first sight, yes. But philosophy is not an answer book to life's problems, it is a way of thinking about them.

Consider that mission statement. Some philosophers have suggested that there is no grand purpose to life and therefore by extension to our organizations. We are an accidental life-form, so we might as well just enjoy it and survive as long as we can do so. Which, of course, raises the further question, What is enjoyment? Apply that to a business, and you might argue that as long as the business exists we should first make sure that it survives, then make as much money as we can and let those who have the power keep the majority of it for themselves. Many businesses appear to have adopted this philosophy.

Many philosophers, however, have worried over this idea of enjoyment. Aristotle called it *eudaimonia*, which is usually translated as "happiness," a mistranslation that has worked its way into the American Declaration of Independence as one of the inalienable and self-evident rights of all citizens. What Aristotle was talking about is more accurately translated as "flourishing," which still doesn't answer the question. Unpacked a bit more, it means doing your best with what you are best at. On one level Aristotle seems to be anticipating, albeit more elegantly, the concept of core competences, or Tom Peters's injunction to "Stick to the Knitting."

Going deeper, the concept of *eudaimonia* suggests that we each, individual or organization, should develop our own special talents and resources as far as we can if we are to get the most out of life. It could go further still, to imply that we ought to discover our own purpose in society, one that we are specially, maybe even uniquely, qualified to perform. Discerning what that might be, and equipping ourselves for it, then becomes our main challenge in life. For leaders of organizations it is no different. In this philosophy, each organization needs its special purpose, a purpose that will surely go further than making the shareholders richer. Leaders must bear in mind that they have an obligation, if they accept this reason for our mortal existence, to ensure that each of those who work with and for them also has the chance to decide on their special purpose and to develop their potential to achieve it. One cannot have one law for oneself and another for the rest. That Declaration of Independence turns out to be a call for the universal right to self-development.

This interpretation of *eudaimonia* might sound a little grandiose to those struggling with the daily minutiae of life and work. But we don't all have to take on the responsibility to change the world. Voltaire, another philosopher, put it nicely: "How infinitesimal is the importance of anything I do, but how infinitely important it is that I do it." Leaders do well to remember that every one of the people working under them is entitled to feel this.

There are, of course, other explanations of why we exist and what our purpose in life ought to be. Christian philosophers might argue that, having been made in the image of God, we are required to be partners in His continuing creation of the universe. If you hold that view it would be incumbent on you, as a leader, to make sure that your organization lived up to its responsibilities to leave a positive imprint on the world, to be careful, yourself, to treat your fellow human beings as also made in the image of God, and to walk the talk of your personal beliefs. The integrity that people increasingly demand of their leaders properly means wholeness; there should be no distinction between your personal beliefs and your behavior, at all times and in all places. Only then can the necessary trust be built, the trust that binds followers to their leaders.

Issue Two: The Social Contract

What is the role of the state, and, by extension, the role of the organization, which is itself a sort of ministate? What should be the relationship of the individual to the larger organization and vice versa? Hobbes thought that the state's only obligation was to stop us harming others. Law and order are essential to any society; after that it is every individual for himself or herself. He didn't, however, expect it to result in a comfortable world. Life would be "nasty, brutish and short." Many businesspeople might therefore stretch the role of the state a little to make life a trifle less brutal, but would prefer to trust the market rather than the government to get things right. Individuals, too, might go for as much liberty as possible in their work, and as much control over their own money and lives as is consistent with a secure environment. Liberty, however, is the enemy of equality, even if they are often bracketed together. Too much liberty breeds selfishness and thus inequality in outcomes.

Marx and his descendants preferred equality to liberty as they looked at its consequences in the economies of the West. They therefore made the state, in countries such as Russia and China, responsible for every aspect of the lives of its citizens. That bred another sort of selfishness, as people left it to the state to look after their neighbors and the environment. Their only responsibility was to themselves within the tiny scope of freedom that was left in their lives. They eventually discovered that they had achieved neither liberty nor equality, and the regimes in most countries such as this have tumbled. They have, however, left a sad legacy. Released from their chains, the people in places such as Russia and China have given free rein to their new freedoms but still without too much concern for others or for the wider society. Unfortunately, the state can no longer take care of these things in the way it used to. There is, as a result, a new vacuum of social concern and involvement in those countries. "It's none of our business," the leaders of organizations say, but it is no one else's either.

The view we hold of the social contract, a key element in political philosophy, will determine what we do about corporate governance, a phrase, incidentally, unknown in China, and the newly fashionable idea of corporate social responsibility. At the organizational level a leader's viewpoint will influence the relations between the organization and its workforce. It is ironic that those corporations that advocate a philosophy of open markets and systems for their country apply a quasi-totalitarian regime to their own organizations, assigning individuals to their roles, organizing their daily lives, and, in some cases, decreeing their futures. It may be done with care, but it does trade a measure of individual liberty for efficiency if not equality. Leaders need to ask themselves whether their view of the social contract is consistent in all aspects of their organization. Liberty does carry responsibilities. If these are ignored, the liberty that leaders cherish may be curtailed in the interests of the wider society. The growth of the regulation regime is one sign that this is already happening.

Democracy is an inefficient system for getting things done, but it does recognize the rights of the individual to have some say in how he or she is to be governed and whom by. If leaders believe in this aspect of the social contract in society they should also find ways to respect these rights in their own organizations. Under existing company standards, providers of the finance have superior rights to those who make the money for those same providers. This seems unbalanced, particularly since most of those so-called owners are not owners in the normal sense of the word. They have bought their shares from other investors and have, typically, no direct association with the organization on the ground. They are more like gamblers at the racecourse, betting on their favorite horses or dogs. But at the racecourse the gamblers don't have the right to sell or destroy the horse if it fails to perform, nor can they sack the trainer. Shareholders can, if they act together. No other recognized social contract gives the rich so much power over ordinary citizens. When it does, it is called a dictatorship.

To rail against dictatorships in foreign countries and ignore those at home because they are more benevolent, more limited in their scope, and thought to be more efficient, is to be inconsistent philosophically. Over time such inconsistency is sensed and increasingly resented. Unions were one response to a manifestly unbalanced social contract in organizations. Now that organizations are increasingly composed of professionals or paraprofessionals we may expect more challenges to the rights of the outside financiers and more insistence on a recognition of the rights of employees to be consulted. Ultimately, there will be pressure from key staff members to have more control over the destiny of their ministate. As it is, the language of rights is beginning to displace the language of property, signs that the social contract is slowly changing.

Issue Three: Justice and Fairness

Most leaders would like to think that they are just and fair in their dealings. They may not be aware of the unthinking prejudices that they bring to this tricky area of social philosophy. Justice turns out to mean several different things. It is just to give people what they deserve, whether it be reward or punishment. Pay for performance is one application of this concept of justice. But it is also just and fair to give people what they need. "From each according to their abilities, to each according to their needs," was what Marx called for, but you don't need to be a Marxist to believe that poverty ought to literally be history, at least in organizations headquartered in the affluent West. To do less is unjust, even if it keeps the costs down.

John Rawls, a much-respected contemporary American philosopher who died recently, argued that the only true justice was to treat all people equally, unless you could imagine yourself standing behind what he called a veil of ignorance and could, without bias, conclude that treating some people unequally might benefit all. For example, it might then be considered just to give doctors special education because we all need their skills.

Would John Rawls's argument justify paying CEOs up to four hundred times the pay of the average worker? Conceivably. But a case would need to be made for such preferential treatment. Or is the justification to be found in their performance? If so, then it could be argued that the same principle of pay for performance should be replicated throughout the organization, unless Rawls's principle comes into play again, justifying unequal treatment by universal benefit. The argument that salaries and conditions have to be comparable with others in similar positions may have a market justification—we could not keep them if we didn't match the other offers they could receive—but it fails to meet either of the other two definitions of justice. They do not necessarily deserve it and they certainly don't need it. It should be no surprise, therefore, that some suspect a rigging of the market in these cases and complain of injustice.

The New Leadership Challenge

Organizations are the new politics. In the institutionalized societies of the affluent world it is organizations of all types that are the drivers of change. We can't rely on governments to lead us. In democracies, governments have to go with the grain of public opinion or they won't be reelected. They inevitably follow rather than lead, articulating and then legalizing what is already beginning to happen where people live and work. More people work in organizations than bother to vote. More now prefer the marketplace to the ballot booth as a way of getting what they want, markets that are served by organizations. In one way or another, even the most independent of us has to rely on organizations to meet many of our needs. Organizations matter. They now matter more than they did, despite the spread of the virtual world, because they are often the best, if not the only, place to express ourselves and demonstrate our competencies outside our nuclear families. In an uncertain and fluctuating world the organization still offers something relatively stable to belong to. For many, the organization is now their principal community.

We must therefore treat the organization as a community, not as a machine with humans to work the parts. *Leadership* is a word borrowed from political theory, *management* from the world of engineering. We speak of managing things, resources, space, or processes. We lead people. Translating people into human resources suggests that they can be managed like forklift trucks, moved around, serviced, and disposed of according to the needs of the organization. You cannot however, properly talk of leading people to be moved, serviced, or disposed of. The language doesn't work, because the concepts don't work in political philosophy. Words are the bugles of social change. The philosophy of organizations is changing in front of our noses.

It will change more. If organizations are going to be the bulwark communities of our new societies, their leaders will increasingly have to articulate the premise of their actions and decisions. They will be increasingly accountable not just to their paymasters but to their inhabitants, their neighbors, and society at large. Transparency will be demanded of them, as it now is of politicians. Their actions will be matched to their words in a kind of ethical audit. Indeed, the new concern with ethics in the boardroom is just one more sign that the operating philosophies of our leaders are now under inspection. What is needed, however, is not a guidebook to good ethics but more exposure to a way of thinking about the underlying quandaries of life. That's doing philosophy. Plato discovered his philosophy by arguing with Socrates, an irritating but wise man. Maybe the future Guardians of our organizations will each need a Socrates to challenge their thinking, and thereby help them to work out what it is that they believe is the basis of a good life, a good society, and a good organization, and then to apply their philosophy to their own lives and organizations. Doing so has to be the real challenge for the leaders of the future.

13

Leadership as a Brand

Dave Ulrich and Norm Smallwood

Dave Ulrich is a professor of business administration at the University of Michigan, where his teaching and research addresses the question of how to create an organization that adds value to employees, customers, and investors. He is also a partner at the RBL Group (www.rbl.net). He has helped generate multiple award-winning national databases on organizations that assess alignment between strategies, human resource practices, and HR competencies. Ulrich has published over one hundred articles and book chapters, and twelve books. Ulrich has also consulted and done research with over half of the Fortune 200 companies.

Norm Smallwood is a recognized authority in developing businesses and their leaders to deliver results and increase value. He is on the faculty of the Executive Education Center at the University of Michigan Business School. He is cofounder (with Dave Ulrich) of the RBL Group, a firm of well-known and broadly experienced management educators and consultants. In 2005, the RBL Group was ranked as the number one leadership development firm in the world by Leadership Excellence.

L eaders matter.
   Research shows—and experience confirms—that organizations with strong and effective leadership at all levels achieve superior business results, whereas organizations with inconsistent leadership achieve inconsistent business results, and organizations with inferior leadership achieve inferior business results. Effective executives can turn fledgling companies into viable competitors;

ineffective executives turn once-competitive companies into take-over targets.

At each level of an organization, a similar leadership impact occurs. The manager of an individual McDonald's franchise shapes it into a restaurant that attracts or repels customers. The vice-president of a finance, IT, or HR function creates or dissipates energy, focus, and ultimately results. The plant manager affects plant productiv-ity, product quality, safety, and production innovation by his or her actions and style. When it comes to business performance and cre-ating value, leadership matters.

Because leadership matters, and because most leaders want to learn how to become more effective, the past twenty years have brought a profusion of creative metaphors and images to describe what it takes to be a successful leader. From fish to cheese, from habits to natural ecosystems, from self-empowerment to servitude, great numbers of leadership thinkers have struggled to distill the essence of what makes an effective leader. Over the years, we have read that leaders need to be transformational and create funda-mental change in their organizations; to be visionary and articulate a point of view about the future; to be primal and release emotional intelligence; to build a pipeline for future leaders; to demonstrate good principles through their behaviors; to lead through science and art; to be resonant and renew oneself and the organization; and to be courageous in taking and making decisions. All of these top-ics have been covered in leadership books in the past five years; they show the array of metaphors for informing leadership thinking and action.

Leaders learn what previous successful leaders have done and adapt lessons from leaders such as Santa Claus, John Wooden, Attila the Hun, Colin Powell, Jack Welch, Rudolf Giuliani, Gandhi, Abraham Lincoln, and Jesus Christ. And yet, the search for the leadership holy grail continues. We continue our quest for how to become more effective leaders and how to create more effective leadership throughout our organizations. In this chapter, it is not our intent to reveal the eternal and inviolable truths of effective leadership; rather, we propose to offer a simple and unique metaphor of leaders and leadership that offers new insights on how to ensure that leaders continue to matter and affirms that they do have real impact on their organizations.

Leadership as a Brand

The concept of brand is known to all—everywhere we go, product brands are pervasive. We buy clothes with the Nike swoosh or the Polo horse and rider. We drive cars that have distinctive styles embodied in their brand and emblems emblazoned on their hoods. Our laptops, notebooks, wallets, pens, and watches are all branded to send a message and maximize differentiation. We choose products in part because their brand reflects our self-identity.

Although product brands are what surround us, the emphasis in the branding business itself has shifted from products to the firms that produce or design them. Today it is less a specific product that entices the customer and more the reputation of the firm. When airports decided to replace their anonymous cafeterias and restaurants with branded firms (for example, Starbucks, McDonalds, or Chili's), revenue in the same locations increased by about 40 percent almost overnight. This result was not specifically because of the products that the branded firms offered, but the *brand* of the firms themselves that communicated value to prospective customers. When a no-name hotel changed ownership to a Hyatt, the same room in the same location with many of the same features earned about 20 percent more per night. We know that brand creates value over generics for both products and firms. Similarly, it is our belief that a firm's brand is sustained and enhanced by the firm's leadership brand.

A leadership brand represents the identity and reputation of leaders throughout a company. Leaders demonstrate a brand when they think and act in ways congruent with the desired product or firm brand. A leadership brand exists when leaders at all levels of an organization demonstrate a consistent reputation for both attributes and results.

Thinking about leadership as a brand instead of simply something leaders do offers a number of insights into leadership effectiveness and into creating sustained and consistent leadership that enhances firm value.

Brand has both core and differential elements. All cars have steering, suspension, cylinders, and other components that make them go. Without quality parts, the car will not work. Many of these core components are invisible to customers, but they are vital elements of the automobile brand. So, although a Yugo and a Lexus have the requisite components to be functioning automobiles, they are very different brands. The pursuit by Lexus of organizational-perfection brand identity leads the company to continually innovate and put into the car features that differentiate it from other cars (such as styling and design), which customers relate to. Likewise, we believe there are core elements of leadership that are generic to any successful leader. Leaders need to think about the future and act in the present, they need to engage individuals and govern organizations, and they need to demonstrate personal qualities that give them credibility. But what differentiates branded leaders is the ability to reflect in their leadership style the attributes and results that customers want to see in their firm. Lexus leaders would be driven to continuous learning and improvement while Yugo leaders would be focused on managing costs and delivering efficiencies. A firm's leadership brand should reflect customer expectations.

Brand focuses on the outside-in. Just as a product or firm brand matters only to the extent that consumers value it, a leadership brand that doesn't result in a firm that is more likely to attract or please consumers is useless. We therefore begin the conversation to define effective leadership for a firm by asking, What would customers want this firm to be known for? What do our leaders need to know, do, and deliver to make that customer-desired identity happen? With this approach, leadership matters not because leaders say so, or because employees will be happy, but because customers and investors will take money out of their wallets and put it into the firm. Leadership brand requires that leadership results be assessed by the extent to which leaders deliver value to customers and investors outside the firm.

Brand evolves over time to meet the changing needs of the marketplace. Brands change with consumers. For years, the Pillsbury Doughboy was a cute, chunky icon of the Pillsbury product line. With today's emphasis on healthy eating choices and lifestyle, however, the Doughboy went on a diet and adapted to current consumer conditions. Similarly, Kentucky Fried Chicken became KFC; the March of Dimes went from curing polio to other childhood diseases; Marriott went from hotels to retirement centers; and Nike has moved from shoes to clothes. Brands evolve, and so do leaders. Successful leaders continually tie their brand or identity to the changing expectations of customers and investors. As customers change, so must the leadership brand.

Brand puts leadership into business terms. Leadership rhetoric is often plagued with ambitious but fuzzy terms such as *transformation, vision, aspiration, character,* and *empowerment.* A leadership brand focuses on quantifiable business terms of customer share and market value. We have argued that the ultimate return on a leadership investment should be a "return on intangibles" (a new ROI for leadership) that shows up in a firm's stock price. When leadership brand connects to customer share or market value, the rationale for leadership investment is much easier to make. For example, when Jack Welch retired and Jeff Immelt replaced him at the helm of General Electric (GE), the two other contenders for the top GE job left to head up other companies—Bob Nardelli went to Home Depot and Jim McNerney went to 3M and then on to Boeing just a few years later. At each move of these top leaders, the stock of the company went up and stayed up in anticipation of their delivering on future results.

Brand is unique, not generic. We have asked participants in training programs to bring along the leadership competency models that they use for 360-degree assessments. We then post them along the wall and ask participants to name the company they match up with. Often they cannot, because the competencies are generic and similar. What company, for example, doesn't include such competencies as "has a vision," "communicates well," "builds teams," and "engages employees" in its assessments? While these generic competencies offer the core elements of leadership, a leadership brand goes further. A leadership brand pushes leaders to move from generic leadership to targeted leadership. In our work we have proposed the "so that" question to move from generic attributes to focused results. At Marriott leaders communicate *so that* customers experience exceptional service—the Marriott brand—while at Pfizer, leaders communicate *so that* innovation can more readily occur—the Pfizer brand. For each competency, if we apply the "so that . . ." statement, we evolve to a specific result that is tied to the strategy or identity of the organization.

Brand turns leadership into specific decisions. Product and firm brands are not random; they are reinforced and sustained by choices in material and design. Likewise, leadership brand is reinforced by dozens of day-to-day decisions. These decisions may be about relationships, resources, strategies, or measures. Leaders are branded when the array of decisions they make on a daily basis reinforce and support a clear identity.

Effective leadership brand must be reflected by leaders at all levels of an organization. A strong brand is universally understood to convey a specific message: Nike communicates athleticism to rich and poor, to athletes in training and athletes in mind only. In the same way, a firm's leadership brand cannot be something that the top leaders in an organization do while others watch—or worse, do something else. Instead, it must engage and be reflected by leaders at every level of the organization. Organizations with an effective leadership brand have leaders throughout the organization that "be," "know," and "do" the leadership identity. If a leader two or three layers down in the organization does not reflect the desired brand, that leader dilutes or pollutes an entire segment of the organization, affecting employee, customer, and investor response to the firm and under-mining performance. Leaders that do not reflect the firm's leader-ship brand must be identified and upgraded—or removed.

Brand is sustainable, not tied to any individual person. Leadership brand is not tied to any one person, no matter how charismatic or talented—it is embedded throughout the organization. When Bob Nardelli took the reins at Home Depot, he brought with him a dis-ciplined, aggressive, and engaging style. This style was soon cap-tured throughout the Home Depot network of stores. The company began to adapt the leadership brand he modeled. It was reinforced through the company's financial management, information tech-nology, and human resource processes and systems. When money, data, and people are institutionalized consistent with the leader-ship brand, they communicate and reinforce that brand. We have worked in companies in which a top leader wants to be "the" leader, the one who embodies the brand of the firm, leaving oth-ers to emulate him or her rather than execute a defined, consumer-centric leadership brand. The ultimate test of the success of a leader is when he or she leaves. Is the leadership brand effective enough and broadly executed enough to be recognized by the leader's successor?

Brand must have efficacy or it will not last. Unfulfilled promises are worse than no promises. Hotels that guarantee full refunds for any service faux pas often cannot live up to those expectations, and their brand promise is violated. More patron complaints are regis-tered in a high-end restaurant than in a diner, because the expec-tations of the patrons are higher in the high-end restaurant. Leaders who declare a leadership brand must live and breathe it or they will create cynicism and lose credibility. Leadership brand efficacy occurs when employees, customers, and investors believe—and see—that promises made at the top are promises that will be kept.

Branded Leadership Matters

When firms have a leadership brand, they win on multiple dimensions.

They win with investors because investors will grant higher market value for similar earnings, often called intangibles. Quality of management or leadership gives investors confidence in the future, leading to a higher share price. General Electric, for example, has a reputation for great leaders. Those who leave GE to lead other firms carry that leadership brand with them and often create intangible market value. Of course, as we noted earlier, if the perceived brand value is not rooted in reality, or if the brand does not transfer to the demands of the new consumers, the brand image fades. But branded leaders are often in firms that have a higher price to earnings ratio than others in their industry.

Firms with branded leadership win with customers because the customers have confidence that the leaders at every level of the organization will respond to their needs in a consistent and appropriate way. Nordstrom wins in the service game because its leaders are branded with a service mentality at all levels of the organization. They don't have to ask for permission to serve customers, they just do it as a part of who they are. And customers respond with very high customer share. Targeted customers who spend $1000 every six months on products Nordstrom sells buy a larger percent of their products at Nordstrom because of the service brand that is embedded among all Nordstrom leaders.

Finally, firms with branded leadership win with employees. When a consistent and effective leadership brand exists in an organization, employees know what to expect and the productivity- and engagement-draining dissonance is eliminated. One leader told us that he treated his best customers as if they were his best employees and his best employees as if they were his best customers. If a firm makes a customer brand promise of timely and responsive behavior, the same brand should be reflected in employee relations.

Herman Miller wants to be branded as the innovator in the office furniture business by consistently creating innovative products and services for its customers. In extending and consistently applying the leadership brand, that same spirit of innovation resonates in how management treats employees—offering creative and flexible approaches to employee terms and conditions of work, work settings for employees, and work processes.

Building Leadership Brand

In the past few years, we have worked to define how leaders can build their personal brand to be consistent with the firm's brand, thus creating leadership market value. More recently, our work with excellent firms has helped us identify six steps to creating branded leadership within a firm.

Step 1: *Create a need for leadership brand.* Before making investments in creating a leadership brand, the senior team needs to recognize that investing in a leadership brand will help the company's financial and customer performance. Although some senior leaders will immediately understand that creating a leadership brand can deliver much the same value as a firm or product brand, others may want something more substantial. Here are a few ways to gather the data you'll need to create a need for leadership brand:

- Plot your company's earnings and stock price versus those of your largest competitor. How have you done? If your price to earnings ratio has exceeded the industry average over a significant period of time, you probably have a favorable leadership brand. If not, or if it has declined in recent quarters or years, you may be losing intangible value tied to your leadership brand.

- Identify the leadership brand for your company. Ask yourselves, What are the top three things we want to be known for by our best customers in the future? and

What attributes and results do we need to exhibit in order to achieve that reputation? Once there is consensus on these attributes, identify the extent to which your current leaders possess them in their day-to-day behaviors.

- Review your growth strategy and pose the question, Do we have enough leaders with the right skills to deliver this strategy? To deliver on strategic aspirations requires money, technology, product innovation, and leadership. Which of these key ingredients is missing? Often firms have better access to capital than to leadership.

Step 2: *Articulate a declaration of leadership.* In the Declaration of Independence, the signers stated their beliefs by way of a clear statement ("We hold these truths to be self evident. . . .") that rallied both their intellectual and emotional energy. It gave them clarity about why they wanted change and what they wanted from the change. Likewise, we believe that branded leadership is more effective with a declaration of leadership. This declaration states clearly and succinctly what leaders should know, do, and deliver. It combines attributes and competencies of leaders and their results. For a company's leadership brand, it sets the standards of what leaders at all levels should know and the results they should deliver. At a personal level, a declaration of leadership brand articulates the personal reputation that a leader aspires to, what he or she wants to be known for. Because the organization and individual brand statements are aligned to results, they are not generic but instead are crafted for the situation. And, like the Declaration of Independence, they offer both an intellectual and an emotional roadmap for personal and institutional leadership.

Step 3: *Assess leaders against the leadership brand standard.* With a clearly articulated declaration of leadership, a standard is set that can now be assessed. Leadership assessment requires collecting perceptual and objective data on leaders' behaviors and results. Because personal assessments are rarely accurate, data also should be collected from multiple stakeholders in a 360-degree assessment with input from superiors, peers, and subordinates or, even better, in a 720-degree assessment that includes these individuals plus key stakeholders outside the corporation (such as suppliers, customers, investors, community members, and so on). An assessment should be tracked over time to look for patterns—not events—and to build the next generation of leaders.

Step 4: *Invest in leaders to enhance brand.* Using data from an assessment, investments can be made to enhance the leadership brand. There are three general types of leadership investment: training, on-the-job experience, and off-the-job experience. Training offers structured learning experiences in which individuals may learn academic principles and apply them in structured settings. On-the-job experience allows individuals to learn from their day-to-day experiences. These experiences may be more structured with coaches, mentors, and task forces or less structured through job assignments and presentation opportunities. Off-the-job experience also offers leaders a great source of learning. Serving on not-for-profit boards, doing community service, and being engaged in other off-the-job activities builds relationship and leadership skills.

Step 5: *Measure the quality of leadership and the impact of leadership investments.* Measurement of leadership investments is critical so that appropriate resources are invested in next-generation leaders in effective ways. Measurement starts with asking about the business case for why leadership matters: Why are we investing in leadership brand? What results do we expect to see as a result of this investment? Often this means tracking things such as employee engagement, customer share, or investor intangibles. Measurement may also focus on behaviors that leaders demonstrate. Too often, however, this is where the measurement stops. Therefore, the initial business case should include a plan for routine measurement and assessment of results, followed by adjustments, as necessary, to investment strategy to ensure that appropriate results are being achieved.

Step 6: *Publicize the leadership brand in ways that encourage continuity.* In the first five steps we have focused on ensuring that our leaders have efficacy to deliver on the leadership brand proposition. To ensure brand recognition, however, we must develop awareness that these investments are worth it. The major aim of this awareness campaign is to build stakeholder confidence in the future of the organization. The CEO should be the brand manager of the company leadership brand, and he or she should take the lead in building brand awareness. This is done by ensuring that employees, customers, analysts, and investors understand the leadership brand, what leaders are doing to build the brand, and the results that have been achieved as a result of the investment.

Leadership Matters

At the beginning of this chapter, we made the assertion that leaders matter. But just as leaders matter to organizations, so too does leadership—specifically, the brand of leadership—matter to organizations. Branded leadership helps turn the desire for leadership into the actions required to make it happen throughout the organization—in a way that is aligned with the organization's strategy.

Further, branded leadership offers insights on what those who are invested in building leadership throughout a company should pay attention to. For those who want to become more effective leaders—in our experience, most anyone who is in a position of leadership—branded leadership provides a clear roadmap of what they should know, what they should do, and what they should be. What is your firm's leadership brand?

14

Regaining Public Trust
A Leadership Challenge

Ken Blanchard and Dennis Carey

Ken Blanchard is coauthor of The One Minute Manager *and chairman and chief spiritual officer of The Ken Blanchard Companies.*

Dennis Carey is a partner of Spencer Stuart and founder of G100, an exclusive club for CEOs only.

As long as we can remember, the American free enterprise system has made us proud. It has generated more wealth per capita for U.S. citizens than any other economic system in the history of the world—and all with little government interference, regulation, and politicization. Except for laws that require boards to exercise their fiduciary duties of care and loyalty, public corporations—and of course private corporations—have been left to operate on a relatively unfettered basis. And it worked well.

The general consensus was that with public companies, it was the board's responsibility, with management at its side, to self-monitor and self-police. Until recently, the only federal and state regulatory interventions related mostly to social issues regarding equity, fair employment, and environmental protection.

The Problem: Ethical Lapses

In the late 1990s, rampant excesses and findings of fraudulent activity started coming to light. It all began with Enron, WorldCom, TYCO, Adelphia, and the professional firms that serve them, from accounting and compensation advisers to outside legal counsel and investment banking firms. When the long-standing belief that corporations could self-regulate was exploded, politicians—feeling immense pressure from their constituents to fix things—began devising rules to discourage ethical lapses and ensure that proper ethical practices were adhered to. The Sarbanes-Oxley Act of 2002 represented a seismic shift to government regulation of boards and their management.

As if outside regulation was not hard enough to get used to, the press aggressively stepped in and questioned the credibility of CEOs. As a result, for the first time in history, CEOs began to appear below politicians in public opinion polls. Worse, for the first time in corporate history, directors were being sued personally for the misdeeds of others in management. The Disney shareholder schism and the unprecedented WorldCom settlement, which held directors personally and financially liable, have tilted the scales even further. Now it is becoming harder and harder to get some of the best in the global corporate community to serve on boards.

How can we turn this situation around and regain the trust and respect that American business enjoyed for years, as well as the freedom business had to essentially self-regulate? Current initiatives of whistle-blowing or CEOs issuing a few memos a year fall far short of the ethical revolution that is required to preserve the free enterprise system that has served us so well for so long. Responsibility for reform must start in the boardroom and the office of the CEO.

The Solutions: The Right Target and the Right Kind of Leadership

When we look for solutions for this ethical dilemma, two things leap out at us.[1] First, over the past decade or so, more than ever before, Wall Street and the stockholders it serves have tended to focus on only one target in evaluating a business—the bottom line. Today, when top managers are asked how long they have had their present positions, they often are tempted to talk in terms of quarters rather than years. After all, they are under the gun for bottom-line performance every ninety days. Unfortunately, it might not be too long before they have to talk about weeks. As a result, the impression one often gets is that there is only one reason to be in business—to make money. That has not helped the reputation of the business world one bit. And yet, we all know in our hearts that money alone is not the right target.

Second, leaders who seem to get the most attention in the media are ones who act like leadership is all about them. You'd think that the sheep were only there for the benefit of the shepherd. With these leaders, all the money, recognition, power, and status tend to move up the hierarchy without any concern for anyone else's interests. That surely is not the right kind of leadership.

The Right Target

To us, *profit is the applause you get for taking care of your customers and creating a motivating environment for your people*. Therefore, the right target for values-based, ethically driven companies is the triple bottom line: being the investment of choice, the provider of choice, and the employer of choice. As Jim Collins emphasized in *Good to Great*,[2] the leaders of such organizations have a "both-and" philosophy regarding results and people, not "either-or." They realize that what keeps their cash register going ka-ching, ka-ching, ka-ching for the long haul are Raving Fan customers and Gung Ho people. Without that perspective, the only question that gets attention for decision making is, Is it legal?[3] Other questions about fairness for all involved or legacy (would you like your kids to know what you are thinking about doing or have it published in the local newspaper?) become irrelevant. Hitting the numbers is all that counts. We think a bigger target that includes both results and people is needed. After all, the best reasons to pursue excellence or grow profitably are to do more good for your customers and create more opportunities for your people.

The Right Kind of Leadership

To rebuild trust and confidence in our free enterprise system, CEOs and their boards must expel any signs of self-serving leadership and aggressively adopt and drive a servant leadership point of view throughout their organizations. When we suggest servant leadership as a solution to the ethical dilemma facing business today, we get befuddled looks. First, most businesspeople don't think those two words go together. How can you lead and serve at the same time? Second, the term *servant leadership* conjures up thoughts of the inmates running the prison, or leaders trying to please everybody, or some kind of religious initiative. These misconceptions are easily overcome when people understand that there are two aspects of servant leadership: vision and direction, and implementation.

Vision and Direction

Leadership is about going somewhere. Great leadership that both leads and serves focuses first on developing a compelling vision and a clear sense of where the enterprise is heading. This is where the "lead" part of servant leadership comes in, and it is crucial. According to Ken Blanchard and Jesse Stoner in *Full Steam Ahead! Unleash the Power of Vision in Your Company and Your Life*,[4] a compelling vision tells people in your organization who you are (your purpose), where you're going (your picture of the future), and what will guide your journey (your values). For example, when Walt Disney started his theme parks, he said they were in the happiness business. Disney's picture of the future was that all guests leaving one of their parks would have the same smile on their faces as they had when they entered, and the behavior of their cast members (employees) would be driven by their rank-ordered values of safety, courtesy, the "show," and efficiency.

The traditional hierarchical pyramid, with the CEO and board at the top, is well-suited for this visionary-direction aspect of leadership. Clear vision and direction start with top management and must be communicated throughout the organization by the leadership. While top management should involve people in shaping direction, the ultimate responsibility for having a vision and communicating it throughout the organization remains with the higher-ups and cannot be delegated.

Implementation

Once vision is set, established goals and strategies can be placed in a higher-order context, and the second role of servant leadership—implementation—begins. This is when the "serve" part of servant leadership comes into play.

It is during implementation that organizations run by self-serving leaders get into trouble. The traditional pyramid is kept alive and well, with the self-serving leaders on the top and customers at the bottom of the hierarchy uncared for by unmotivated people who act like victims and go, "Quack, quack, quack!" because they are not empowered to take initiative and soar like eagles. All the energy in the organization moves up the hierarchy as people try to please their bosses. The bureaucracy rules, and policies and procedures carry the day.

Customers can always identify a bureaucracy run by self-serving leaders when they have a problem and are confronted by ducks who quack, "It's our policy. I didn't make the rules—I just work here! You want to talk to my supervisor? Quack, quack, quack, quack, quack." Yet customers don't care who the boss is. The only people they care about are the ones who answer the phone, greet them, write up their orders, make their deliveries, or respond to their complaints. They want top service, and they want it fast. But that will never happen if you treat your people as though they are unimportant and don't have brains.

How do you create an organization in which ducks are busted and eagles can soar? The traditional hierarchy must be turned upside-down, so the people who are closest to the customers are at the top. In this scenario, leaders serve the needs of the people, cheerleading and supporting them to soar like eagles so they can accomplish the established goals and live according to the vision. Pleasing everyone is not the intent; serving the vision and direction is.

Restoring Trust and Respect to American Business

Why will servant leadership help restore trust and respect to American business and its leadership? There are several reasons.

One reason is that in practice, servant leadership focuses on the triple bottom line by providing better service and motivating people more. Organizations led by servant leaders are more likely to take better care of their customers. Today, if you don't take care of your customers, somebody else is ready, willing, and able to do it. The only thing your competition can't steal from you is the relationship your people have with your customers. Under servant leadership these relationships can really grow, because the people closest to the customer are given the power and motivation to soar like eagles rather than quack like ducks.

Ken had a beautiful example of eagle behavior when he was leaving for a trip that would take him to four different cities:

> At the airport I realized I had forgotten my driver's license. Not having time to get it and make the flight, I had to be creative.
>
> Only one of my books has my picture on the cover: *Everyone's a Coach*, which I wrote with Don Shula, the legendary NFL football coach.[5] When I got to the airport I ran into the bookstore and, luckily, they had a copy of our book. The first airline I had to go to was Southwest. As I was checking my bag at the curb, the porter asked to see my I.D. I said, "I feel bad. I don't have a driver's license or a passport. Will this do?" And I showed him the cover of the book. He shouted out, "The

man knows Shula! Put him in first class!" (Of course, Southwest doesn't have a first class.) Everybody started to high-five me. I was escorted through security and treated like a hero. Unfortunately, things did not go so smoothly at the other airlines, which were staffed by ducks who quacked, "You'd better talk to my supervisor."

This great experience with Southwest Airlines was a direct result of servant leadership. Herb Kelleher, who cofounded Southwest, set the whole organization up to empower everyone—including the frontline baggage-check folks—to make decisions, use their brains, and be servant leaders who could carry out the vision of high-quality customer service. The result is better service, motivated people, and guess what? A better bottom line than any of the other airlines. The triple bottom line comes through again.

Another reason why servant leadership will help restore trust and respect for American business is that organizations led by servant leaders ward off unethical behavior. Companies work more effectively and ethically if clear vision and values are established up front, as they are with servant leadership.

When everyone is clear on the vision and values, there is less confusion when wrongdoing occurs. At these times, it becomes clear to everyone—especially the offender—that anyone involved had made a premeditated decision to go against the agreed upon values, and therefore the responsibility or accountability will rest clearly in his or her court. The intent here is not to place blame; the intent is to serve the vision and direction and get people back on track. In this environment, whistle-blowers are valued, because the leadership of the organization wants to know about and correct any instance in which people are not "walking the talk."

Without clearly established guidelines for behavior, people are left to their own values and interests—thus creating a free-for-all operating style and culture.[6] As the Bible says, "Where there is no vision, the people are unrestrained" (Proverbs 29:18). The *Tao Te*

Ching affirms, "If the sage governs with vision, then his people would not go wrong." When unethical leadership occurs in companies, it is often the result of the moral confusion created by the organization's lack of clearly established guidelines, which a compelling vision provides. For example, after concerns were raised about Tylenol and Vioxx, the quick responses by Johnson & Johnson and Merck to withdraw these products illustrated how clear, rank-ordered values can guide decision making.

How Have Corporate Leaders Been Doing as Servant Leaders?

We believe the boards and CEOs of most public companies—and, for that matter, private companies—in our country could do better with both aspects of servant leadership—vision and direction, and implementation. First let's look at the visionary role. Based on our combined experience of more than fifty years working with business leaders throughout the country, we estimate that less than 10 percent of businesses in America have a clear vision that includes visible, rank-ordered corporate values that are widely distributed and used for decision making. This is where the ethical trouble begins and if unchecked, mushrooms.

Even if a company has a compelling vision, it can run into trouble with the implementation role of servant leadership if the CEO and board are self-serving. As we said before, when that occurs the hierarchy remains alive and well and all the energy in the organization—as well as money, recognition, power, and status—moves up the hierarchy, away from the frontline people and customers.

If it is true that too many CEOs and boards have not been good servant leaders, what have they been doing? The CEOs have been off running the organization while the board has not been actively involved in governance. Unfortunately, many boards have had the philosophy that there should only be two agenda items at every board meeting. The first is, Should we fire the CEO? If the answer to that question is Yes, the second agenda item should be, Who should be on the selection committee to pick the new CEO? If the answer to the first question is No, the second agenda item should be, How can we support the CEO and his initiatives?

As a result of this philosophy, such boards have become "seagull managers." They are not around or involved much until there is a big problem. Then they fly in, make a lot of noise, dump on everyone—especially the CEO—and then fly out. This style has backfired, and now not just these boards, but all boards, are being forced to micromanage compliance to the Sarbanes-Oxley Act.

While some time on compliance is necessary and certainly was occasionally lacking, it is now crowding out what should be, in the spirit of servant leadership, two of the fundamental functions of a board. The first function is making sure that a compelling vision is in place that tells everyone who the company is, where it is going, and what will guide its journey. Second, boards must encourage corporate leaders to become model citizens who help equip, cheerlead, support, and encourage everyone throughout the organization to live according to the vision. During this implementation phase, leaders have to become almost like third-grade teachers, repeating the purpose, picture of the future, and values "over and over and over again" until people throughout the organization act like owners of the vision and, most important, get the values "right, right, right."

Summary

The stakes are high. The image of American business has been tarnished and the opportunity to be self-regulated is being threatened by quick-fix regulations that could impede rather than encourage business progress. But the solution for future leaders may be found in servant leadership. The solution is simple in concept but challenging in implementation.

CEOs and their boards can regain the public trust by focusing on the triple bottom line, shouting the merits of servant leadership from the rooftops, and championing more values-based, ethically driven companies. Rather than permitting self-serving leaders to survive—or worse, rewarding their egocentric behavior—corporations can cultivate and reward servant leaders. Charged with establishing clear, compelling visions for their companies, these leaders can inspire people to live the company values through their own exemplary behavior. Making decisions in accordance with agreed upon, rank-ordered values, these leaders can "walk the talk," showing everyone throughout the organization what the vision looks like in action.

Are you up for the challenge? Are you ready to serve rather than be served?

Endnotes

1. In *Customer Mania* (New York: Free Press, 2004) Ken Blanchard, Jim Ballard, and Fred Finch talked about four key steps to building a company the right way: (1) set your sights on the right target and vision, (2) treat your customers right, (3) treat your people right, and (4) have the right kind of leadership. Treating your customers and people right is implicit in the triple bottom line.

2. Jim Collins, *Good to Great* (New York: HarperCollins, 2001).

3. In *The Power of Ethical Management* (New York: William Morrow, 1988), Ken Blanchard and Norman Vincent Peale wrote about The Ethics Check, a series of questions used to guide ethical decision making.

4. Ken Blanchard and Jesse Stoner, *Full Steam Ahead: Unleash the Power of Vision in Your Company and Your Life* (San Francisco: Berrett-Koehler, 2003).

5. Ken Blanchard and Don Shula, *Everyone's a Coach: Five Business Strategies for High-Performance Coaching* (Grand Rapids, MI: Zondervan, 1995).

6. Drea Zigarmi, senior author of *The Leader Within: Learning Enough About Yourself to Lead Others* (Upper Saddle River, NJ: Prentice-Hall, 2005), contends that a moral dilemma exists when there are

no guidelines for decision making, forcing an individual to rely on his or her own values and beliefs. An ethical dilemma arises when the organization has clearly established guidelines for behavior, and the individual must consciously decide to go along with or violate those guidelines.

15

Leading New Age Professionals

Marshall Goldsmith

Marshall Goldsmith been recognized by the American Management Association as one of fifty great thinkers who have influenced the field of management and by Business Week *as one of the most influential practitioners in the history of leadership development. He was ranked in* The Wall Street Journal *as one of the top ten executive educators, listed in* Forbes *as one of five most-respected executive coaches, and described by* The Economist *as one of the most credible thought leaders in the new era of business. Along with* The Leader of the Future 2, *Goldsmith is the author or coeditor of twenty-two books, including the upcoming* What Got You Here, Won't Get You There. *In 2006, Alliant International University named their school of management and organizational psychology the Marshall Goldsmith School of Management.*

Over the past twenty-five years, the role of leadership in large organizations, particularly in the United States, has been transforming. Several trends that were beginning to be discussed when we published the first edition of *The Leader of the Future* (1996) not only have continued, they have accelerated. More and more organizations are beginning to realize that a large part of their value is being created by smart, hard-working, highly motivated, dedicated professionals. Several trends are causing managers at all levels to revisit their assumptions about what leadership means, and what work means, in a rapidly changing high-pressure, insecure professional world.

In the early 1980s I had the opportunity to work as a consultant in several of America's largest organizations. In those days, I often thought that corporate managers and professionals were lazy. In most corporate headquarters buildings I could have shot a cannonball down the hall at 5:00 P.M. and not hit anyone! Professionals and managers were working thirty-five to forty hours per week. They were taking four-to-five-week vacations. They enjoyed incredible security, great benefits, lifetime health care, and guaranteed pensions.

Those days are gone! Today I am amazed at how hard corporate managers and professionals work. What happened?

The Changing World of Professional Work

Five factors have converged to create a new world of professional work.

• *Increased differentiation in compensation.* Many studies and reports in the press have highlighted the huge compensation increases of CEOs relative to the general population of employees. A much less-noticed change is the salary increase in almost all managerial and professional jobs relative to the general population of employees. As CEOs have enjoyed massive increases in pay, other C-level officers—the next level down—have also noticed large increases in compensation. This trend has continued down throughout organizations, from vice presidents to directors. Although middle managers and staff professionals have not had the relative increase in compensation enjoyed by executives, they have still been moving ahead at a much faster pace than the general population.

Recently, in a conversation involving the CFO of a Fortune 500 company, I received an example of the impact of increased compensation. When one of his direct reports complained that, "I didn't go to work in a major corporation to work this hard. If I had wanted to put in this many hours, I would have worked in a professional services firm," the CFO replied, "You are getting paid as much as a partner in one of the top professional services firms. If you don't want to work like one, why don't you either take a demotion or leave?"

Higher salaries come with higher expectations. The "bottom line" pressure from shareholders has only gone up. As top managers and professionals are being paid more money, they are being given greater expectations. Managers expect their subordinate managers and professionals to earn their pay increases.

• *Decreased job security.* In the early 1980s I did a study of dismissals at IBM. Although IBM would always fire employees who committed ethical violations, almost no one was fired because of poor performance. In other words, if you wore a white shirt, showed up, and achieved minimal expectations, you had a job for your entire career. As IBM's corporate profits began to disappear, its CEO John Akers faced increased pressure from stockholders to change the corporation. His hesitation to move away from IBM's "full-employment practice" was one of the factors that led to his eventual dismissal. IBM's lack of tough performance standards was not that unusual in the United States—the same story could have been observed at AT&T, Kodak, and many other huge companies of that era.

In today's competitive world, job security for managers and professionals seems a distant dream. Along with the greater "carrot" of increased rewards, managers and professionals live with the greater "stick" of losing their jobs. Overall, the professional work ethic has increased in a world in which the value of performing can bring greater rewards, while the cost of nonperformance can bring severe and immediate punishment.

There has also been a marked decline in mid-level work—a "hollowing-out" of the middle class. The lack of mid-level jobs has further increased the distance between society's economic winners and losers.

• *Decreased health care and pension security.* In the past ten years the concept of guaranteed lifetime health care and pension in the United States has been greatly eroded. Employees in steel companies, airlines, and now automotive suppliers are facing the reality of losing part—or all—of the benefits that they thought were a given. The relative losses in benefits for managers and professionals can be even greater than the losses faced by wage-earning employees. Even companies that are retaining pension benefits (such as IBM) are moving away from "defined benefit" plans that provide guaranteed, inflation-proof income security.

As the probability of guaranteed lifetime health care has started to go away, the cost of health care has escalated. As corporate pensions have become more suspect, the certainty of even collecting social security has diminished. These changes have caused many professionals to feel like they are "on their own," even if they work for large companies. Not only do they face pressure to keep their jobs today, they feel the need to save enough money to provide for their own retirements as they grow older.

• *Global competition.* Ten years ago global outsourcing was largely limited to manufacturing or lower-level service jobs. In the future, many more managerial and professional jobs can and will be outsourced. In the 1950s managers and professionals in the United States had a huge competitive advantage. Although business was largely conducted in English, relatively few people around the world spoke fluent English. To add to our advantage, only an incredibly small percentage of the populations in China, India, or Eastern Europe had professional educations that were competitive with those in the United States or Western Europe.

Today, millions of smart, highly educated, hard-working non-American professionals—who speak fluent English—are flooding the job market. They are willing to work for salaries that are much lower than the wages paid to Americans. They are more than happy to work long hours. Global competition has helped further fuel the job insecurity and job pressure experienced by professionals in the United States. The fact that American, European, and Japanese workers earn more than workers in developing countries has led to increased pressure to ensure that their higher-paying jobs are justified by staffing with workers who are making great contributions.

• *New technology.* Many years ago there was an illusion that new technology would lead to more "leisure time." For today's managers and professionals, this can seem like a quaint joke. New technology has created a "24-7" mind-set. Even professionals who are walking down the street, on trains, or in restaurants can be seen using cell phones or PDAs to communicate with their coworkers. New technology has gone hand-in-hand with globalization to create a world where work never stops. It has also begun to blur the distinction between home and the workplace.

The five changes that we have discussed have created a new breed of professional employee—more driven and hard-working, yet more insecure, than ever before. Leading these new professionals will be one of the key challenges for the leader of the future.

What New Age Professionals Want from Leaders

As corporations' expectations of their professionals have increased, the professionals' expectations of their leaders have also increased. In an Accenture-sponsored study involving two hundred specially selected future leaders from 120 companies around the world, we were given the opportunity to ask very bright young professionals to describe what they wanted from their ideal "global leader of the future."[1] Their answers described a world in which leadership was more challenging, yet potentially more rewarding, than ever before. Peter Drucker often talked about the importance of effectively leading knowledge workers—professionals who know more about what they are doing than their boss. In leading new age professionals, it is important to be able to "invert the pyramid" and look at leadership from the perspective of the wants and needs of the professional, as opposed to the perspective of the skills of the leader. In other words, the leader of the future may be judged more by the gifts he or she *provides* than the gifts that he or she *possesses*.

• *Encourage their passion.* When professionals were working thirty to forty hours per week and taking four to five weeks of vacation, it was not as important that they love what they did. When professionals are working as much as they are today—and will be in the future—loving their work is critical. Professionals need to look forward to going to work in the morning! The leaders of the future need to identify, support, and encourage passion in their professional employees. Leaders also need to "lead by example" and demonstrate this same passion in their love for leadership. When we asked high-potential future leaders why they stayed with their companies, "I love working here!" was a top-ranked response.

• *Enhance their ability.* As job security has decreased and global competition has increased, the need to continually update and refine skills has become critical in maintaining professional careers. Leaders of the future will need to look beyond the skills needed for today and help professionals learn the skills that will be needed for tomorrow. One company that is renowned for educating its professionals has noted, "We cannot ensure your lifetime employment, but we can help ensure your lifetime employability." Top professionals will often be willing to accept less money for more growth. Loyalty will be gained through *learning*, not just *earning*.

• *Value their time.* As professionals have less and less time available, the value of their time increases. When asked to describe the qualities of leaders they do not respect, one of the most common answers from professionals is, "I hate it when leaders waste my time!" It is hard enough working fifty to eighty hours a week and doing what *does* matter. It is incredibly painful to work that much and then end up wasting time on doing what does not matter. Leaders will need to increase skills in protecting professionals from unneeded meetings and bureaucracy that neither encourage their passion or enhance their ability.

• *Build their network.* Professionals in the future will realize that their only security will come from their abilities and their networks. By enabling professionals to establish strong networks inside—and even outside—the company, organizations can gain a huge competitive advantage and loyalty. Professional networking enables members of the network to expand their knowledge and bring back new knowledge to the organization. As multiple career changes become the norm, companies will begin to experience professionals leaving and then returning to the company. A role model for providing positive networking is the noted strategy consulting firm McKinsey and Company. McKinsey goes out of its way to provide a network for previous members of the firm. As any roster of executives in the United States shows, many of these former McKinsey consultants go on to become leaders in major corporations—and customers of McKinsey. The company's loyalty to former employees helps lead to loyalty from future customers.

• *Support their dreams.* The best professionals are working for far more than money. They have a dream of making a meaningful contribution in their field. I recently heard Eric Schmidt, the CEO of Google, explain why (after their IPO) he was not afraid that many of their best people (who were going to be very rich) were going to leave. He noted that Google wanted to be the world's leader in providing information, and that any professional who wanted to be the best in the field would want to work there. He pointed out that these professionals had a dream, and that Google wanted to be the place that could enable them to best support that dream. Leaders in the past have asked, "What can you do to help our company achieve its dream?" Leaders in the future will also ask, "What can our company do to help you achieve your dream?"

• *Expand their contribution.* As more and more professionals become "free agents," organizations will need to provide them with opportunities that they cannot provide for themselves. As was mentioned earlier, Google can provide the resources and infrastructure to help professionals become the best in their field, which they could not do on their own. Large pharmaceutical companies can provide professionals with the R&D support that they cannot get on their own. Two of the most important needs of hard-working professionals are happiness and meaning. Leaders need to encourage passion to create an environment in which hard-working professionals are happy and want to come to work. Leaders will also need to show how the organization can help the professional make a larger contribution to the world. When people have 24-7 lifestyles they may not have much of a chance to find meaning and the opportunity to make a contribution outside of work. If this is the case, their major opportunity to find meaning and make a positive difference will come from inside of work. No one wants to put in endless hours on trivia. Leaders will need to help professionals make a real difference in their professions and in the world.

In summary, leading the managers and professionals of the future will be a challenging yet rewarding job. Leaders will need to go beyond looking at the work to be done and consider the human doing the work. They will need to understand the incredible pressures that have been brought about by globalization, technology, and competition. They will need to appreciate the hard work and sacrifice needed for professional success in a much tougher world. Leaders will need to realize that as work becomes even more important, and organizations become even more important, they will become even more important—in helping to shape the quality of life and the futures of the professionals they lead.

Endnote

1. M. Goldsmith, C. Greenberg, A. Robertson, and M. Hu-Chan, *Global Leadership: The Next Generation* (Upper Saddle River, NJ: Prentice-Hall, 2003).

16

Tomorrow's Leader

Srikumar S. Rao

Srikumar S. Rao conceived Creativity and Personal Mastery, a pioneering course that is one of the highest-rated at Columbia Business School and London Business School. It is believed to be the only course at a top business school to have its own alumni association. He also created the Advanced Leadership Clinic, a unique and intensive leadership workshop offered to senior executives. His book, Are YOU Ready to Succeed? Unconventional Strategies for Achieving Personal Mastery in Business and Life, *was published by Hyperion.*

Rao has been featured and quoted widely in the media and is the Louis and Johanna Vorzimer Professor of Marketing at the C. W. Post campus of Long Island University and an adjunct faculty member of London Business School and Columbia Business School. More information on his work is available at www.areyoureadytosucceed.com.

Business is changing. Although this is hardly an original observation, what few realize is the extent to which and speed with which it is doing so.

What are some of the more important factors driving this change? First, the way in which business is transacted is changing. Technology—the Internet, new methods of communication, faster and more customized manufacturing, and so on—is a principal cause, but not the only one. Second, the breadth of the playing field in which business takes place is increasing enormously. A tiny bookstore in a suburb of Manila can take a sale away from Borders. Third, consumer expectations are changing, and consumers are becoming much more demanding. At the same time, employees and their expectations are changing. They expect more from work and want to contribute in different ways. Another important factor is that interdependence is becoming greater and much more complex. A U.S. company may have a research laboratory in Bangalore developing prototype products for Australia. The interdependence goes beyond business relationships to encompass governments, nongovernmental organizations, and other parts of the citizen sector. Last, the pace of change has accelerated so rapidly that size is no longer a protective buffer. Multibillion dollar companies often see their competitive positions erode within months.

Leadership then is a hot area for management thinkers and writers, for good reason: in this new world, our organizations—commercial, not-for-profit, and government—need leaders with different skills and a richer set of them to lead us into the future.

And I know what the successful leader of the future will be like. I am not guessing. I know.

I know this not because I am brilliant or a prescient thinker or in possession of a time machine that can reveal the future, but because I have been unequivocally told this by the people who know. The people who know are the bright graduates of some of our best business schools who are entering the workplace and are very clear about the kind of person who can command their unquestioned allegiance.

Let me explain.

I have taught a course called Creativity and Personal Mastery for many years at schools such as Columbia Business School and the London Business School, and to executives in other forums. It is a deeply introspective course, and those who take it spend enormous amounts of time contemplating the workplace and how they would like it to be. They think about leadership styles they would like to develop and what they would like to see in their hierarchical superiors.

Hundreds of students and executives have shared their opinions with me. Are there variations? Sure there are. But the composite picture that emerges is startlingly clear and quite unambiguous. The successful leader of the future is one who can create systems that bring into being organizations that command a deep allegiance from employees, and from others who interact with the organizations, such as customers and suppliers.

In discussing this new type of leader, I speak mainly from the perspective of for-profit business organizations, but intuitive changes can readily be made to adjust to the needs of other types of organizations. Also, much of what I reveal concerns organizational culture and values.

So what is the task that lies ahead for the successful leader of the future?

Set an Inspiring Mission

While this may not seem relevant to leadership, mission is actually crucial. The leader sets the organization's mission, and if this mission does not resonate deeply, then those being led will merely go through the motions. Many of our present organizations have exemplary missions that exist primarily in framed statements in the boardroom and in company brochures. This does not work. The mission should resonate *and* it should be crystal clear to all that it is indeed *the* guiding principle of the organization.

Nobody gets passionate about maximizing shareholder value, or gaining market share, or reaching market dominance, or achieving set revenues or earnings increases. In fact, a leader who puts any of these, or similar, metrics forward immediately and silently loses much support.

Here is what I have learned: the purpose of a business is to ensure that every person who comes into contact with it reaches his or her highest potential. This includes employees, customers, suppliers, lenders, shareholders, and the community at large. Such an assertion immediately raises a host of questions:

What is meant by "highest potential"?

How is it measured?

Who should define and measure it?

How should conflicts be resolved?

How can this be turned into actionable steps?

All of these are very legitimate questions, and sincere persons can hold varying views when it comes to the answers—even diametrically opposed views. It is not important that there be agreement or disagreement. *What is important is that this is the arena in which the debate should be taking place.*

A leader trying to formulate his or her company's mission in line with this purpose will find an unbelievable degree of engagement at all levels.

Pursue Profits After Mission

Profits are the lifeblood of a successful business. None of the people who have shared their thoughts with me have anything against healthy profits. What they are against is a primary focus on profit. Viktor Frankl postulated that success and happiness cannot be pursued—they must ensue as unintended side effects of one's personal dedication to a course greater than oneself.

In like fashion, profits are the inevitable by-product of a business successfully run in accordance with a mission and purpose as described earlier.

Compensate Fairly

Hardly any discussion of leadership even broaches this topic, but it is hugely important. Leaders of the future will not seek monstrous compensation. In fact they will turn down offers of excessive remuneration and go out of their way to ensure that their emoluments are not disproportionate relative to others and the average at the company.

There are pragmatic reasons for this. The chief's compensation—monetary as well as in the form of perquisites—is closely scrutinized. Any perception of excess immediately signals that this is a person prone to self-serving. None of his or her dictums to husband company resources or control costs carries any real weight, and many employees psychically distance themselves from such a leader. A leader certainly cannot generate a loyal following with that baggage.

There are also ethical reasons. In a complex modern organization, it is by no means clear who really adds value and how much. Outsized compensation for the person on top simply reflects where power has been amassed, and is a misuse of that power. This is seldom spoken of but is always recognized, and the resentment it generates chips away at the very fiber of an organization.

The following comments from one of my students are highly instructive. They are also representative of the thoughts of many:

> Say a company is in trouble. The board decides that they need a "strong leader." To get him they offer a huge signing bonus, a large block of stock or options and other compensation that is frequently hidden. The implicit assumption is that money is the major factor that makes the job worth considering. And this has a chilling effect on everyone else in the entire company. Everyone starts thinking in terms of what they, too, can extract from the company.
>
> It never occurs to the board members that the message they are sending is deeply flawed and dangerous. That maybe it is incumbent on them to find a person who thinks that rescuing a corporation with a storied past is a privilege. That there are people who would consider saving thousands of jobs and careers a reward in

itself. They never find such persons because they never look for them. They never look for them because they think that money is the only way to motivate someone.

When they put someone like that at the top, the person immediately hires a whole bunch of others exactly like him. Carried to an extreme, this is what brings people like Al Dunlap to the top job of major corporations. Our system is broken.

Leaders who cannot induce a deep and inherent respect by virtue of being who they are cannot easily direct their followers. They then have to resort to "fear and greed" mechanisms to ensure behavioral compliance. Sometimes such mechanisms work, sometimes they don't. But their presence does explain why so many of our largest companies have highly toxic environments.

Eliminate Demotivators and Obstructions

It is supposedly the job of a leader to "motivate" the rank and file, to fire them up with enthusiasm and get them to whole-heartedly work toward achieving organizational goals. Motivation is done through pep speeches, individual exhortation, incentive structures, evaluation mechanisms, and similar methods. Great "motivators" are in much demand.

The reality is less pleasant and can be downright ugly. Everybody perceives that the emperor is naked, but few will proclaim that he has no clothes. Much of what is lauded as "motivation" is actually sophisticated manipulation to get unwilling workers to do what they are not particularly interested in doing. The carrots are incentives of various kinds, and the sticks are threats of firing, demotion, and loss of compensation. Such "motivation" may be okay when used on animals in a behavioral science laboratory. It is downright demeaning when applied to human beings.

If the mission of an organization is carefully constructed and totally authentic, the vast majority of employees will enthusiastically rally around it. No great effort is needed to engender "motivation." It is already built in and an integral part of the psyches of employees.

The function of a leader is *not* to motivate his or her employees. The function of a leader is to identify what is demotivating the employees and get rid of it. This is *not* semantic hairsplitting. It is a profoundly different philosophical approach, and I have seen near unanimity on this point. This is where tomorrow's leaders will spend a good chunk, if not the majority, of their time. Management structures and workplace procedures that were once helpful can easily ossify into obstructions. The leader constantly examines these and breaks up the obstructions as quickly as possible.

Be of Service, Not Self-Aggrandizing

The role of the leader is to be of service. He or she is constantly seeking ways to help all employees become more fulfilled, at work and as individuals. Part of this is the leader's effort to systematically identify and remove demotivating factors, as mentioned earlier. Another part of it is to encourage individuals to live up to the very best that they are capable of.

Such exhortation differs from the traditional pep talk aimed at reinforcing particular behaviors. The difference is in the intent. The leader we are talking about *genuinely cares* about the employee and whether or not the employee is fulfilled. It really matters to the leader that the desired behavior is manifested from conviction rather than fear or compliance.

There is no better way for leaders to establish their credentials than to walk their talk. If they demonstrate that they will cheerfully do whatever needs doing in any part of the organization, they gain immense moral stature and authority. When Bill Pollard, as CEO of Service Master, mops the floor; when David Neeleman, CEO of Jet Blue, serves coffee to passengers as a temporary part of the flight crew; when N. R. Narayana Murthy, as CEO of Infosys Technologies, stands in line in the cafeteria holding his own tray; and when

Alex von Bidder, managing partner of the Four Seasons restaurant in New York, personally serves a customer, they all send very powerful messages.

Bear in mind that such CEO behavior does not shape company culture when it is a gesture or a PR stunt. It only works when it is the outward manifestation of the kind of person the CEO really is. It was not for nothing that Mahatma Gandhi personally cleaned toilets, and insisted his wife do the same, when he was developing his movement in South Africa. That was where he started building up the immense bank of respect and goodwill that eventually enabled him to sway an entire country and command the unquestioned commitment of tens of millions of people. The "cost-cutting" CEO who cancels free coffee and newspaper subscriptions while acquiring a bigger corporate jet and hiring a better-known personal chef never commands great loyalty.

Demonstrate a Commitment to Community

It would be wonderful if all members of an organization were like "family," and some companies unctuously proclaim this is true of them. This is unrealistic, given the size and geographical dispersion of modern companies. It is, however, possible for members of an organization to form a close-knit community. The effective leader, the one who is tomorrow's hope, knows this and makes sure that he or she strengthens the community feeling and sense of belonging. There are several aspects to this:

1. *Care in separation:* A community cares for its own. Before a member is cast out every effort is made to give that member a chance to integrate into the community and live up to its norms. Codes of conduct are clear. If a violation could seriously harm the community, retribution is swift and sure. Otherwise, the member is cut considerable slack and given rehabilitative help.

2. *Shared suffering:* When bad times roll around, as they inevitably do, the community rallies around itself and distributes the pain. Burdens are shared in line with the ability to bear them. The leader ensures, for example, that first-class travel and expense accounts are eliminated before layoffs begin. He or she makes sure that salary reductions start at the top with highly compensated members taking proportionately greater cuts. The weakest members of the community are extended the greatest protection. There are never any golden parachutes at the top, and if the ship goes down, the captain remains on the bridge till everyone else is off.

3. *Diversity:* Certain shared values are a given. Outside this, it is a dull community in which all the houses are built and painted the same way. Diversity is what makes a community vibrant. Cross-fertilization builds strength in the next generation. The leader goes out of his or her way to ensure that diversity flourishes and tolerance is high.

4. *Bench strength:* A community built around—or dependent on—a single individual is unstable and will dissipate easily when that individual goes. The leader makes sure that there are many others capable of snatching the banner if he or she falls. Each person who grabs the banner should be able to count on the support of the community. This can happen only if everyone bears allegiance to the mission. So the leader makes sure that the mission is always alive and in the forefront of community consciousness.

Make a Commitment to Learning and Justice

There always will be complaints. There always will be bitching and moaning. This comes with the territory in any company, and the leader knows this. What is important is the *nature* of this grumbling. In moribund organizations persons might complain about how cold the coffee is. In vibrant organizations persons might complain about how long it takes to get approval for a new marketing strategy.

"Satisfaction" measures are largely meaningless. Much more important is that all individuals feel that they are in an environment in which (1) they are learning and (2) there is justice. When employees feel that they are in a situation in which they are developing their skills and are confident that they will be given a fair shake, when they are also committed to the company mission, then powerful energies are released.

When this occurs across the board, magic happens and the momentum is unstoppable. The effective leader knows this all too well and spends all his or her time making sure that the company offers innumerable opportunities for growth in many different areas and that there are mechanisms in place that swiftly and openly address any perceived inequities.

Mistakes are rarely a problem as long as they are acknowledged and addressed. The leader is not driven by ego but by a sincere desire to nurture the organization and keep it healthy.

The successful leader of the future, then, sets an inspiring mission, pursues profits secondarily to that mission, and makes sure that compensation is fair at all levels. This leader eliminates demotivating obstacles and is of service to his or her followers, not self-aggrandizing, and demonstrates a commitment to community, learning, and justice.

And this, my students tell me, is the sort of leader for whom they will gladly lay their heads on the rail.

17

Challenges for Leaders in the Years Ahead

Sally Helgesen

Sally Helgesen is an author, keynote speaker, and leadership development consultant. Her books include The Female Advantage: Women's Ways of Leadership, *the classic in its field, and* The Web of Inclusion: A New Architecture for Building Great Organizations, *chosen by* The Wall Street Journal *as one of the best books of all time on leadership. She is also a contributor to* Strategy + Business *magazine.*

B y 1996, when the first *Leader of the Future* was published, the stable and highly efficient hierarchies that had served the industrial era were rapidly becoming outdated. Top-down technologies of control were being supplanted by web-like technologies of opportunity, which had the effect of distributing knowledge and power more broadly in organizations and in society as a whole.

As a result, the dominant model of leadership was being challenged. The command-and-control, my-way-or-the-highway heroic leader who had stood unquestioned at the top of the organizational pyramid and relied on positional power and charisma to keep his troops in line was increasingly perceived as a figure of weakness rather than a figure of strength, a testament to the old order and a hindrance to the new. So the primary task that faced leaders in 1996 was the need to understand the nature of the new technological and economic order, and to help their organizations adapt to it.

Meeting this challenge required a certain humility from leaders. It also required that they recognize the true nature and source of one of the most ubiquitous buzzwords of those years, *empowerment*. Although in many organizations "empowerment" remained an empty slogan mouthed by executives who did not believe it actually existed, empowerment was not a management fad but a real phenomenon. Whether organizational leaders liked it or not, people in the ranks were in fact being empowered by a new technological architecture, and by the increasing value and amount of the knowledge they carried around in their heads. Only leaders who really understood the nature of this shift, and had the grace to work within its parameters, were positioned to meet the challenges that lay ahead.

Yet as the industrial economy morphed into the knowledge economy, and as networks eroded and blasted apart formerly closed and orderly structures, many leaders continued to rely on positional power as the sole basis for their authority and to insist upon the primacy of their own perceptions. In doing so, they not only failed to exhibit the humility required by the new era but also failed to comprehend how and why the world around them had changed. Such leaders were increasingly viewed as inappropriate and even dangerous to those in their organizations whom the new technologies had vested with increasing value, and who therefore chafed at the exercise of mere positional power.

The weakness of purely positional definitions of leadership was demonstrated most dramatically in the series of scandals that began unfolding in rapid succession over the ten years since 1996. These scandals have given this period its most lasting epithet: the Enron Era. In every arena—corporate, legal, accounting, financial, political, governmental, military, medical, regulatory, charitable, and religious—prominent and often previously admired leaders were undermined and challenged by those they formerly viewed as subordinates whose job it was to simply listen, or by stakeholders whose role had always been relatively detached. Although ethical problems were clearly a major factor in this unfolding saga, these scandals were also and most profoundly the consequence of the shift to a new economic and technological order. Many leaders whose attitudes, presumptions, and self-perceptions were outdated by this shift were punished more rapidly and severely than anyone could have foreseen in 1996.

Demographics also played a role in the reversal of fortunes that many had imagined to be secure. It has often been noted that the most visible and effective whistle-blowers in the scandals of the past ten years were disproportionately women: at Enron itself, at World-Com, within the FBI, and within that most ancient and cautionary of hierarchies, the Catholic Church. This suggests not that women have superior ethics, as some commentators have maintained, but rather that women have been more acutely attuned to the abuse of purely positional power, and more ready to take action when they perceive it.

This readiness is the understandable consequence of women having been latecomers to the values and beliefs of the old hierarchical system, and of not having thoroughly assimilated its presumptions. As outsiders to traditional organizations, and as harbingers and beneficiaries of the new order, women often had fresh eyes to discern what was going wrong while remaining remote enough from centers of power to speak truth as they saw it. Thus demographics as well as technology and economics played a part in transforming the way in which leadership has been understood over the past ten years.

In an essay published in the 1996 version of *The Leader of the Future*, I made precisely this point. However, I had no way of knowing at the time how quickly and ruthlessly those leaders who failed to adjust to the changing environment would be punished. Most were pushed from their positions by the actions of perceived underlings who understood their leaders' portfolios better than the leaders did themselves, and whose sense of awe for their overlords was diminished by their own technological empowerment. The consequences of their actions now define our organizational environment, placing limits on it while also opening up new opportunities.

And so in 2006, cautioned by scandals that continue to unfold, leaders face an even more complex set of challenges than they confronted ten years ago. Yet these challenges are nevertheless rooted in the same transformative factors that gave shape to the past decade: the diffusion of knowledge, the widespread access to powerful and cheap networked technologies, and the demographic rise of what are still sometimes referred to as "nontraditional" workers. Thus the challenges that confront leaders in the years ahead will intensify the conditions of the present environment, and the consequences for those who fail to perceive these challenges may be even more punishing.

I see this intensification occurring in several distinct arenas, each of which presents challenges for leaders in the years ahead. These primary challenges can be defined as follows: the need to foster inclusion, the need to build sustainability, and the need to redefine diversity to focus on values.

Let's look at each in turn.

Fostering inclusion. Organizations used to be defined by clear boundaries. It was easy to say who was a part of one and who was not, who fell inside the circle and who remained outside. At the same time, true power in organizations resided within a tight core of insiders who made the decisions—the heads. Those who executed these decisions—the hands—had little power, and were often viewed as interchangeable parts, following the factory model.

This situation has changed. On one hand, the definition of *stakeholder* has become far more expansive, now including customers, clients, suppliers, distributors, investors and their advisers, the local community, the global community, and those who absorb the environmental and economic impact of an organization's decisions. On the other hand, the diffusion of knowledge has expanded the decision-making pool within the organization, requiring that more decisions be made in the units so that specialized and embedded knowledge can be put to use. Thus managing by inclusion—expanding the definition of who matters and bringing more voices into the decision-making process—has become a precondition for success.

Virtually all of the organizations that found themselves beset by scandal in the past ten years failed to understand this. They remained places in which a tight core of insiders continued to monopolize every major decision, and did so in isolation from any voices that might dissent. The consequences of this kind of obsolete insider perspective are evident everywhere, and the spectacle has not been edifying for many leaders and organizations. From cronyism and incompetence in government agencies to the seeming surprise of American auto manufacturers caught unaware yet again by a mismatch between available product and the reality of energy prices, the common thread is the obtuseness and inadequacy of leaders who restrict decision making to a narrow and insufficient base and insulate themselves from anyone who might ask a challenging question.

The pharmaceutical industry provides some vivid examples. In many companies, the operative idea for the past decade has been seeding regulatory agencies with insiders who then have the power to "benefit" the industry as a whole by making it easier to get products to market. This insider approach may have proved successful in the short term, but has had disastrous consequences over time. Diminishing regulatory oversight led to drugs being distributed before they were adequately tested, with catastrophic consequences for the bottom line of several prestigious and formerly highly profitable organizations (not to mention for those who may have bought these drugs). In each case, leaders failed to understand the extent to which a transparent environment fostered by empowered consumers with far-reaching access to information could exact revenge upon those whose deepest impulse is to exclude any voices that might prove skeptical—or even merely urge caution.

Building sustainability. The example above points to another challenge that faces leaders in the years ahead: building a model of enterprise that can be sustained over the long haul. In American organizations in particular, the structural imperative to focus on the short term as defined by the quarterly statement has led some for-profit organizations to ignore the long-term or even medium-term consequences of their actions. In addition, the increasing pressure on nonprofits and government agencies to operate "more like a business" often causes them to become vulnerable to a similar approach.

As a result, only organizations that almost entirely dominate their market (the Microsofts, the Intels) have been able to afford the long-term investment that is required to maintain consistently positive results over time. However, the imperative to dominate the market leads to other problems, since achieving such a position often exacerbates a leader's belief in his or her superior understanding of the environment being confronted.

Practicing inclusion—understanding that stakeholders of every variety must be factored into every decision—is necessary for building sustainability over the long term. Looking again at the example of U.S. automakers, we can see the long-term consequences of refusing to do so. With the recent and courageous exception of Ford, the inner circle of leaders in these companies have traditionally viewed environmental restrictions as something to be fiercely and unquestioningly fought. This focus has blinded them to the broader picture, in which the adverse effects of overdependence on petroleum define the common future for manufacturers as well as consumers. Instead of battling restrictions or lobbying for trade sanctions that punish competitors who have acknowledged this reality, leaders in the industry would have been wiser to put their efforts into reforming an economic system that punishes long-term thinking.

Redefining diversity to focus on values. In 1996, diversity was still an issue to which many businesses paid only lip service. In 2006, it is recognized by virtually all forward-thinking organizations as an inarguable business imperative. For example, Jeffrey Immelt, the CEO of General Electric (and a leader who perhaps not coincidentally has articulated an awareness of the need to build sustainable growth in a company formerly famous for its fierce focus on short-term financials), summed up the situation at a recent forum of The

Business Council. Declaring that diversity is one of *the* two major issues that will face GE in the future, Immelt noted that his company has a pool of 50 million highly educated potential traditional workers from which to draw from worldwide—and 150 million highly educated nontraditional workers.

Given the extent to which organizations now depend on having a broad base of talent and creativity, we can see why diversity has moved to the forefront of concern. But how do we define diversity? For the past decade, we have defined it demographically, as a phenomenon shaped primarily by the fact that women, Asians, Hispanics, and those of African ancestry now make up the majority of the available workforce. Diversity thus has been simply an acknowledgment of gender and ethnic differences, with some consideration of age and sexual orientation thrown into the mix.

But diversity in the contentious, technologically empowered, niche-focused social environment that is emerging in the twenty-first century requires a more expansive definition, one that admits the extreme variety in opinion and outlook that now characterizes our highly diverse population. Even such workplace fundamentals as what constitutes an acceptable work ethic or how individuals define and pursue satisfaction on the job are increasingly open to interpretation and debate. The rich and challenging diversity of opinion manifest in the workplace, of course, simply reflects the rich and challenging diversity of opinion we find in our larger society, where people are ever-more fiercely divided along political, religious, ideological, sectarian, economic, and social lines. In such a climate, and given the extent to which the information that shapes opinion is both more fragmented and more likely to mirror and reinforce sharply held viewpoints, consensus on any issue can seem almost impossible to achieve.

In the organizations of the late industrial years, leaders could forge consensus—could indeed embody it—by asserting the power of their position, and could do so with little risk of being challenged. In today's more skeptical, individualistic, and empowered landscape, this strategy is doomed to failure. Leaders in the years ahead will be able to manage the contentiousness around them only by uniting diverse factions behind a strong and overarching vision. Thus Peter Drucker's original insight about the centrality of vision in what he chose to call Post-Capitalist Society is being vindicated by today's diverse circumstances. When people are free to disagree on basics, and eager to defend their right to do so, vision rather than the charism of power must be the glue that holds contending elements together. Only those leaders who can bring wildly (and proudly) diverse segments together through the clear and inspiring articulation of a larger vision will be able to leverage the power of diversity, rather than sinking under its fractious weight.

18

Leadership Judgment at the Front Line

Noel M. Tichy and Chris DeRose

Noel M. Tichy is a professor of organizational behavior and human resource management at the Ross School of Business at the University of Michigan, where he is the director of the Global Business Partnership. Professor Tichy is the author of numerous books and articles. His most recent books are The Ethical Challenge; The Cycle of Leadership, *with Nancy Cardwell; and* The Leadership Engine, *with Eli Cohen.*

Chris DeRose is a researcher and consultant in the area of organizational change and leadership. He assists business leaders in improving their organization's growth and profitability while concurrently developing the next generation of leadership. He has been an associate of the Global Business Partnership, a department of the Stephen M. Ross School of Business at the University of Michigan. He also teaches executive education with Noel Tichy at the Business School. In addition, DeRose is a partner with Action Learning Associates. DeRose has co-authored book chapters, development handbooks, and articles for publications such as Fortune *magazine,* Training & Development, Journal of Cost Management, *and* Australian Human Resources Journal.

Trilogy Software, an Austin, Texas, company founded by Stanford dropout Joe Liemandt, is a prototypical company for the knowledge economy. Selling complex enterprise software, Trilogy is an extremely successful private enterprise that partners with many *Fortune* 50 companies. Since its founding, it has relied on hiring the best and brightest computer scientists from top schools. In a *Harvard*

Business Review article, we chronicled how Joe Liemandt created Trilogy University, a three-month orientation "boot camp," to simultaneously indoctrinate these hotshot new hires while creating the next generation of products.[1] Today, Trilogy runs its university in Bangalore, India, because the bulk of its hiring is at the top Indian and Chinese universities, and new recruits create products for a global market.

Trilogy's workers fit the old stereotype of the knowledge worker— the highly trained engineering and computer science graduate. The importance of knowledge workers such as these cannot be disputed, but we see the emergence of a new breed of knowledge workers.

Intuit, the Mountain View, California, company, also produces software. Its *Turbo Tax*, *Quicken*, *QuickBooks*, and other software solutions serve both small enterprises and individual consumers. As with Trilogy, computer scientists play a vital role in developing its products. Unlike Trilogy, however, Intuit relies heavily on specialists to support accountants and retail customers. These knowledge workers don't necessarily hail from top universities or write complex computer code. They are frontline leaders and agents working in call centers, often paid an hourly rate. Intuit has learned that these call service agents can have a critical impact on customers and sales by both identifying customer needs and solving after-sale problems.

At Intuit, frontline leaders take responsibility for sharing best practices and creating new knowledge about customer needs. For example, one frontline manager developed a process in which customer service agents now meet several times a week to discuss common customer problems and role play responses. By doing so, they not only share knowledge but also creatively come up with newer and more innovative ideas to enhance the customer's experience. As a result, there has been a nearly 40 percent increase in the measure of customer satisfaction.

Intuit demonstrates how knowledge creation increasingly is shifting to the customer interface. Companies such as Toyota and Southwest Airlines have long known that frontline problem solving produces better business results and customer satisfaction. Today, however, customer-focused companies are discovering that front-line employees not only must solve problems, they also must adaptively create new solutions based on an intimate understanding of local customers or specific companies.

Best Buy, the leading North American consumer electronics retailer with over seven hundred stores, is another example. A front-line associate in one of Best Buy's California stores knew that the area surrounding his store had a large number of real estate agents. After several failures to sell digital cameras to real estate agents, the associate researched their needs. Having been trained to diagnose customer problems and empowered to create his own solutions, he realized that real estate agents needed to take pictures and then e-mail or print on the spot, often from their cars. He assembled a bundle of products and software that would enable an agent to snap a digital photo, produce the photo with a mobile printer that fit easily in any backseat, or e-mail the picture from a laptop or PDA. After the product bundle became a hot seller in the area, one of the agents invited the Best Buy associate to present to the real estate agents at a monthly meeting at the local Chamber of Commerce. The associate's innovation resulted in thousands of dollars of incremental sales and a group of new customers who continued to shop at Best Buy.

The stories at Best Buy and Intuit demonstrate the impact that frontline associates have when they exercise good judgment and come up with innovative solutions to customer opportunities. We are collaborating with these companies in developing frontline leadership capacity for customer-centric knowledge creation. The specific solutions these front-line leaders provided their customers could not be anticipated in advance. Instead, leaders had to be adaptive, weigh their options, and figure out how to please their customers. As companies strive to differentiate themselves with inundated consumers, more and more are realizing that knowledge is created at the customer interface, not at headquarters or in isolated development groups. This requires the full engagement and intellect of frontline associates. It can only happen with top-down support, a clearly articulated strategy with strong enablers at all levels of the organization, and intensive training and development of frontline leaders and their associates.

Creating a Framework for Judgment Calls

When Peter Drucker presciently introduced the world to the concept of knowledge workers, he urged managers to treat knowledge workers as assets rather than costs. Drucker's line of thinking has been popularized to the point that it can be found in an enormous volume of corporate reports and management writing. Drucker asked a fundamental question that, despite the increased attention, organizations still struggle with: What is needed to increase [knowledge worker's] productivity and to convert their increased productivity into performance capacity for the organization?

As already noted, organizations such as Best Buy and Intuit have been discovering knowledge workers in a place where many companies rarely look: among hourly, frontline associates. Such companies rely on frontline associates to be more than service workers applying routines and rules to every customer interaction. Instead, they expect frontline employees to apply specialized knowledge of local customer preferences and technological know-how. For Best Buy, it is no surprise to see an associate innovate a new marketing campaign for local Vietnamese customers or figure out how to triple sales of voice-over-Internet protocol products. At Intuit, call center agents routinely help accountants not only use their software but also interpret and apply accounting rules in the process.

In their bid to create a differentiated customer experience, Best Buy and Intuit are realizing that the key to answering Drucker's question lies in enabling knowledge workers at the front lines to make good judgment calls. The process starts with the CEO and senior leaders setting clear direction for the organization and defining the role and scope of contribution expected of frontline leaders. The senior leadership is ultimately responsible for setting the strategy, reinforcing desired values, energizing the organization, and making tough calls on resource allocation and staffing. In short, the senior leaders are responsible for developing a "teachable point of view," which is taught throughout their organizations (Figure 18.1). Our work at both Intuit and Best Buy started with helping the senior teams develop such a teachable point of view.

At Best Buy, there are now hundreds of stories describing how frontline employees dynamically created customer solutions. Innovative approaches to problems as diverse as ethnic marketing programs, tailored product displays, and new product introductions have been identified and implemented directly by frontline associates.

This could only happen because Brad Anderson, Best Buy's CEO, defined the organization's strategy around "customer centricity," a

Figure 18.1. A Teachable Point of View.

Ideas
Great companies are built on central ideas. By passing the ideas to others and teaching others how to develop good ideas, leaders create organizations that are finely tuned toward delivering success.

Values
Winning leaders articulate values explicitly and shape values that support business ideas.

Ideas — Values

E^3
Emotional
Energy/Edge

Energy
Winning leaders are motivated, and they motivate others about change and transition. Leaders energize others when they personally interact with them.

Edge
Leadership is about making tough yes-no decisions. Winning leaders face reality, and they make decisions about people, products, businesses, customers, and suppliers.

concept that we helped Best Buy's leadership team frame in partnership with Larry Selden from Columbia University. In Brad's judgment, the strategy that had made Best Buy the leading consumer electronics seller in North America and a top performing stock would not sustain the company's success. Best Buy had focused on mass market retail efficiency and solid merchandising. This was an inherently product- and process-focused strategy that would not differentiate Best Buy against competitors such as Wal-Mart, Dell, and Amazon that were aggressively targeting consumer electronics.

Brad created a burning platform for his top 160 leaders at an offsite in 2002 when he showed a distressing video of actual customers leaving Best Buy stores angry and upset, telling the interviewers of their plans to spend their money at competitors because Best Buy had failed to meet their needs. The transformation Brad called for required focusing the company on creating local, tailored solutions for customers. This was a strategy that would only work if frontline associates understood customer problems and had the tools, autonomy, and creativity to solve customer needs. As Brad challenged his team, "None of this happens if we don't have the right culture and the right people with the right training and values to solve customer problems." We then spent the next three days in a workshop with the corporate officer team preparing them to directly teach thousands of Best Buy leaders and share the new teachable point of view for building a customer-centric organization.

Overcoming Technical, Political, and Cultural Challenges

The CEO, as in Best Buy's case, can create the conditions for enabling frontline leaders to fully implement a customer-centered strategy. After more than two years of hard work, this remains an awesome challenge for Best Buy. It has required a massive revolution, as the company historically was built on strong centralization, with employees at its Minnesota headquarters setting strategy and passing down direction for the troops to follow. Today, the "troops" are expected to act as local field generals, generating solutions and new knowledge. Best Buy continues to invert the organizational pyramid, empowering employees to demand headquarter's support for once centrally controlled functions such as merchandising, information systems, and training.

It has been easiest for Best Buy to identify and work on the technical issues in making this transformation. The information, skills, and tools to make good judgments have required new information systems that are still being overhauled more than two years after the transformation began. The company is also providing each store with a local profit-and-loss statement, good customer data, and performance management tools. Similarly, the career paths, compensation systems, merchandising programs, and numerous other facets of the business have had to be entirely rethought.

At Intuit the focus is on simplifying the technical challenges call center agents face in trying to find information, execute company processes, and share knowledge with one another. Intuit has engaged frontline associates directly in identifying and changing how the company works to support better customer interactions. Intuit is reducing the bureaucracy that stands in the way of letting customer agents focus on customers and make good judgments.

One thing that makes the frontline leaders at Best Buy and Intuit different from service workers in many industries is that they are held accountable for making decisions that not only delight customers but also keep their companies profitable. They are expected to practice sound business judgment, not give away the store. At Best Buy, training on understanding a store's profit-and-loss statement, return on invested capital, and organic growth drivers has been given to part-time, hourly associates.

Such technical fixes are a vital first step, but political considerations are usually far more difficult to manage. Increasing trust in frontline associates feels unnatural to many ambitious, highly educated executives. Some executives fear that increased accountability and

autonomy at the front lines will potentially reduce their own influence and authority. In many cases, such a change does create a profound power shift away from centralized groups. At Best Buy, the
merchant team responsible for buying products and setting prices
was accustomed to setting policy with the stores. Similarly, the visual
merchandising group had long set standardized controls severely limiting the extent to which local employees could change the look and
feel of their stores. Ultimately, Best Buy's seven-hundred-plus stores
will be able to tailor their merchandise selection and already have
much more latitude and local expertise in creating end-caps (the displays at the end of the aisles that drive a high percentage of sales)
and product displays.

Political leadership will be essential in determining Best Buy's
long-term success with its customer-centricity strategy; not all leaders at headquarters will have the skills to work in the new organization, and some will lack the desire to share power with frontline
associates. It will require Brad Anderson's personal involvement and
the resolve of Best Buy's management team to upend its traditional
business approach. Those in power are likely to have vested interests and will test the senior team's determination. In some cases,
executives who disliked the new approach and what they perceived
to be their diminished stature have already left the company.

David Novak, the CEO of Yum! Brands, also confronted the
challenge of creating political alignment across his organization of
more than seven hundred thousand employees. Instead of offering
customers just one choice in a restaurant, Yum! wanted to combine
two or more of its brands—Pizza Hut, Taco Bell, Long John Silver's,
A&W, and KFC—under the same roof. If mom wanted chicken,
she could have it while the kids ate tacos. As Novak was testing the
idea with his franchise leaders, he got a rude awakening from one
of his largest operators. The franchise requests for information,
Novak learned, were being passed from person to person with long
delays and little follow-through from Yum!'s corporate office. Novak
had been working hard to create a frontline-focused culture and
avoid arrogance in the executive ranks. He ultimately built a new

operations team that was more focused on frontline requests, and the company successfully deployed the multibranding strategy. What Novak saw first-hand, however, is a disconnection between senior leadership rhetoric and frontline reality that trains many frontline leaders to be skeptical of corporate leaders and less caring about their customers.

By standing firm on implementing the technical and political changes required to enable frontline leaders, as Brad Anderson and David Novak did, senior leaders make it much more likely that a lasting cultural change will occur. Developing judgment capability at the front lines takes time and patience when frontline leaders make mistakes. For example, in a California Best Buy store recently, an associate proudly showed off his inventory of plasma televisions and the displays he had created. He energetically admitted, however, that he had made several bad decisions—he was carrying too much inventory and had the display set up incorrectly to drive sales of his high-margin products, resulting in a lower return on invested capital than he needed. The associate knew his errors and had a fix already in place. Early in Best Buy's transformation, a senior executive may have seen the associate's mistakes as signs of failure and proof that inventories and displays should be centrally controlled. The executive, more familiar with scale operations than local innovation, likely would have taken the financial cost of the mistakes and multiplied it across all of Best Buy's stores to demonstrate that the company could not afford such errors in judgment. Today, with Best Buy's cultural change well under way, most executives realize that this was a local mistake and not likely to be replicated in this store or elsewhere. They see this as an invaluable investment in developing good business judgment in leaders at all levels.

Virtuous Teaching Cycles

Creating an environment that encourages teaching and learning is central to developing frontline leaders. As with the teachable point of view, the process must start at the top of the organization. Senior leaders must routinely bypass the chain of command to have direct dialogues with frontline employees. These are opportunities for senior leaders to create virtuous teaching cycles (VTCs). In a VTC, the teacher is also a learner, and the learner becomes a teacher. Best Buy store managers run morning "chalk talk" sessions in which they both teach and learn from the associates. In many Best Buy stores twenty to thirty associates are paid an extra hour a day to come in early and review the prior day's P&L and customer segment performance and to share ideas for improving performance in the future. These are highly interactive virtuous teaching cycles with everyone generating new knowledge to improve performance (Figure 18.2).

The VTC is a stark contrast to top-down traditional models of cascading the strategy through the organizational hierarchy. If knowledge is created at the customer interface, the old approach not only creates more alienated associates, it destroys knowledge and blocks the generation of new customer interface knowledge.

The need for VTCs extends well beyond the top of the organization. As Intuit and Best Buy have discovered, it can be even more important for the managers who lead frontline associates to create

Figure 18.2. Virtuous Teaching Cycle.

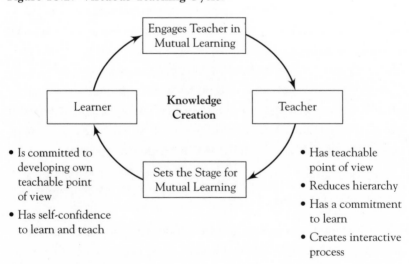

VTCs. As these managers develop the judgment capability of their associates, they must foster an environment that encourages sensible risk taking. Rather than practice command-and-control leadership in which they tell their associates what to do, they must instead encourage employees to come up with their own ideas based on customer insight. This needs to be genuine, not a paternalistic approach. When an employee brings an idea to a manager, the manager can no longer dismiss it by saying "We've tried that already" or "I just don't think that will work." Instead, he or she must coach the individual by testing the thought process. The manager must ask whether the idea is based on sound customer insight and good business understanding, and if the employee has a rigorous approach for testing the idea.

In short, Best Buy is teaching its frontline associates how to be knowledge workers. The company has trained tens of thousands of people to apply a version of the scientific method as they attempt to innovate on a local level. Associates are expected to create a hypothesis based on the financial and customer impacts of their innovation, create a time-bounded test, and then measure to verify the results. Using this methodology, an employee suggested offering gift cards to kids under eighteen who are having birthdays or who get all As on their report cards. Figuring that mom would want to reward the kids on this special day, it seemed possible that giving them a $5 gift card would be enough to lure mom and the kids into a Best Buy store. This simple idea—which started with frontline employees—has had a massive return. Entering the store with a $5 gift card awarded for an excellent report card, a typical family spends $60 during a visit. Those who come in for a birthday use the gift card to kickstart average purchases of $160.

Similarly, at Intuit, a call center manager created a VTC with his associates when examining the success metrics the team was using. The manager worked with the team to identify the vital metrics to measure team effectiveness and now assembles the team weekly to diagnose progress and share practices for improving each agent's customer impact.

Teaching Frontline Managers to Teach

Another thing that distinguishes Best Buy and Intuit is the enormous investment each company has made in teaching frontline managers how to coach and teach their associates. At Best Buy, thousands of employees have participated in workshops teaching everything from financial basics to customer segmentation approaches to frontline leadership (Figure 18.3).

Intuit has required its call center managers to become teachers. We launched the process with a rigorous three-day workshop designed to prepare frontline managers to be more effective teachers of frontline agents. Following the workshop, each frontline manager conducted his or her own disciplined, highly interactive workshop for groups of frontline leaders. No consultants or staff personnel were allowed to teach. At the end of the three days the frontline leaders had new concepts and tools for enhancing the effectiveness of their call center agents. The frontline leaders identified how they could better structure their work to deliver the business strategy, how they could eliminate unnecessary activities, and how they could reshape goal setting and performance management. The frontline leaders also engaged the agents to provide input on companywide initiatives to streamline operational processes. As knowledge creation increasingly moves to the front lines, Intuit recognizes that its managers must be more skilled than ever in leadership fundamentals.

The Frontline Challenge

When most people picture knowledge workers, they think of engineers, scientists, or service professionals, not hourly sales people or call center agents. However, as numerous companies increasingly attempt to differentiate themselves through their service, they are recognizing that the best strategy is creating judgment capability at the front lines (see Figure 18.4).

The paradox of shifting power to the front lines is that it requires senior leaders to use their authority to overcome the technical,

Figure 18.3. Intuit's Frontline Leader Process.

Intuit's investment in developing the judgment capability of front-line leaders requires them to attend two workshop sessions, teach their own teams, implement new work routines, and execute a knowledge-creation project.

Step 1: Three-Day Workshop

Frontline leaders are

- Immersed in the strategy, values, and vision and taught how to translate them to their area
- Immersed in business acumen
- Taught to focus on creating a team teachable point of view and using operating mechanisms as virtuous teaching cycles
- Taught how different employee styles and capabilities may be deployed
- Prepared to teach

Step 2: Frontline Leaders Teach

- Frontline leaders who attended the three-day workshop are required to teach—they personally re-create the workshop they attended, doing all of the teaching themselves.
- The process develops their ongoing teaching and coaching capability.

Step 3: Knowledge-Creation Project

- Frontline leaders work with their team of frontline associates to share knowledge and implement a project with measurable business impact.

Step 4: Two-Day Follow-Up Workshop

- Frontline leaders share results and best practices with one another.
- Frontline leaders continue learning on business acumen, company support processes, frontline leadership, and performance management.

Figure 18.4. How to Get Started: Steps in Building Judgment Capacity at the Customer Interface.

Step 1: Teach the CEO and top team: This typically takes a three-day workshop to help the team articulate and align on a new teachable point of view for the future success of the organization.

Step 2: Cascade teach to everyone: The top team then becomes the direct teachers for the next level. At Best Buy, 160 officers ran their several-day workshops, involving thousands of employees in transforming the business. At Intuit, the top two hundred leaders followed a similar process.

Step 3: Transform the headquarters and infrastructure: The transformation to support frontline leadership cannot happen without radical change of the traditional mind-set and infrastructure. At Best Buy, prior success had been built on headquarters' command-and-control approach with standard operating procedures. Knowledge creation was assumed to occur at headquarters and then parceled out in directives to the thousands of associates in the stores. Best Buy's new approach has required turning that paradigm on its head, supporting the store managers and frontline associates to generate customer-centric knowledge in the stores. Transformations of this scale often lead to removing executives who cannot lead the change by redesigning the information, financial, and human resource systems.

Step 4: Develop frontline leadership capacity to teach and lead VTCs: typically, a huge investment is needed in teaching and learning at the front line. Development workshops are usually required to prepare frontline leaders to be teachers and learners, as well as to improve their customer knowledge and business acumen. New mechanisms for teaching and learning, such as Best Buy's "chalk talks," are also needed. As Best Buy and Intuit demonstrate, the payoff for these investments is ongoing, given that the front line is where value is created for the customer.

political, and cultural barriers that often stand in the way. Companies must actively invest in creating the support systems that enable frontline leaders to make good judgment calls. When they do, they realize that frontline leaders are those most skilled in making local decisions to simultaneously delight customers and protect the bottom line.

Endnote

1. Noel Tichy, "Leadership Boot Camp," *Harvard Business Review,* April 2001.

Bibliography

Selden, Larry, and Colvin, Geoffrey. *Angel Customers & Demon Customers.* New York: Portfolio, 2003.

Tichy, Noel, and Cardwell, Nancy. *The Cycle of Leadership: How Great Leaders Teach Their Companies to Win.* New York: HarperCollins, 2002.

Tichy, Noel, and Cohen, Eli. *The Leadership Engine.* New York: HarperCollins, 1997.

Tichy, Noel, and DeRose, Chris. "Roger Enrico's Master Class." *Fortune Magazine,* November 27, 1995.

Tichy, Noel, and DeRose, Chris. "Launching Cycles of Leadership." *Optimize,* August 2002.

Tichy, Noel, and Sherman, Stratford. *Control Your Destiny or Someone Else Will.* New York: Doubleday/Currency, 1993.

19

It's Not Just the Leader's Vision

Jim Kouzes and Barry Posner

Jim Kouzes and Barry Posner are the authors of the award-winning and best-selling book, The Leadership Challenge, *with over 1.4 million copies sold in over sixteen different languages. They have coauthored over a dozen books and developed the highly acclaimed* Leadership Practices Inventory (LPI), *a 360-degree questionnaire assessing leadership behavior, which is one of the most widely used leadership assessment instruments in the world. More than three hundred doctoral dissertations and academic research projects have been based on their* Five Practices of Exemplary Leadership *model.*

Currently an Executive Fellow at the Center for Innovation and Entrepreneurship at Santa Clara University, Jim Kouzes is a popular seminar and conference speaker, named by the Wall Street Journal *as one of the twelve best executive educators in the United States. He is also the 2006 recipient of the Golden Gavel award from Toastmasters International. Barry Posner is dean of the Leavey School of Business and professor of leadership at Santa Clara University, where he has received numerous teaching and innovation awards. An internationally renowned scholar and educator, Barry is also the author or coauthor of more than one hundred research-and-practitioner-focused articles.*

At some point during all this talk over the years about the importance of being future-oriented, leaders got the sense that they were the ones who had to be the "visionaries." Often with the

---

Adapted from a chapter in the book *A Leader's Legacy* by James M. Kouzes and Barry Z. Posner. Copyright 2006 Jossey-Bass. Reprinted with permission of John Wiley & Sons.

encouragement of a lot of leadership developers, including us, leaders came to assume that if others expected them to be forward-looking, then they have to go off all alone into the wilderness, climb to the top of some mountain, sit in a lotus position, wait for a revelation, and then go out and announce to the world what they foresee. Leaders have assumed that it's *their* vision that matters, and if it's *their* vision, then *they* have to create it.

Wrong! This is *not* what constituents expect. Yes, leaders are expected to be forward-looking, but they aren't expected to be prescient or clairvoyant. Exemplary leadership is not about uttering divinely inspired revelations. It's not about being a prophet. It's actually much simpler than that.

What people really want to hear is *not* the leader's vision. They want to hear about *their own* aspirations. They want to hear how their dreams will come true and their hopes will be fulfilled. They want to see themselves in the picture of the future that the leader is painting. The very best leaders understand that it's about inspiring a *shared* vision, not about selling their own idiosyncratic view of the world.

Maybe your constituents don't tell you this quite so directly. Maybe they don't tell you this at all. But we're quite certain that very few grown adults like to be told in so many words, "Here is where we're going, so get on board with it." No matter how dressed up it is in all kinds of fine and fancy language, most adults don't like being told where to go and what to do. They want to feel part of the process.

Buddy Blanton, a principal program manager at Rockwell Collins Display Systems, learned this lesson first-hand. He got his team together one morning to give him feedback on his leadership approach. He specifically wanted to learn how he could be more effective in creating a shared vision. What they told him helped him understand that it's the process and not just the vision that's critical in getting people all on the same page.

> One of the team members that I most respect . . . spoke first. She is very good at telling it like it is, but in a

constructive manner. She provided me the following feedback: "You have all of the right skills," she said. "You have global vision and understanding. You are a good, sincere listener. You are optimistic, and you command respect and trust of your team and your colleagues. You are open and candid, and you are never shy about saying what needs to be said to team members." Then she gave me this advice, "You would benefit by helping us, as a team, to understand how you got to your vision. We want to walk with you while you create the goals and vision so we all get to the end vision together."

Another team member said that sharing this road-map would help him to feel more able to take the initiative to resolve issues independently. A couple of other team members stated that this communication would help them to understand the realism of the goals. One of the team members said that they would like to be a part of the vision-building process so they could learn how to better build visions for their team.

I looked at the group. It was clear that they were in agreement that they wanted to be a part of the vision-sharing and development process. We launched into a discussion on our vision for the program, and each person contributed to the discussion.

Previously, I believed that the team would benefit more by my setting the roadmap and vision and then just letting them give me feedback when they thought that I was off base—which they have done on numerous occasions. From our discussion, it was clear that the team wants to be included in the process. I asked them if it would be useful if we got together every two weeks to discuss and build our program vision, similar to what we did that day. The feedback was a resounding "Yes."

The vast majority of us are just like Buddy's team members. We want to walk *with* our leaders. We want to dream with them. We want to invent with them. We want to be involved in creating our own futures. This doesn't mean you have to do exactly what Buddy did, but it does mean that you have to stop taking the view that visions come from the top down. You have to stop seeing it as a monologue, and you have to start engaging others in a collective dialogue about the future.

Let's take a look at some data we have collected from the use of our *Leadership Practices Inventory (LPI)* and see what it tells us. The LPI is a 360-degree assessment instrument or questionnaire that leaders and organizations use to measure leadership competencies. The inventory consists of thirty behavioral statements assessing five practices of exemplary leadership, with six statements measuring each practice. Participants assess themselves according to how often they engage in each desired behavior, and other "observers"—typically selected by the leaders—also can rate the leaders on how frequently the leaders engage in each behavior. Of the six statements on the LPI that measure a leader's ability to "inspire a shared vision," three, or 50 percent, are among the four lowest scoring items in the *entire* thirty-item inventory. That makes "inspire a shared vision" the weakest leadership competency according to our research. Here are the three "inspire a shared vision" behaviors on which leaders perform the poorest:

- I describe a compelling image of what our future could be like.

- I appeal to others to share an exciting dream of the future.

- I show others how their long-term interests can be realized by enlisting in a common vision.

Examine these three statements for a moment. What do you notice? Do you see that each of these is about how well a leader engages others in the vision? Do you see that these statements are about "us" and not "me," "we" and not "I"? The underlying reason for such poor ratings on the practice of "inspiring a shared vision" is that leaders really struggle with communicating an image of the future that draws others in. It's not that leaders don't have a personal conviction about the future or spend time thinking about it; it's just that they don't effectively speak to what others see and feel about it.

To be able to describe a compelling image of the future, you have to be able to grasp hold of what *others* want and need. To appeal to others and to show them how their interests will be served, you have to know *their* hopes, dreams, motives, and interests.

That means you have to know your constituents, and you have to speak to them in language they will find engaging. If you're trying to mobilize people to move in a particular direction, then you've got to talk about that future destination in ways that others find appealing. It's got to be something that *they* care about as much, or even more, than you do.

Getting others excited about future possibilities is not about creating better PowerPoint presentations. It's not about better public-speaking skills, although that would help. And it's certainly not about being more charming or charismatic.

It's about intimacy. It's about familiarity. It's about empathy. The kind of communication needed to enlist others in a common vision requires understanding constituents at a much deeper level than we normally find comfortable. It requires understanding others' strongest yearnings and their deepest fears. It requires a profound awareness of their joys and their sorrows. It requires experiencing life as they experience it.

Being able to do this is not magic, nor is it rocket science. It's really all about listening very, very closely to what other people want.

Now some of you at this point may be saying to yourselves, "All well and good, but what about breakthrough innovations? Aren't leaders supposed to focus on the next new thing? Nobody ever said they wanted an airplane or telephone or personal computer!" True, but people did say they wanted to travel faster to more distant places, connect more easily with their friends and family, and work more productively.

We'd submit that these innovations were not and are not the result of hermits who come up with ideas in isolation. They are, in fact, the result of superb and attentive listening. They are the result of being more attuned to the environment. They are the result of a greater appreciation of people's aspirations.

And what if people don't know what they need? This is all the more reason to be a stellar listener. Listening is not just about the words. It's also about what is unspoken. It's about reading between the lines. It's about paying attention.

What breakthrough innovators and exemplary leaders understand is that *all* of us want a tomorrow that is better than today. We don't necessarily all want exactly the same thing, but whatever we want, we want it to be an improvement. The critical skill is in discovering just what "new and improved" means to others.

If you're going to stir the souls of your constituents, if you are going to lift them to a higher level of performance, then this is what you need to know: it's *not* the leader's vision, it's the *people's* vision that matters most.

Part V

The Quality and Character of the Leader of the Future

20

Leading in the Knowledge Worker Age

Stephen R. Covey

An internationally respected leadership authority, family expert, teacher, organizational consultant, and author, Stephen R. Covey dedicates his life to teaching principle-centered living and leadership to individuals, families, and organizations. Holder of an M.B.A. degree from Harvard and a doctorate from Brigham Young University, Covey is author of the international best-seller, The 7 Habits of Highly Effective People, *named the "#1 Most Influential Business Book of the Twentieth Century," and other best-sellers that include* First Things First, Principle-Centered Leadership, *and* The 7 Habits of Highly Effective Families.

A recipient of awards ranging from International Man of Peace to the National Fatherhood Award, Covey is continually engaged in the pursuit of knowledge and understanding, through reading and through interaction with the diverse, inspirational people he encounters the world over.

When I was a young man, I had an experience with a leader that profoundly shaped the rest of my life. I had decided to take a break in my education to give some extended volunteer service. An invitation came to go to England. Just four-and-one-half months after my arrival, the president of the organization I was volunteering with came to me and said, "I have a new assignment for you. I want you to travel around the country and train local leaders." I was shocked. *Who was I* to train leaders two and three times my age? Sensing my doubt, he simply looked me in the eye and said, "I have great confidence in you. You can do this. I will give you materials to help you prepare to teach these leaders and to facilitate their sharing best practices with one another."

His confidence, his ability to see more in me than I saw in myself, his willingness to entrust me with responsibility that would stretch me to my full potential unlocked something inside me. I accepted the assignment and gave my best. It tapped me physically, mentally, emotionally, spiritually. I grew. I saw others grow. I saw patterns in basic leadership principles. By the time I returned home, I had begun to discover the work I wanted to devote my life to: unleashing human potential. I found my "voice." And it was my leader who inspired me to find it.

I realized in time that I wasn't the only one he treated this way. His affirmation of others, his ability to unite us in a vision toward our work that inspired and motivated us, his pattern of providing resources to enable and empower us as true leaders with account-ability and stewardship became the norm in our entire organization. We began to lead and serve others in the same way, and the results were remarkable.

I've realized since then that the principles that guided his lead-ership are common to great leadership in any organization—regard-less of the level or formal position of the person. My teaching, consulting, and leadership experience in business; university; vol-unteer and church organizations; and especially in my own family—have taught me that leadership influence is governed by princi-ples. When you live by them, your influence and moral authority increase, and you are often given even greater formal authority.

Ultimately, I learned that leadership is not a formal position; it is a choice to deal with people in a way that communicates to them their worth and potential so clearly that they will come to see it in themselves.

Management and Leadership

Literally hundreds of books on leadership have come out in recent years. This indicates how vital the subject is. Leadership really is the *enabling* art. The purpose of school is to educate children, but if you have bad leadership, you have bad education. The purpose of medicine is to help people get well, but if you have bad leadership, you'll have bad medicine. We could give illustration after illustration to show that leadership is the highest of the arts, simply because it *enables* all the other arts and professions to work. This is particularly true for a family.

I've spent a lifetime studying, teaching, and writing on both leadership and management. These collective experiences have reinforced in me the understanding that both management *and* leadership are vital—and that either one without the other is insufficient. At times in my life, I've fallen into the trap of overemphasizing leadership and neglecting the importance of management. I'm sure this is because it's become so evident to me that most organizations, families included, are vastly overmanaged and desperately underled. This gap has been a major motivating force in my professional work, and has led me to focus on principles of leadership. Nevertheless, I've been powerfully reminded of the vital part that management plays.

I learned (painfully) that you can't "lead" things. You can't lead inventories and cash flow and costs. You can't lead information, time, structures, processes, facilities, and tools. You have to manage them. Why? Because things don't have the power and freedom to choose. Only people do. So you *lead* (empower) people. You *manage and control* things. The problem is, the organizational legacy we've all inherited says you *do* need to manage and control *people*.

The Thing Mind-Set of the Industrial Age

We live in a Knowledge Worker Age but operate our organizations in a controlling Industrial Age model that absolutely suppresses the release of human potential. The mind-set of the Industrial Age that still dominates today's workplace will simply not work in the Knowledge Worker Age and new economy. Here's why.

The main assets and primary drivers of economic prosperity in the Industrial Age were machines and capital—*things*. People were necessary but replaceable. You could control and churn through manual workers with little consequence—supply exceeded demand. You just got more able bodies that would comply with strict procedures. People were like things—you could be efficient with them. When all you want is a person's body, and you don't really want their mind, heart, or spirit (all inhibitors to the free-flowing processes of the machine age), you have reduced a person to a thing.

So many of our modern management practices come from the Industrial Age:

- It gave us the belief that you have to control and manage people.

- It gave us our view of accounting, which makes people an expense and machines assets. Think about it. People are put on the P&L statement as an expense; equipment is put on the balance sheet as an investment.

- It gave us our carrot and stick motivational philosophy—the Great Jackass technique that motivates with a carrot in front (reward) and drives with a stick from behind (fear and punishment).

- It gave us centralized budgeting—in which trends are extrapolated into the future and hierarchies and bureaucracies are formed to drive "getting the numbers"— an obsolete reactive process that produces "kiss-up" cultures bent on "spending it so we won't lose it next year" and protecting the backside of your department.

All of these practices and many, many more came from the Industrial Age—working with manual workers.

The problem is, managers today are still applying the Industrial Age control model to knowledge workers. Because many in positions of authority do not see the true worth and potential of their people and do not possess a complete, accurate understanding of human nature, *they manage people as they do things.* This lack of understanding also prevents them from tapping into the highest motivations, talents, and genius of people. What happens when you treat people like things today? It insults and alienates them, depersonalizes work, and creates low-trust, unionized, litigious cultures. What happens when you treat your teenage children like things? It insults and alienates; depersonalizes precious family relationships; and creates low trust, contention, and rebellion.

To further illustrate—I frequently ask large audiences, "How many agree that the vast majority of the workforce in your organization possesses far more talent, intelligence, capability, and creativity than their present jobs require or even allow?" The overwhelming majority of the people raise their hands, and this is true of groups all over the world. About the same percentage acknowledge that they are under immense pressure to produce more for less. Just think about it. People face a new and increasing expectation to produce more for less in a terribly complex world, yet are simply not allowed to use a significant portion of their talents and intelligence.

Can you imagine the personal and organizational cost of failing to fully engage the passion, talent, and intelligence of the workforce in this new reality? It is far greater than all taxes, interest charges, and labor costs put together!

The Power of a Paradigm

Author John Gardner once said, "Most ailing organizations have developed a functional blindness to their own defects. They are not suffering because they cannot resolve their problems, but because they cannot *see* their problems."[1] Einstein put it this way: "The significant problems we face cannot be solved at the same level of thinking we were at when we created them."

These statements underscore one of the most profound learnings of my life—if you want to make *minor,* incremental changes and improvements, work on practices, behavior, or attitude. But if you want to make significant, quantum improvement, work on *paradigms*. The word *paradigm* stems from the Greek word *paradeigma*, originally a scientific term but commonly used today to mean a perception, assumption, theory, frame of reference, or lens through which one views the world. It's like a map of a territory or city. If inaccurate, it will make no difference how hard you try to find your destination or how positively you think—you'll stay lost. If accurate, then diligence and attitude matter. But not until.

The new Knowledge Worker Age is based on a new paradigm, one entirely different from the *thing* paradigm of the Industrial Age. Let's call it the Whole-Person Paradigm.

The Whole-Person Paradigm

At the core, there is one simple, overarching reason why so many people remain unsatisfied in their work and why most organizations fail to draw out the greatest talent, ingenuity, and creativity of their people and never become truly great, enduring organizations. It stems from *an incomplete paradigm of who we are—our fundamental view of human nature*.

The fundamental reality is that human beings are not *things* needing to be motivated and controlled; they are four dimensional—they have body, mind, heart, and spirit.

If you study all philosophy and religion, both Western and Eastern, from the beginning of recorded history, you'll basically find the same four dimensions: the physical-economic, the mental, the social-emotional, and the spiritual. Different words are often used, but they reflect the same four universal dimensions of life. They also represent *the four basic needs and motivations of all people*: to live (survival), to love (relationships), to learn (growth and development), and to leave a legacy (meaning and contribution).

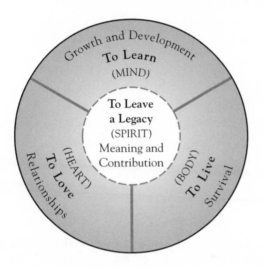

People Have Choices

So what's the direct connection between the controlling "thing" (part person) paradigm that dominates today's workplace and the inability of managers and organizations to inspire their people to volunteer their best talents and contributions? The answer is simple. People make choices. Consciously or subconsciously, people decide how much of themselves they will give to their work depending on how they are treated and their opportunities to use *all four* parts of their nature. These choices range from rebelling or quitting to creative excitement.

CHOICES

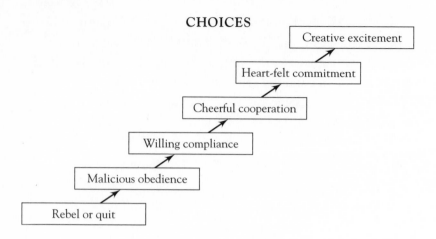

If you neglect any one of the four parts of human nature, in effect, you turn a person into a thing, and what do you do with things? You have to control, manage, and carrot-and-stick them to motivate them. Unless you value people and enable them to contribute in all four areas—"pay me fairly" (body), "treat me kindly" (heart), "use me creatively" (mind), "in principled ways that serve mankind" (spirit)—they'll rarely choose to give of themselves above the bottom three categories of choices shown in the figure—rebel or quit, maliciously obey (meaning they'll do it but hope it doesn't work), or at best willingly comply. But in today's Knowledge Worker Age, only an individual who is respected as a whole person in a whole job makes one of the upper three choices—cheerful cooperation, heart-felt commitment, or creative excitement.

Can you begin to see the how the core problems in the workplace today and the core solution to those problems lie in our paradigm of human nature? Can you see how many of the solutions to the problems in our homes and communities lie in this same paradigm? This Industrial Age "thing" paradigm and all the practices that flow from it are the modern-day equivalent of bloodletting.

Peter Drucker, one of the greatest management thinkers of our time, spoke of this new reality in the following way:

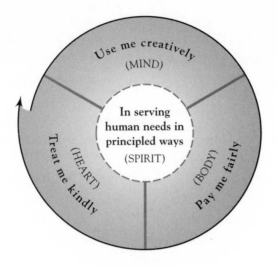

In a few hundred years, when the history of our time is written from a long-term perspective, I think it very probable that the most important event those historians will remember is not technology, not the Internet, not e-commerce—but the unprecedented change in the human condition. For the first time—and I mean that literally—substantial and rapidly growing numbers of people have choices. For the first time, people have had to manage themselves.

And we are totally unprepared for it.[2]

The Call of a New Era

I have written much over the years on *effectiveness*. Being effective as individuals and organizations is no longer an option in today's world—it's the price of entry to the playing field. But surviving, thriving, innovating, excelling, and leading in this new reality will require us to build on and reach beyond effectiveness. The call and need of a new era is for *greatness*. It's for *fulfillment, passionate execution,* and *significant contribution*. These are on a different plane or dimension. They are different in kind—just as *significance* is different in *kind*, not in *degree*, from success. Tapping into the higher reaches of human genius and motivation—what we could call *voice*—requires a new mind-set, a new skill set, a new tool set—a new habit.

The pathway to the enormously promising side of today's reality stands in stark contrast to the pain and frustration many are experiencing. In fact this pathway is a timeless reality. It is the voice of the human spirit—full of hope and intelligence, resilient by nature, boundless in its potential to serve the common good. This voice also encompasses the soul of organizations that will survive, thrive, and have a profound impact on the future of the world.

Voice is *unique personal significance*—significance that is revealed as we face our greatest challenges and that makes us equal to them.

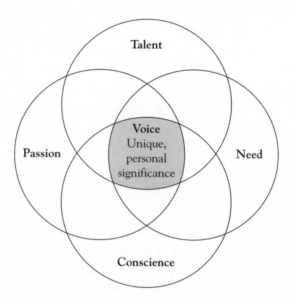

As illustrated in the diagram, voice lies at the nexus of *talent* (your natural gifts and strengths), *passion* (those things that naturally energize, excite, motivate, and inspire you), *need* (including what the world needs enough to pay you for), and *conscience* (that still, small voice within that assures you of what is right and that prompts you to actually do it). When you engage in work that taps your talent (mind) and fuels your passion (heart)—that rises out of a great need in the world (body) that you feel drawn by conscience to meet (spirit)—therein lies your voice, your calling, your soul's code.

Leadership in the Knowledge Worker Age will be characterized by those who find their own voice and who, regardless of formal position, inspire others to find their voice. It is leadership when people communicate to others their worth and potential so clearly they will come to see it in themselves. Therein lies a bright and limitless future.

Endnotes

1. John Gardner, *Self Renewal* (New York: Harper, 1965).
2. Peter F. Drucker, "Managing Knowledge Means Managing Oneself," *Leader to Leader*, Spring 2000, 16, 8–10.

21

Are the Best Leaders Like Professors?

Teaching, Asking Questions, and Evidence-Based Management

Jeffrey Pfeffer

Jeffrey Pfeffer is the Thomas D. Dee II Professor of Organizational Behavior at Stanford University's Graduate School of Business. He served on the faculties of the business schools at the University of Illinois and the University of California at Berkeley before coming to Stanford in 1979. He is the author or coauthor of eleven books, including The Knowing-Doing Gap: How Smart Companies Turn Knowledge into Action, *and* Hard Facts, Dangerous Half-Truths, and Total Nonsense: Profiting from Evidence-Based Management. *He has also published more than one hundred articles and book chapters. Pfeffer serves on the board of directors of SonoSite, UniCru, and Audible Magic, and has given management seminars in twenty-eight countries and for numerous organizations and associations in the United States.*

W hen Harrah's chief executive Phil Satre chose Gary Loveman to become the company's chief operating officer in 1998, many observers considered this to be a risky and unobvious decision. After all, Harrah's is a multibillion-dollar operator of casinos and associated facilities such as hotels, restaurants, and entertainment, and Loveman was a thirty-eight-year-old untenured professor in the service management group at Harvard Business School. As Loveman himself acknowledges, at that time he had direct experience managing no one except for some research assistants and a fraction of an administrative assistant, and he was going to now try to run a company that at the time had almost forty thousand employees and operated numerous large properties across a number of locations in different states. Loveman commented that a number of Harrah's executives thought they were much better qualified than he for the job. He wryly noted that since he had taken a two-year leave from Harvard, many people inside the company expected his tenure there to be like a kidney stone, painful but temporary. When Loveman was actually successful at the COO job and a few years later succeeded Satre as CEO of Harrah's, many observers were surprised. Some have continued to be surprised as Harrah's has outperformed its competitors in the gambling industry and in 2005 completed a large merger with Caesar's that leaves Harrah's with more than a hundred thousand employees and revenues of about $7.5 billion in 2005.

But people actually shouldn't have been surprised by Loveman's success at all. The skills that Loveman had developed as a Harvard Business School professor, albeit to a level of unusual proficiency, are actually precisely the skills that leaders of large corporations need. As I watch organizational leaders produce remarkable transformations and lead change at companies such as Harrah's and DaVita, the $2.2 billion revenue operator of kidney dialysis centers, I am increasingly convinced that organizations would be well-served to rethink both the qualities that they are looking for in their leaders and their selection process for choosing people for senior positions. Rethinking what makes a good leader and changing how they choose their senior leaders might help companies avoid the ever-shortening tenure of senior managers around the world who can't seem to perform adequately in meeting today's competitive challenges.

The Qualities Needed in the Leader of the Future

Research by Henry Mintzberg, John Kotter, and others that is now more than thirty years old has described what managers actually do, which mostly is communicate with others in short, unstructured interactions to motivate, coach, and influence them to do what needs to be done.[1,2] Yet somehow many people still see the leader's role as that of being a great, insightful decision maker and strategist, and as knowing a lot about the details of operations. In short—all of the literature on empowerment and decentralization notwithstanding—leaders are often seen as some sort of überexecutive, possessed of more knowledge, more technical skill, perhaps more of everything, than other executives in the company. Rakesh Khurana has described the results of this idealization of the skills of the leader in the context of the executive succession process as looking for a corporate savior.[3] Khurana has noted that what this often means in practice is seeking someone who has already served as a CEO or president of "a high-performing and well-regarded company," not some academic like Gary Loveman.[4]

At first glance, Kent Thiry, the CEO of what was then called Total Renal Care (the company now called DaVita) and a company that was almost on the verge of bankruptcy in late 1999 when he was hired, and Joe Mello, the chief operating officer he brought in a few months later, might look to be more conventional choices as leaders. After all, both had led a smaller, successful dialysis company called Vivra that had done pretty well. However Thiry had just spent two years losing about half of his investment and the investment of some private equity groups in an unsuccessful effort at building a managed care company—perhaps not a typical job experience to immediately precede appointment as CEO of a large company facing a crisis situation, and not something that one might expect would predict a very successful turnaround.

A number of other noteworthy business leaders also do not seem to fit the conventional mold. James Goodnight, the cofounder and long-time CEO of SAS Institute, the enormously successful privately owned software company with revenues over $1.5 billion, certainly doesn't look like the typical CEO at first, or maybe even at second, glance. Goodnight has a Ph.D. in statistics, a degree that prepared him to be an academic, is not particularly loud or charismatic, and refers to the physical facilities of SAS as a "campus," consistent with his more academic orientation. He prefers to do programming to running a large organization and has talked frequently about not being a technological visionary like Bill Gates, able to tell the future. Instead, Goodnight tries to guide the company by just listening to customers and giving them what they want. Herb Kelleher, the legendary CEO of Southwest Airlines who was once called by *Fortune* America's best CEO, was a corporate attorney with no previous experience in airline industry operations.

Upon some reflection, however, it appears that many of these successful executives share some qualities that are actually extremely useful in leading large, complex organizations facing numerous and often unpredictable competitive challenges. Many of these qualities and behaviors are more commonly associated with professors and teaching than with leading large organizations, but they are extremely useful nonetheless. Let's look at a few of those less frequently considered leadership qualities and why they are so helpful.

The Ability to Teach Others

DaVita operates more than six hundred dialysis centers in thirty-seven states. Harrah's operated almost twenty casinos when Loveman arrived, and now, with its merger with Caesar's, operates more than forty facilities both in the United States and internationally. Southwest Airlines has thousands of employees operating flights all over the United States. And SAS Institute, with most of its product development located in Cary, North Carolina, has a core software product that has more than three million lines of code, and the company offers a number of products in a range of vertical and horizontal markets. The point is that in none of these cases, nor in most other organizations of any size, is it possible for the leader to know everything about everything—either about every business issue or about what is going on everywhere at all moments.

That leaves two choices for senior executives. One choice is to try to micromanage in an effort to obtain a feeling of control over a complex and unpredictable world, something I suspect all of us have experienced in our careers and not particularly liked. A second alternative is to try to build the competence and skill of others in managing and leading. Of course, leaders want the skills of others to develop in ways such that their resulting actions are consistent with the organization's vision, values, and business model. This latter choice of helping others do their own work more effectively involves the leader "teaching" others how to think about business issues and decision making.

Harrah's, for instance, is justly famous for its focus on facts and evidence and its insistence that people run small experiments—on promotions, marketing campaigns, whatever—before they implement any program on a large scale. But this focus on facts, evidence, and experiments is largely a way of thinking about how to go about solving business problems. Loveman's task when he arrived at the company was *not* to gather all the data or even do all the analyses, and certainly not to make all the decisions himself, but rather to impart, through his questioning and through his own example as a role model, a way of thinking about business that others could learn and implement in their own activities. In other words, just as in the Harvard Business School classroom Loveman tried to teach his students how to think about business decisions and issues, that is precisely what he had to do with his numerous managers in the various facilities and functions—people who also needed to learn a more analytical, disciplined way of making business decisions and thinking about how to beat the competition.

Or consider DaVita. Kidney dialysis is a business under constant cost pressures from Medicare and from the private insurers and hospitals who contract with the companies to provide dialysis services. But many, maybe the majority, of the geographically dispersed centers are run by registered nurses, people who are health care providers first and foremost and who may have never had formal training in analyzing budgets or thinking about labor productivity. Many of these nurses, however, are fantastic managers of people and have built devoted teams in their centers. Moreover, for a company interested in the quality of patient care, their long experience in nephrology is extremely helpful. Joe Mello and Kent Thiry's answer to this challenge of having skilled health care practitioners with great values and interpersonal skills but possibly little business acumen has been to build DaVita University (DVU), an extensive set of training and communication activities that touches all of the management structure. New facility administrators come to DVU to learn basic skills such as Microsoft Excel and also the basics of the business of running a facility, including profit and loss, budgeting, scheduling labor, and so forth. There is then subsequent training in business skills. DaVita's ability to deliver the highest quality of care in the industry while also continually improving its labor productivity over the past five years is the direct result of facility leaders learning, on an ongoing and continuous basis, how to be better decision makers and more effective executives. Presentations and programs of instruction are relentlessly evaluated and updated, just as good courses should be, to ensure that the desired learnings are being taught and that people find the educational experience engaging.

Asking Good Questions

Professors and academics ask questions—inquiry is what science is about after all, and asking questions is very much part of the Socratic method used in teaching at places such as Harvard Business School, for instance. But as Kent Thiry of DaVita has commented, "A question well asked is half answered." The insight is that if you can ask the right insightful and intelligent questions, there is a chance that you and others can find the answers to them with some effort and, by so doing, come up with some useful and innovative insights. By contrast, great and complete answers to not very interesting, insightful, or useful questions won't get you or your organization very far.

Gary Loveman had worked for Harrah's as a consultant and had done executive education with their senior team. He knew enough about the basics of the business and the challenges Harrah's faced to be able to ask questions that caused others to think about the business and how to make it more effective in creative and different ways. Mello, Thiry, and their colleagues at DaVita had enough experience and training as engineers and consultants—Thiry had started his career at Bain, Mello's background was in industrial engineering— to ask questions that focused people on the key success factors to improve clinical care and produce better financial results. To observe Thiry or Loveman in action is to see leaders who are continually asking questions of themselves and others, who also listen carefully to the answers, and who through their inquiry seek to impart this spirit of learning and exploration throughout their companies. This behavior is part and parcel of the process of continuous improvement, but it is also an extremely powerful way of focusing attention and of teaching people how to be better decision makers and leaders themselves through the dialogue the questions engender.

Using Evidence-Based Decision Making

Academics, at least most of them, try to emphasize facts, rigorous thought, and patterns of inquiry, in contrast with the casual benchmarking, recourse to ideology, or acting on the basis of habit that characterizes so much of business today. It seems obvious that business decisions will be better if they are based on the facts rather than on conventional wisdom, what others are doing, or belief.

Conventional wisdom in the gaming industry was that companies needed to attract the high rollers, the people who dropped a fortune at the roulette wheel or the poker table; that the best way to get people into the casino was to offer them free or reduced-price rooms; and that "attractions"—edifices that looked like Paris, Luxor, New York, or Venice and built at a cost of billions—were more important than the guest experience in producing satisfied customers and repeat business. Harrah's has challenged all of this, finding that the most profitable customers were people who lived nearby and who gambled regularly as a form of entertainment. These people

were more interested in meals and free chips than in rooms. And
Harrah's found that by reducing employee turnover and providing
a better customer service experience, and by capturing data on its
customers so that attention and service could be focused differen-
tially according to the value of those customers, great improvements
in margins and profitability could be achieved without spending billions on physical plant and equipment.

SAS Institute is so devoted to fact-based decision making that it
uses its own software to help it decide on adding or cutting particular exercise classes and how to best organize and deliver its generous
benefits. DaVita's mantra of "no brag, just facts" represents an interest in learning and understanding what is really going on in the quality of care and in its business operations. As Joe Mello explained, the
company is so committed to learning about what is important that
it will sometimes put a measure on a report and leave it blank when
there aren't the systems or ability to yet gather it—as a way of
reminding people of the urgent need to get the additional information that can be helpful in improving operations and care.

Working Through Others

Teachers, particularly the best teachers, understand that teaching
and learning are two different and, believe it or not, empirically disconnected processes. By different processes I mean that teaching is
something that the instructor does, learning is something the students do. By empirically disconnected I mean that the evidence
shows that there is essentially *no* relationship between the quality
of instruction, as measured for instance by instructor ratings, and
the amount students learn, as measured for instance by performance
on standardized tests.[5] In a similar fashion, leaders only lead successfully when others follow—leading is an activity that the leader
does, but it amounts to nothing if others aren't themselves motivated and convinced about what they themselves need to do.

This absence of control of the outcomes in a classroom environment, and the need to work through and with others to accom-

plish learning, is very relevant experience for working through the thousands of others one will need to make something happen in a large, complex corporation. There has been a lot of discussion, and empirical evidence, about the downside of executive hubris, a quality that has led CEOs to grossly overpay for acquisitions, as one example, and also to be closed to new information that might have prevented decision errors as another. Let me suggest that there is no more humbling experience than trying to get others to learn, and teaching is also an experience that helps people learn how to get things done through and with the cooperation of others.

Some Implications for the Selection Process

There is a second lesson in the choice of a Harvard academic to lead a company, or someone who just recently has not done particularly well in a business venture. In many instances, selecting leaders today is a process of evaluating resumes—what jobs or positions people have held, and, albeit less frequently because reliable information on this aspect is much harder to come by in today's litigious world, how they have performed in those positions. In many cases, what organizations evaluate most are educational and other credentials, job background, and relevant work experience to see if the right boxes have been checked.

This seems sensible, until you think about it for a moment. Consider the U.S. Army's leadership mantra, "be, know, do." Fundamental to the Army's concept of leadership and leadership development is the fact that leadership is a manifestation of the individual and that person's essential nature and qualities—so what is fundamental is who and how that person is, his or her "being." The Army's leadership development, particularly at West Point, is about the development of character, the "be" component of leadership, as well as providing knowledge and practice in leadership roles.

To make the obvious point, you won't learn much, if anything, about people's character or essential nature from their resumes, from what positions they have held, or from what education and background they have acquired. Kent Thiry of DaVita is a person who believes deeply and passionately in organizations as caring communities—borrowing from the Three Musketeers, he often shouts "one for all and all for one"—and also is committed to providing the best patient care possible to people who are, after all, the mothers, fathers, parents, sisters, brothers, and friends of others who care about them and their health and survival. But one might not necessarily predict that level of caring and concern for patients or the attachment to the idea of community—DaVita is referred to as a village—based on Thiry's education at Harvard Business School or his early experience as a Bain consultant.

We overemphasize resumes—what people have done—at the expense of who they are, what drives them, what their interests and capabilities are—in other words, what they might do. To take another example, consider Roger Martin, the immensely talented and successful dean of the business school at the University of Toronto. Roger Martin has an M.B.A. degree from Harvard and was one of the founding partners of the strategy consulting firm Monitor. A Canadian by origin, he was drawn to the challenge of reinvigorating the Rotman School at Toronto and building its quality, impact, and visibility. But there was nothing in Martin's background or training—he didn't even have a Ph.D.—to suggest that he would wind up teaching quite successfully, something that many deans don't even bother doing because they are too busy doing their dean job. Nor was there anything to suggest that Martin, even more surprisingly, would be a prolific author, writing not only a book but also numerous articles for publications such as *Harvard Business Review* and columns in various magazines and newspapers.[6] In fact, Martin has published more work than many of his dean counterparts at other schools, some of whom have Ph.D. degrees and other credentials that might lead one to expect they would actually publish more. Talking to Roger Martin reveals a person with an extremely high level of intellectual curiosity and a person of enormous energy and commitment to the educational and research process. Martin's essential self predicts a lot more about his activities of writing and teaching than does his absence of a Ph.D. or his previous practical experience helping to run a consulting firm.

I certainly am not suggesting that resumes and experience are irrelevant. To the contrary, usually it is the case that the best predictor of future behavior is past behavior. The problem is that resumes and what we typically look at when we hire don't speak to behavior at all—only to a set of positions that people have occupied.

While discussing with my class on power in organizations a case I had written on him, Gary Loveman explained how finishing a Ph.D. degree in economics at MIT and then succeeding as a professor in the demanding environment of Harvard Business School did reveal something about him—that he is a deeply competitive person. He likes to win and has shown the ability to do so in the past, for instance at MIT, overcoming a slow start in a quantitatively oriented doctoral program to eventually earn a prestigious fellowship. Loveman has used that lesson about the importance of character and essential being in his own hiring. He has commented that when he hires people, he wants to select people who have excelled at some domain of activity in their lives. He doesn't particularly care what the specific activity is—he wants to know that people have experienced success and the need to push themselves to excel in a competitive environment.

In a very similar fashion, DaVita's hiring process and its performance evaluation screen not just for ability and accomplishment but also for cultural fit and the individual's values and beliefs. People who can learn, care about patients and their teammates, and have energy and intelligence can accomplish great things. Obviously relevant job experience is also important, but it is what people have done and who they are, not just the roles they have been able to attain, that also matter.

The Importance of Inquiry and Curiosity in Leadership

We live in a world in which intellectual capital is increasingly important for business success, particularly in the developed economies. There is much attention, or at least talk, paid to building "learning organizations."[7] But there is surprisingly little attention to building organizations designed to actually encourage learning.

My colleague at Stanford's Engineering School, Robert Sutton, codirector of the Center for Work, Technology, and Organization, talks about "the attitude of wisdom," knowing what you know and knowing what you don't know, being able to take action based on always imperfect knowledge while remaining open to inquiry and learning as you and your organization gain experience. He has argued that it is precisely this attitude that has helped make a company he works with, IDEO Product Development, such a successful, innovative, and award-winning product design firm.

If we take the idea of learning seriously, if we believe that the attitude of wisdom is important, and if we are serious about developing intellectual capital, then the argument that some of the characteristics we associate with university professors are also useful for corporate leaders should not seem that surprising. However, old habits die hard, and the tough, sometimes abusive, and often egomaniacal leader remains a surprisingly seductive model for corporations in contemporary society. As we cast about for alternative templates for what effective leader behavior is and what great leaders in the future might look like, this chapter has argued that considering the qualities of particularly effective professors or teachers is not a bad place to start. Teachers impart a spirit of inquiry and learning and a quest for continually improving mastery—and that seems to be precisely the sort of mind-set that is useful given current competitive business conditions.

Endnotes

1. Henry Mintzberg, *The Nature of Managerial Work* (New York: Harper and Row, 1973).

2. John Kotter, *The General Managers* (New York: Free Press, 1982).

3. Rakesh Khurana, *Searching for a Corporate Savior* (Princeton, NJ: Princeton University Press, 2002).

4. Khurana, *Searching for a Corporate Savior*, p. 20.

5. H. Attiyeh and K. G. Lumsden, "Some Modern Myths in Teaching Economics: The U.K. Experience," *American Economic Review*, 1972, *62*, 429–433.

6. The book, *The Responsibility Virus* (New York: Basic Books, 2002), appeared after he was in his job as dean.

7. Peter Senge, *The Fifth Discipline* (New York: Currency, 1990).

22

The Leader Integrator
An Emerging Role

Usman A. Ghani

A respected international consultant and popular keynote speaker, Usman A. Ghani is CEO of AIMS, LLC, an organization that assists businesses and nonprofits of all sizes in integration and transformation. Applying fresh thinking and refined dynamic business models to reveal the best solutions to complex challenges, Ghani leads powerful leadership development and team-building programs for corporate America and worldwide businesses.

He is also a visiting professor at the University of Texas at Dallas School of Management and is the author of InteGreat, *a forthcoming business book that takes a holistic approach and provides deep insights into the dynamics of business, governance, and strategy.*

In past decades, leadership has often been viewed as a formula—one that most often appeased organizational "wants" rather than attending to their "needs." Some leaders were capable of leading with their hearts while others led with their minds, pushing the "warm, fuzzy" stuff to the side to make room for theories and concepts aimed at strengthening the organization's structure or its impact on the marketplace. Still other leaders were crowned the ultimate "multitaskers," leading first with their hearts, then with their minds and occasionally, at some point, with their souls.

When confronted with problems, traditional leaders often were unwilling to admit mistakes until these had taken their toll, allowing products and services to degrade, customers to complain, employee morale to erode and, in some extreme cases, the companies to fragment or implode. Eroding ethics and sagging integrity have had their own consequences, creating a lack of trust and fleeting accountability that resulted in diminished authenticity—inside and outside the business.

Rather than directing the organization in a holistic manner, these leaders found it easier to focus on finding the answers rather than taking a step back and asking, What's the real question? Instead of developing all parts of the organization, they focused on the quick wins and easy accomplishments, distracting their energy and resources from the ultimate goal of steady development and growth.

Sixty years ago, Peter Drucker was among the first to dissect and examine the role of the leader.[1] In *Managing the Nonprofit Organization*, Drucker described his vision of an effective leader:

> The leaders who work most effectively, it seems to me, never say "I." And that's not because they have trained themselves not to say "I." They don't *think* "I." . . . They understand their job to be to make the team function. They accept the responsibility and don't sidestep it, but "we" gets the credit. . . . This is what creates trust, what enables you to get the task done.[2]

Throughout his writings, Drucker has repeatedly emphasized executive *effectiveness* over efficiency or other leadership characteristics.[3]

Ultimately, the leader of the future will continue to embrace the traditional responsibilities and the effectiveness characteristics Drucker depicted, and he or she also will know when and how far to step outside the box to fine-tune the organization's mission and vision as well as its operation and execution, or to reset the context. The leader of the future will have the agility to move from previous traditions to innovation, the courage to adapt to new or dynamic business models, and the ability to examine issues across the breadth and depth of the organization.

The Leader Integrator

The leader of the future is the Leader Integrator—an individual who breeds multiple perspectives, consciously connecting these perspectives and applying a variety of skills to establish new directions, options, and solutions for the organization. Leader Integrators adapt multiple roles for themselves and seek new talents and new teams to create new directions for their organizations.

As a rule, Leader Integrators move away from the traditional accolades such as, "He is a great visionary" or "She is a strong recruiter" or "He is an astute strategist" or "She is an excellent mentor" or "He is a smart implementer" to *"He brings myriad talents to the table and can effectively bring into play a particular role at an appropriate time."*

The most important characteristics of Leader Integrators include

- Having faith in the power of an idea in action, rather than the idea of power in a person

- Having the ability to be deep listeners, actively seeking multiple perspectives

- Having a relentless predisposition and openness to critique

- Being creative decision makers, weighing a variety of options and possibilities

- Being bridge-builders across multiple disciplines, fields, departments, stakeholders, and so on

- Being visionaries with limitless perspective and an ability to zoom in or zoom out at all times

- Having a strong commitment for continuing learning experiences—to themselves, their employees, their organization, and their organizational partners

- Being steadfast developers of leaders, facilitating others unleashing their potential, and helping everyone discover the leader in themselves and in every situation

Embracing diversity, Leader Integrators eagerly invite a wide variety of experiences, visions, and skill sets into the task of forming and then expanding the corporate vision. As a result, the Leader Integrator not only increases the passion of every worker for his or her contribution to the corporation's direction but also amplifies the workers' personal commitments to the organization.

Harlan Cleveland, a business, educational, social, and political leader, sees leadership from an integration perspective, calling it the "get-it-all-together" profession:

> "How can we be different together?" . . . sums up a prime dilemma of our time. . . . Helping the many think of themselves as one, selling a wholeness that can incorporate diversity will be a central challenge for many different kinds of leaders in the 21st century. . . . The threat to robust cultures (those that can meld the best of the new with the best of the old) comes from both extremes: an unthinking attachment to what has already been thought or done, and an overenthusiastic espousal of what is new because it is new.[4]

Compare the role of the Leader Integrator to that of the traditional leader. Whereas a traditional leader generally focuses on "one slender slice" of the organization at a time, the Leader Integrator "sees the whole pizza," so to speak, arranging each slice to establish new directions and aligning, motivating, and inspiring people to generate a new collective meaning. As Lou Gerstner described his early days as CEO of IBM:

> We needed to rebuild the fundamental strategy of the company. . . . [T]he unique opportunity for IBM—our distinctive competence—was an ability to integrate all the parts for our customers. . . . However, before I could integrate for our customers [in 160-plus countries], I first had to integrate IBM! . . . I turned my attention to three areas . . . organization, brand image, and compensation. . . .[5]

As an archetypal Leader Integrator, Gerstner applied his vision across the corporate landscape, discerning the areas needing his attention first and then, as he became familiar with the corporation and his people, identifying the next levels of consequence—organization, branding, compensation, and so on.

Much like a consummate multitasker, the Leader Integrator is constantly evolving and expanding his or her arena of activity and spheres of influence. Susan Hockfield, president of the Massachusetts Institute of Technology, in a recent address defined the expanded scope of MIT's future direction:

> I have been impressed by the volume of collaborative activity between MIT and other area universities, such as the exceptional joint program in Health Sciences and Technology established by MIT and Harvard 35 years ago. Structuring collaboration across departments within one school is a non-trivial task; building collaborations across institutions poses even greater challenges. But MIT will actively foster these collaborations because many of the most important opportunities before us require skills and resources that no single institution can deliver.
>
> I have drawn the circle of collaboration around departments and schools within MIT and then enlarged

it to include our academic and medical colleagues. Of course, I must enlarge the circle further to include the critically important collaborations between the academy and industry.[6]

Think of the Leader Integrator in the role of a Broadway musical director, maintaining the synergy of the various actors, singers, dancers, and other performers while combining and mixing these elements and then reframing them in new formats conceived to move performance to a higher level.

Three Model Leader Integrators in Corporate America

Within the modern business environment, the nature of leadership challenges continues to evolve, requiring leaders to reach beyond traditional scopes of influence to guide the growth of their organizations. Let us consider three examples of Leader Integrators and the indelible imprint they have made on their organizations as well as on society.

Lou V. Gerstner, Former Chairman and CEO of IBM Corporation

It was once believed the greatest leaders were those individuals with "guts," and the gutsiest must therefore be the most successful. Next, it was believed the greatest leaders were the great "minds" of their times. Then, as the "heart" began to emerge as the driver of passion, leaders with "hearts" were at the forefront. Over time, the "backbone," the "sixth sense," and "soul" were also emphasized as central to the leadership role.[7]

Lou Gerstner's success at IBM was not attributable to these or any other leadership traits. His success was due, in part, to his "wholeness"—his ability to lead the organization by bringing all faculties, thoughts, and feelings into focus and applying each to bring about richer, more effective outcomes.

As he describes in his book *Who Says Elephants Can't Dance?*, Gerstner focused on four critical decisions as he began devising a survival strategy for the struggling IBM: (1) to keep the company together, (2) to change the fundamental economic model, (3) to reengineer how IBM did business, and (4) to sell unproductive assets in order to raise capital.[8]

When Gerstner took IBM's helm, his Leader Integrator instincts immediately took over, helping him resist the knee-jerk responses that would have destroyed the company. He was able instead to focus on day-to-day execution, stabilizing the company as he sought growth strategies that would leverage IBM's unique position in the industry. Using the "pizza analogy" mentioned earlier, Gerstner focused on the whole pizza, rather than obsessing on a single slice, and—in the interim—he built a team of people who were ready to try to do things in very new and different ways.

As the Leader Integrator continues to refine and refurbish the organization's vision and mission, he or she is also focusing on sustainability and succession—the defining difference that has, for whatever reason, escaped much of modern leadership.

At his retirement, Gerstner said this: "I want IBMers to think and act like long-term shareholders—to feel the pressure from the marketplace to deploy assets and forge strategies that create competitive advantage."[9] Then he added, "If you ask me today what single accomplishment I am most proud of in all my years at IBM, I would tell you it is this—that as I retire, my successor is a longtime IBMer, and so are the heads of all of our major business units."[10]

Indeed, Gerstner's role as a Leader Integrator allowed him to see the value—to the corporation and to its employees—of being succeeded by someone from inside the corporation rather than someone totally unknown to the organization from another city, another state, or another industry.

Oprah Winfrey, Chairman of Harpo Inc.[11]

Taking on multiple professional and social roles—news anchor, talk show host, entrepreneur, magazine editor, business executive, and social advocate—Oprah Winfrey has uniquely positioned herself as a Leader Integrator with the ability to see through multiple lenses and to have an impact on many of the environments under her observation.

Obviously, as the media offers immediate mega-audiences for Winfrey's initiatives—such as her overwhelmingly successful book club and her efforts to improve educational opportunities for the underclass—she has leveraged the reach of her organization and has been able to focus on the real rather than the mundane. This vision, replacing the typical short-term, sensational issues addressed by others in her genre, has lifted Winfrey and company far above her competitors, many of which eventually foundered and failed.

Winfrey, who has continued to respect diversity in all its venues, generates initiatives to address issues that resonate with her audiences as well as much of the country and, as a result, this Leader Integrator has redefined standards for her genre and ultimately is working to redefine overarching media standards as well.

As chairman of Harpo Inc., Winfrey serves as

- Institution-builder, crafting a new definition of the media industry that others are adopting

- Motivator to her staff, as well as role model

- Hope and inspiration to audiences around the world

- Innovator for her organization as well as for the entire television industry

- Connector of desperate entities with a common purpose and meaning

As a team builder, Winfrey has created an entire organization, as described by Professor Nancy Koehn of Harvard Business School, as a place where employees are incredibly committed and where turnover—an issue hurting many corporations, including those with strong brand names—is minimal. "They all breathe and think they have a very important mission they are fulfilling as an organization," Koehn wrote. "They have very important precepts for how they engage with that mission and execute it, day to day."[12]

Said Winfrey in case "Oprah Winfrey":

> I have already done the work of creating a team of people who understand not to propose a show idea to me unless there is an intention behind the idea. Tell me what the intention is first so we know that the intention is in line with [Harpo's] mission. It's a broad mission, to transform the way people see themselves, to uplift, to enlighten, to encourage, to entertain. So you get a really broad canvas in which to do that, but whatever show idea you're bringing me has to fit into that category.[13]

In the mode of the classic Leader Integrator, Winfrey continues to perceive and plan for future shifts in the entertainment industry as she seeks to address deep social issues, not just those affecting women and minorities but those truly of a global reach. Winfrey views these forecasted trends as unique opportunities to develop in new directions and to leverage and appropriate resources to continue her social impact across diverse and disparate elements.

By redefining directions and goals across people, problems, and processes, Winfrey has maintained and increased every skill in her leadership arsenal as she has simultaneously strengthened her organization. And she continues to grow.

Herbert W. Kelleher, Founder and Chairman, Southwest Airlines[14]

Long noted for his strategic successes within a capricious and fragile industry, Herb Kelleher provides an unquestioned model of the Leader Integrator, taking on roles, either simultaneously or individually, as

- Coach to his employees

- Careful listener to his board

- Challenger and creator of new business concepts

- Operational manager for execution and evaluating the business

- Visionary in thinking long term when most think there is no long term, or when current hyperactivity blinds most from admitting there is a clear blue sky

Unlike the traditional leader, who rushes to gather only the "low-hanging fruit," Kelleher continues to mine the marketplace for those unique opportunities that push and pull the boundaries of the Southwest business model to meet the demands of each new decade. As he built the business, he also built a culture of loyalty, in which employees immediately became part of a family whose pride far exceeded temptations to jump ship when tough sledding occurred.

Soon after the airline industry suffered the first blow of the 9/11 tragedy, for example, numerous passengers were seeking to change or cancel their prepurchased tickets. Many airlines were charging $100 to make these alterations. Kelleher, however, thought beyond the current stages of panic, deciding that frightened passengers should not be penalized, and instead offered a full refund without penalty. The loyalty Southwest had built with its passengers paid off. While several did ask for refunds, most did not. A few even sent their tickets to Southwest with a note saying, "Take this money and put it back into the company." The result: Southwest did more than just survive during a time that brought near-death experiences to some long-established brands within the industry.

Instead of cutting costs to the bone in order to enhance profitability, Kelleher on numerous occasions opted to refine processes and optimize the full potential of the company's workforce. Once this was accomplished, opportunities to explore pent-up demand and unmet needs presented themselves, and these in turn would encourage expansion of services and eventually new business.

Ultimately, the three Leader Integrators mentioned here have served in multiple capacities and worn many hats in their diverse organizations. However, all of them embraced the roles of change agent, visionary, transformer, culture builder, synergistic catalyst, and many others for their organizations. In the face of tradition, they ventured far outside the proverbial box to explore unique options and, in their wake, have developed loyal teams and successors to continue their work.

The Leader of the Future

By disposition, the Leader Integrator works with an inclusive attitude, incorporating individual viewpoints as well as commonalities across different personality types and thoughts. It is *the idea and the thought process* that is most important to the Leader Integrator, who actually seeks out diversity to enrich every process.

Leader Integrators—the leaders of the future—consistently escape the bonds of tradition to incorporate many levels and many domains within their vision. They have the ability to translate challenges into opportunities and the future into present reality as they continue to move the corporation forward. Over time, Leader Integrators positively influence the culture of all their communities.

Any discussion of the leader of the future also must include a cursory examination of the development opportunities for Leader Integrators. Initially, these uniquely talented individuals were born as self-styled integrators from chief executives whose burning desire was to do something bigger—and different. Today, however, the advantages of integration have been distinctly clarified to the point that organizations should not be asking themselves if Leader Integrators are vital to their survival but, rather, When will development of the next generation of Leader Integrators begin?

Endnotes

1. See Peter F. Drucker, *Concept of the Corporation* (New York: John Day, 1946).

2. Peter F. Drucker, *Managing the Nonprofit Organization: Principle and Practices* (New York: HarperCollins, 1990), 18–19.

3. Peter F. Drucker, *The Effective Executive* (New York: Harper & Row, 1967). This book (and the supporting films with the same title from BNA Communications) tremendously inspired the author as a young adult in the 1970s.

4. Cleveland, Harlan, *Nobody in Charge: Essays on the Future of Leadership* (San Francisco: Jossey-Bass, 2002).

5. Louis V. Gerstner Jr., *Who Says Elephants Can't Dance?* (New York: HarperCollins, 2002), 83.

6. Susan Hockfield, speech to Greater Boston Chamber of Commerce, *MIT Speeches and Essays*, September 14, 2005, http://web.mit.edu/hockfield/speech-commerce2005.html. Authorial comment: Harvard and MIT have traditionally seen themselves as "rivals," but the new MIT president views these two institutions *collectively as a community* in the *larger social sector.*

7. Each role has had its unveiling at times when its need was felt. Each defined its distinctive role, vis-à-vis what prevailed then, and each had its devout followers. For more examples, see Lee Bolman, *Leading with Soul* (San Francisco: Jossey-Bass, 2001); Sigmund Ginsburg, *Managing with Passion* (New York: Wiley, 1996); Daniel Goleman,

Emotional Intelligence (New York: Bantam, 1995); Sharon Good, *Managing with a* Heart (New York: Excalibur, 1994); Regina McNamara, A Spine *Is a Terrible Thing to Waste* (Cheshire, CT: Kelsco Press, 1999); and Kenichi Ohmae, *The* Mind *of the Strategist* (New York: McGraw-Hill, 1982).

8. Gerstner, *Who Says Elephants Can't Dance?*

9. Gerstner, *Who Says Elephants Can't Dance?*, 96.

10. Gerstner, *Who Says Elephants Can't Dance?*, 73.

11. Material is from the author's research and from excerpts from *Harvard Business School Case: Oprah Winfrey*, by Nancy Koehn and Erica Helms; revised edition, June 1, 2005.

12. Martha Lagace, "Oprah: A Case Study Comes Alive," *HBS Working Knowledge*, February 20, 2006. Available at http://hbswk.hbs.edu/item.jhtml?id=5214&t=leadership.

13. Lagace, "Oprah: A Case Study Comes Alive."

14. Based on notes from the author's personal interviews with Herb Kelleher in 1991 and subsequent follow-up through numerous articles related to Kelleher and to Southwest Airlines.

23

Leadership Competencies
A Provocative New Look

Edgar H. Schein

*Edgar H. Schein has been a prolific researcher, writer, teacher, and con-
sultant. Besides his numerous articles in professional journals he has
authored fourteen books, including* Organizational Psychology, Career
Dynamics, Organizational Culture and Leadership, Process Consultation Vol. 1 *and* Vol. 2, Process Consultation Revisited, *and* The Corporate Culture Survival Guide. *At present he is a Sloan Fellows
Professor of Management Emeritus and serves on the boards of Massachusetts Audubon and the Boston Lyric Opera.*

*Schein has received many honors and awards for his writing, includ-
ing the Lifetime Achievement Award in Workplace Learning and Per-
formance of the American Society of Training Directors, the Everett
Cherington Hughes Award for Career Scholarship from the Careers
Division of the Academy of Management, and the Marion Gislason
Award for Leadership in Executive Development from the BU School of
Management Executive Development Roundtable.*

The identification of leadership competencies has become virtually an obsession. There are long lists and short lists, but they all
have something in common—they are all based on *psychology*, individual or social. Whereas individual psychologists are obsessed with
characterological traits such as "integrity," and competencies such as
"emotional intelligence" (under which label one sometimes finds
dozens of other traits and characteristics which then appear in surveys
that produce complex profiles of the person), social psychologists

are obsessed with relational competencies such as "servant mentality," "listening skills," "team building," and the like—many of which overlap with emotional intelligence.

Recently I attended a session in an organization in which the HR professionals asked senior management to reduce the list of over one hundred (!) competencies identified by a well-known leadership consulting firm to the ten or so that might apply most in this particular organization. I noted that the executives had trouble differentiating such a large number and saw overlaps and relationships among them that made ranking and rating difficult. As we left the meeting, one participant asked, "Am I nuts or is this all 'smoke and mirrors?'"

I don't believe the desire to identify leadership competencies is smoke and mirrors. I think it is an honest attempt from a psychological point of view to make sense of what it is that leaders do and must be good at. The problem that I see is that it is *too* psychological. Most of us admit that leadership is a *relational* concept and is very *contextual*, but we do not take that insight to its logical conclusion, namely that it is not always about the leader but about the culture and environment in which the leader operates. Yet leaders are individual human beings, so we need some way of characterizing what we would like them to be like and what we think they should be good at. How do we bring these two points of view together?

I believe that we have missed something in the exclusive focus on psychology. We have missed the cultural breadth and depth of what creates leaders in the first place, and we have overlooked the reality that what leaders do that is unique is to manage culture. To remedy this bias I will propose and discuss just three *broad* "competencies," though they are actually broader than competencies—they are really roles and attitudes. I have previously proposed these as necessary for organization development professionals,[1] but, as I think about it, they are even more relevant to leaders.

An effective leader should

- Think like an *anthropologist*
- Have the skills of a *family therapist*
- Cultivate and trust *artistic* instincts

Think Like an Anthropologist

Leaders who think like anthropologists would realize several very important things. First, they would realize that they are leaders by virtue of their basic fit into the cultural milieu in which they grew up and in which they are now operating. It is all well and good to note that leaders "create" and "change" cultures, as I have argued in the past,[2] but first they must realize that to change culture you must thoroughly understand the culture that created you and legitimized you. For example, how many leaders who are convinced that they have to be assertive, visionary, and emotionally competent are aware that those very traits are mostly central to the U.S. culture and that they might not be acceptable in leaders in many Asian or Latin cultures? In other words, leaders must be culturally self-conscious and be aware of the cultural layers in their own personalities.

Second, leaders who think like anthropologists would be conscious of the cultural variations among countries and companies, and among occupational subgroups within their companies. This consciousness would inform their thinking about three major problems that are facing most organizations:

1. To what degree is there alignment between the technological state of the environment and the organizational stage of maturity and its culture?[3] Especially important is the recognition that what is needed in a young company in a new technology differs greatly from what an older company in a mature market needs.

2. To what extent is the culture of the organization adapted to the stage of technology and the level of organizational maturity? An organization with a young culture of innovation that now exists in a mature market in which a dominant technology has been accepted will fail, as Digital Equipment did in the mid-1990s.[4]

3. To what extent are the subcultures within the organization aligned with the strategic requirements of the organization based on points 1 and 2? One of the most common problems within organizations is the failure to recognize that "silos" are not just organizational units, but subcultures that have just as much difficulty communicating with each other as do the French and Germans.[5]

Third, leaders with an anthropological attitude would be culturally humble. They would realize that cultures can be well or poorly adapted to the internal and external requirements that the organization faces, but that there is no such thing as a better culture in absolute terms. This is probably the hardest thing for leaders to accept, in part because the role requires self-assurance more than humility. But the self-assurance can derive from insight into cultural dynamics and the ability to manage cultural processes.

Fourth, if they thought like anthropologists, leaders would stop making nonsensical statements like "I am going to institute a culture of service," or "We are going to become a more team-oriented culture." They would realize that cultures cannot be instituted or imposed or created. Leaders can impose (coerce) new *behaviors* based on new *values*, but these become shared assumptions, that is, *new cultural components*, only if they actually work better in helping the organization achieve its goals and make life for the employees more manageable. "Imposed cultures" only last as long as the coercive tactics of the leaders.

Thinking like an anthropologist does not require training in the methodology of the field. Leaders do not have to be ethnographers who gain a deep understanding of a culture by hanging around, developing informants, and keeping field notes. But leaders have to have a personal sense that they are the creation of the cultures of their countries, families, occupations, and reference groups, and that culture plays a huge role in the capacity of their organizations to perform. Hence, "managing culture" becomes a part of their job, and that, in turn, requires insight into how cultures form and evolve.

Have the Skills of a Family Therapist

What family therapists possess that is essential to leaders is the ability to see systems and to intervene in them. The ability to see systems will derive partly from their thinking like anthropologists, in that cultures are complex systems. What leaders can learn from family therapists is how to create processes that *change* systems in the direction of their strategic goals.

Essential to that learning is that human systems are *role networks*, and one must learn to influence roles more than persons. The psychological bias in leadership literature has put far too much emphasis on interpersonal influence and failed to note that systems can change if roles change without any great personal change. Or to put it another way, role change produces self-induced change in the role occupant, often making it unnecessary for the leader to exert direct interpersonal influence; that is, being "persuasive" may not be as necessary as most theories claim.

Second, leaders must adopt a model of systems health that goes beyond just the economic health of their organization. They must think in terms of fixes that last, have a long-range time perspective, and understand "double-loop" learning, or Bateson's "Deutero-Learning," a concept that grew out of systems-oriented psychiatry.[6]

Third, leaders must understand the dynamics of anxiety and accept the reality of defensive mechanisms in individuals and groups. Any leader who says that resistance to change is "just human nature" displays great naiveté. As any family therapist knows, systems create roles that serve as defenses against crippling anxiety, and that certain kinds of role changes are therefore impossible unless other parts of the role system change. Many "bureaucratic" procedures in organizations are defenses against anxiety, hence serving a positive function.

What the family (systems) therapist learns to do is to discover what parts of the system are least paralyzed by anxiety or are ready to change. This often means working with a part of the system that is not intuitively obvious. The family therapist might work with a teenager who can change, though the illness is in the relationship between the parents. If the teenager learns to reward constructive behavior between his parents, they might change though the therapist has not worked with them directly.

The organizational counterpart would be to use changes in the accounting system to cure a paralyzing communication problem between engineering and manufacturing rather than to deal with them directly. For example, when GE acquired an Italian subsidiary, it was the imposition of the accounting system and the Six Sigma quality program that enabled the deeper cultural differences between the U.S. parent and Italian acquisition to begin to function together effectively.[7]

Cultivate and Trust Artistic Instincts

To fully understand what I mean by this prescription, we need to take a look at the role of the artist in society.[8] One of the main roles of the artist is to stimulate us conceptually and emotionally. This is accomplished by making visible what ordinarily is felt only intuitively, and making it visible in a particularly dramatic fashion. For example, the misuse of power by leaders is something we intellectually know about. But having just returned from attending a performance of Richard Wagner's *Ring of the Nibelungen*, I have a much deeper understanding of how Wotan, the God, by letting his power need compromise his own laws made it inevitable that the gods must die at the end, and that the only feeling that can truly redeem the world is love. What the artist is able to do is to take common and universal human problems and represent them as archetypes and, by that representation, make them more visible.

I am suggesting that leaders must at times do the same thing—they must have visions of what is happening and what should happen, and they must have the communication skills to get their insights across to others. This "competence" is often represented in the psychological models as being persuasive, being clear, being a good communicator and so on, but that misses the point. My point is that artistic intuition must precede all that—the leader must see more deeply and grasp intuitively what may not be obvious or provable.

My colleague Otto Scharmer has captured this very well with his concept of "presencing."[9] In terms of the artistic model, the big question is what is going on within the painter when he or she is standing in front of the empty canvas, or within the composer when he or she first sits down at the piano. Leaders must be in touch with the as yet hidden impulses and insights that will determine what they put on the empty canvas. And to be in touch with that part of their selves, they must learn to trust their intuition, to be prepared to make mistakes and learn from them, just as the artist does not produce a masterpiece every time.

To be a good artist requires more than a desire to create. There are technical skills involved in writing, composing, acting, dancing, and painting. The interesting question then arises, if we think of leadership as being partly an artistic endeavor, what are the technical skills needed to "perform"? I would propose that the most difficult of these skills for leaders is to become reflective and open to learning. This is especially difficult in cultures like that of the United States, where impulsive decisiveness is positively valued.

In many organizations the norm exists that when a project is finished the manager should move as quickly as possible to the next project so that if anything goes wrong later it cannot be associated with that manager. The U.S. Army's "After Action Reviews" are quite unique in forcing management and employees, once a project is finished, to review the whole event and examine it from the point of view of what can be learned about doing it better the next time.[10] Leaders need not only to do their own personal after-action reviews but also to learn how to get their organizations to become reflective and more oriented toward learning from experience.

Finally, it is my impression that artists expose themselves to many kinds of experiences and stimuli. Wagner had read extensively about Norse and Icelandic myths, Greek myths, and German philosophy before writing the poems that became the librettos of *The Ring*. He had been a revolutionary and had seen first-hand how different leaders did or did not handle their roles. He had a very different vision of how society worked as a young man when he started *The Ring* than when he finished it in his mature years.

I think leaders should read more, travel more, attend more theater and music, go to more museums, and generally get out into the world and away from the narrow confines of their organizations. I have been told that some CEOs literally read only in-house reports which, of course, are always going to be biased by that organization's culture and the need of subordinates to tell leaders only stuff that will please them. To have valid artistic intuition requires a degree of openness to what is going on around one.

Conclusion

It would be possible to take the points above and make a checklist out of them. I suspect that there are people in the leadership field who will point out that all of these "competencies" are already on many peoples' lists. But that would miss the point that these competencies only make sense in the broader context of a given culture.

The danger would be that once they are treated as a list, we would tend to think of specific training activities to improve leader competence in each item. That would again miss the point that it is the understanding of the context that creates in the leader the insight into what he or she needs which starts the learning process from within. This is important because imposed teaching does not work as well as self-generated learning.

My argument is that leaders must think of themselves as anthropologists, systems therapists, and artists and to realize that the role requires certain competencies based on their insight into those roles. And this insight leads to a final and critical point—being a leader *is itself a role*. Every person in every kind of formal job or informal situation can take on the role. It is a matter of choice. A CEO can choose to be a leader, in which case the roles of anthropologist, family therapist, and artist apply. But a CEO can also choose not to be a leader, in which case those roles are irrelevant. Similarly, any employee in any organization can choose to be a leader by taking on the roles. By being more of an anthropologist, systems therapist, and artist, that employee will discover how to manage and influence culture, even if he or she does not have a formal leadership position.

So dear reader, you have two choices to make. First, do you or do you not want the leader role? If you don't, then you may not need the insights described in this chapter. Second, if you do choose to be a leader, get to work on developing the attitudes and skills that go with being more anthropological, more systemic, and more artistic.

Endnotes

1. Edgar H. Schein, *DEC Is Dead, Long Live DEC: The Lasting Legacy of Digital Equipment Corporation* (San Francisco: Berrett-Koehler, 2003).

2. Edgar H. Schein, *Organizational Culture and Leadership* (San Francisco: Jossey-Bass, 1985); and Edgar H. Schein, *Organizational Culture and Leadership* (3rd ed.) (New York: Wiley, 2004).

3. Schein, *DEC Is Dead, Long Live DEC*.

4. Edgar H. Schein, "Five Traps for Consulting Psychologists," *Consulting Psychology Journal: Research and Practice*, 2003, 55(2), 75–83.

5. Edgar H. Schein, "Three Cultures of Management: Implications for Organizational Learning, *Sloan Management Review*, 1996, 38(1), 9–20.

6. G. Bateson, *Towards an Ecology of the Mind* (St. Albans, UK: Paladin, 1973).

7. C. Busco, A. Riccaboni, and R. W. Scapens, "Management Accounting Systems and Organizational Culture," paper presented to the European Accounting Association, Munich, Germany, 2001; and C. Busco, A. Riccaboni, and R. W. Scapens, "When Culture Matters: Processes of Organizational Learning and Transformation," *Reflections*, 2002, 4(1), 43–54.

8. Edgar H. Schein, "The Role of Art and the Artist," *Reflections*, 2001, 2(4), 81–83.

9. C. O. Scharmer, "Self-Transcending Knowledge: Sensing and Organizing Around Emerging Opportunities," *Journal of Knowledge Management*, 2001, 5(2), 137–150; and P. Senge, C. O. Scharmer, J. Jaworski, and B. S. Flowers, *Presence: Human Purpose and the Field of the Future* (Cambridge, MA: The Society for Organizational Learning, 2004).

10. M. J. Darling and C. S. Parry, "After-Action Reviews: Linking Reflection and Planning," *Reflections*, 2001, 3(2), 64–72.

24

The Three Elements of Good Leadership in Rapidly Changing Times

Lynn Barendsen and Howard Gardner

Lynn Barendsen is a project manager at the GoodWork Project, where she focuses on the work of young professionals as well as that of social and business entrepreneurs. She has most recently written a chapter in Taking Philanthropy Seriously *(Indiana University Press) and, with Wendy Fischman, she codeveloped the GoodWork Toolkit, designed to help develop a common language that school communities and other institutions can use to define their work and identify their goals.*

Howard Gardner is the Hobbs Professor of Cognition and Education at the Harvard Graduate School of Education. He is a leading thinker on education and human development and has studied and written extensively about intelligence, creativity, and leadership. Over the past decade, in collaboration with Mihaly Csikszentmihalyi and William Damon, Gardner has conducted an empirical study of "Good Work" across the professional landscape: such work is at once excellent, ethical, and engaging. Gardner's most recent books include Leading Minds: An Anatomy of Leadership; Good Work: When Excellence and Ethics Meet, *and* Changing Minds: The Art and Science of Changing Our Own and Other People's Minds.

For support of the GoodWork Project we would like to thank The Christian Johnson Endeavor Foundation, The Hewlett Foundation, The Atlantic Philanthropies, Louise and Claude Rosenberg, and Jeffrey Epstein. We thank Rush Kidder for his contributions to our thinking.

What does it mean to be a "good" leader? What are the traits of good leaders across time, and how do these leaders adjust to rapidly changing times? Over the past decade, we and our fellow researchers on the GoodWork Project have interviewed over twelve hundred individuals in a variety of professions, at different levels in their careers.[1] Our research suggests that the best leaders are individuals who, in their work, exhibit three distinct meanings of good: (1) an Excellent technical and professional quality and competence, (2) an Ethical orientation, and (3) a completely Engaged sense of fulfillment and meaningfulness. We think of these as three "E's," intertwined in the DNA of our best leaders.

John Gardner: Living the Three E's

One example of such a leader is the late John Gardner, an expert on the subject of leadership. Gardner served six different U.S. presidents, he was Secretary of Health, Education and Welfare, founder of Common Cause, founder of the National Urban Coalition, and president of the Carnegie Corporation. He authored numerous books during his lifetime, including *Excellence*, *Self-Renewal*, and *On Leadership*.

As part of our study, we interviewed John Gardner in 1999 and again in 2000. Gardner sought excellence in every domain—he memorably observed that excellence in plumbing was as important as excellence in philosophy. But excellence was not a single level, to be reached and maintained; rather, in his view, excellence must be continually renewed. According to Gardner, reaching a high level of success or meeting high personal standards can actually harbor risks:

> I had already written the book on excellence or I was toward having written it, and becoming aware of this other dimension of vitality and stagnation, and I went to an institution, which again I won't name, but it was

of unquestioned quality, and yet some things in it were just foreboding of stagnation. I mean that if they *didn't* mend it, they were going to be dead in the water. And I thought, gee, excellence isn't enough. And a curious thing about some of these great, highly developed fields is that they can be on the edge of stagnation and still so good that you can't help admire them. But they're weaving their shroud. They are not building for the future.[2]

In his own career, Gardner certainly did not stagnate. He continually evolved, from professor to foundation president to high-level official to social reformer, actively pursuing change as soon as he started to feel too comfortable in any one setting. Gardner constantly pushed himself to move beyond his current level of excellence. In our study, we have confirmed that sustaining excellent and ethical work is difficult, once meaningful engagement begins to fray. As he told us,

> I began to think about renewal while I was at Carnegie, and I wrote the book while I was at Carnegie, and it was really the principle of renewal plus the confidence I had that led me to take the government job. For a good year before I was offered the job, I had real feelings that my situation was too comfortable. I knew all the answers to being a foundation president in New York City. I was able to open practically any door and deal with my problems, and that's not a good sign. I mean, you know that life isn't like that, so if you begin to feel that way, something's closing in on you.

To paraphrase Gardner, once success has been achieved, work may cease to be engaging.

As we construe it, ethical work is socially responsible work, work that takes its consequences into account and adjusts accordingly.

Asked about leadership, Gardner responded in ethical terms. In his view, leadership goes hand-in-hand with thinking beyond oneself:

> I began to think about, How do you develop leaders? And it clearly traces back to childhood and early development of a sense of responsibility for the other. And you can't lead if you don't give a damn about the other. Leaders are people who are thinking; even if they are not thinking in kindly or beneficial ways, they are thinking about other people. They are relating themselves to the group. When I began to work on community building, same thing. You go back to people's early involvement with the group and their relation to it. And a lot of the breakdowns in individual performance that lead to delinquency and so forth and so on are people who never learned, never developed any bond with the group. No feedback from the group to govern the individual's behavior because they discounted that.

In Gardner's view, ethical work, without excellence, is equally ineffective. For example, he describes "bad" nonprofits, mismanaged organizations that stumble along, trying to do good and yet lacking innovation and expertise. These nonprofits are "bad,"

> in the sense of pious continuance of not competent or creative work, which in a way is damaging. Damaging because it uses up well-meaning dollars, because it breeds discouragement in people who just feel "We're working so hard and we're just not getting anywhere." And I think there's a fair amount of that in the nonprofit world. And there's something about lofty ideals that are at odds with clean-cut self-evaluation. You know, "How can you criticize us when our ideals are so great?" That's why I

like that cartoon of Peanuts on the pitcher's mound saying, "How can we lose when we're so sincere?"

John Gardner helps us to contextualize the three "E's" of good
leadership. Leadership without excellence, even well-intentioned
leadership, results in mediocrity. Leadership without ethics is
encountered in every sphere, from politics to business to the nonprofit world. Leadership without engagement simply cannot be sustained, and eventually results in burnout or in compromised work.

Current Conditions That Complexify the Task of Leadership

Strong counterforces threaten excellence, ethics, and engagement
in organizations. Indeed, in an era of rapid change, even the identification of that which is good can be difficult. These powerful
forces either must be controlled or they will control us. In the following text, we comment on three conditions that challenge efforts
to achieve good work: the forces of globalization, the struggle to
raise funds in a market-saturated milieu, and the scarcity of positive
examples of leadership.

Globalization

Over the past few decades, we have come to recognize forces that
constitute globalization. In this era, all manner of entities—cur-
rencies, customs, commodities, and communicable diseases, to name
a few—circulate around the world with enormous speed, and without regard to boundaries and borders of any sort. Events that occur
in areas as remote as North Korea, Afghanistan, or the Silicon Val-
ley exert almost immediate effects on populations thousands of
miles away. Because many of these factors are difficult to understand,
let alone to control, it is easy to lose one's ethical bearings—and
thus sacrifice the chance to do good work.

Jill Ker Conway, teacher, author, and feminist historian, served as president of Smith College for ten years. For his book *Shared Values for a Troubled World*, our colleague Rushworth Kidder interviewed Conway. During the interview at her home in a Boston suburb, Conway described one of the problems associated with globalization:

> I just came back from a board meeting of a major international service company. . . . Everybody knows the world is one world: they trade twenty-four hours a day in many different currencies, and you would not have to persuade anybody there that we live in a single global environment. But when I go out to dinner in a suburb like this, it is not apparent to people at all.[3]

Although globalization is an indisputable fact, the multifaceted ways in which it affects every one of us are not always obvious. And, therefore, motivating individuals to acknowledge and act while keeping global conditions in mind is challenging. Conway describes a world so "complicated that it is impossible to imagine any oversight [that is, careful supervision—editor's note] by professionals."[4] When asked about a solution to these issues, Conway points directly to ethical leadership: "Young ones learn their ethics from the adult generation. So we have to model a greater ethical concern."[5]

William Drayton is the founder of Ashoka, one of the very first organizations designed to fund social entrepreneurs (individuals who approach social problems with entrepreneurial spirit and business sense). Ashoka seeks out leaders who will tackle social issues of global consequence. Most of the Ashoka Fellows come from and serve the third world, including many countries that fail to thrive in the global economy. To be selected as an Ashoka Fellow, applicants go through an intensive screening process. Drayton emphasizes the ethical component to this evaluation:

> One of our four criteria is ethical fiber for selecting fellows, and ditto for staff. It's not accidental, it's very care-

fully thought through, as we think that values are absolutely critical. They're critical for efficacy. You can't get people to change the primary patterns in what they do in their lives, which involves all sorts of subtle power changes, unless they trust you. You can't lead people if they don't trust you. And I don't believe that you can fake it. . . . We can't build a fellowship, which absolutely requires openness and trust and mutual respect, if even a tiny number of people were not trustworthy. . . . we just don't want to add to [the] supply of untrustworthy public figures.

According to Drayton, finding and funding these new leaders will accelerate the process of positive social change:

We want people who have society's interests at heart. That's why we are here. We're not a social welfare program for bright people. . . . We're trying . . . to speed up the rate of change and democratization in the world. And these folks just happen to be the single most critical component to that change.

Drayton is one of many leaders determined to use globalization to positive effect. Ashoka seeks out social entrepreneurs who have developed solutions that may be replicated worldwide. Here, "ethical fiber" is described as one element that is used not so much to *combat* globalization but rather to turn the fact of our smaller, faster world into positive results.

One solution, then, to the challenge globalization poses to leadership is to embrace it—to see it as a strength, rather than as an obstacle. Muhammad Yunus, professor of economics in Bangladesh and social entrepreneur par excellence, started the Grameen Bank—an institution that pioneered microcredit lending (providing very small loans to individuals with little or no credit history).

Like other successful leaders, Yunus often sees possibility where others see complication. His perspective envisions the empowerment of underserved populations—with globalization as a great equalizer:

> Borders will be relics of the past. . . . The closeness will come. . . . What you've got in Washington, I'll have in a tiny township with a population of 403—because I've got access to information. So you're not so big any more. You can't come and tell me, "You don't know what's going on in tiny countries; you have to be in Washington to find out." I say, "You're crazy: I know everything!"[6]

Market Pressures

Obtaining sufficient funding is a perpetual problem, especially for those leaders whose vocation is explicitly the pursuit of good work. Many such individuals work for nonprofit institutions, such as hospitals or universities, or for the over one million nongovernmental organizations that have sprung up in the past half century. The issue of survival is exacerbated today because nonprofit organizations are expected to follow business models—to have business plans, to produce "deliverables," and to be accountable in terms of numbers of pregnancies prevented, new audience members secured, or engineers graduated, for example. Forget for a moment that such quantitative measures may be inappropriate, given the mission and mode of operation of the particular nonprofit organizations. Monetary pressures cross professional boundaries—everyone has a bottom line to which he or she is held accountable.

Derek Bok, the president of Harvard University from 1971 to 1991 and an interim president as of July 1, 2006, has written extensively on this topic in *Universities in the Marketplace*. The influences acting upon the university, making it an increasingly commercial venture, are numerous:

> [C]ommercialization turns out to have multiple causes. Financial cutbacks undoubtedly acted as a spur to profit-

seeking for some universities and some departments. The spirit of private enterprise and entrepreneurship that became so prominent in the 1980s helped encourage and legitimate such initiatives. A lack of clarity about academic values opened the door even wider. Keener competition gave still further impetus. But none of these stimuli would have borne such abundant fruit had it not been for the rapid growth of money-making opportunities provided by a more technologically sophisticated, knowledge-based economy.[7]

As president of a well-regarded university, Bok set very high standards for the leaders of our institutions of higher learning—standards of ethics and excellence. This example is particularly important because tomorrow's leaders are being molded within these institutions. Here they will witness and learn a great deal about leadership—of varying qualities.

New leaders—and in particular, innovative leaders, those who are busy trying to establish new models for change—need a specific type of support. Drayton describes the issue as follows:

> Entrepreneurs need loyalty. They need partners who will understand that they . . . are the golden goose. You don't need this if you're putting in the fifteenth department store or another school. . . . But you do when you're fundamentally changing the pattern, because that entrepreneurial mind-set is constantly going after every little change. And it's changing the idea. They're evolving it. If you don't invest in the entrepreneur, forget it. It's going to fail. Most foundations and governments have very little sense of who the entrepreneur is or why they've got to invest for ten years in the entrepreneur and help him or her through this long cycle. The time frame is also completely wrong. And the entrepreneur needs a large sum of money, not little dribs and drabs. . . . There is a

complete misfit between what the entrepreneur needs
and what these institutions provide.

When new leaders are forced to spend an inordinate amount of
time seeking funding, their work suffers. Time spent fundraising
necessitates time away from work, and quality of work may suffer as
a result. Sometimes, funding pressures can result in less-than-honest
practices—what we term "compromised work." Some individuals
may spin the truth to make projects more attractive to potential
funders, while others may take more drastic measures. In our study
of young professionals, in particular, we often heard the justification
of improper (if not frankly illegal) means in service of noble ends
or long-term goals. (The theory: once power and position have been
achieved, one will miraculously be transferred into a paragon of
virtue.[8]) Market forces, such as funding pressures, constitute a
perennial challenge to today's leaders.

One solution, especially apt for entrepreneurial leaders, is to provide long-term funding. In the past few years, this support has
become possible due to the emergence of venture philanthropy.
Often entrepreneurs themselves, venture philanthropists understand
the mind-set and the needs of these creative leaders and are therefore more inclined and more able to give them the long-term support they require. As one venture philanthropist describes it, the
funding process really becomes a collaborative relationship:

> [E]ngaged philanthropy relies on collaboration and real
> shared decision making. . . . It depends a lot on trust, and
> trust takes time, so we make long-term investments that
> allow for the engagement to grow organically over the
> time that we're working with a particular group. I don't
> think you can do engaged philanthropy well if you just
> make a one-time grant.

Such general, long-term support can indeed free entrepreneurial leaders to carry out good work. But this happy ending can only

come about if the venture philanthropist respects the operation of the nonprofit and does not attempt to micromanage the organization or distort its mission. It is great for venture philanthropists to become engaged, but it is risky if this engagement threatens the excellence or the ethics of the funded organization.

Scarcity of Positive Examples

Leadership also can be threatened by a dearth of positive models. In a very basic sense, young people learn by example. When the individuals who are garnering public attention are successful by dint of dishonest means, or in the news because their corrupt actions have been pardoned, many young people are likely to follow suit. And when the flaws of even the most impressive leaders are sensationalized in the media, future leaders may come to believe that good work—excellent, ethical, engaging work—is impossible.

As a long-time leader in the field of education, Bok has garnered much admiration for his attention to ethical issues and the very impressive standards embodied by him and his wife, the philosopher Sissela Bok. In his interview with Rushworth Kidder, Bok makes an explicit connection between ethics and leadership. Referring to major social concerns (poverty, crime, welfare, public education), Bok argues that solutions to these issues must go beyond changes in policy and beyond acquisition of knowledge. Change must begin with the ethical qualities of our leaders, many of whom frequent our university settings:

> [E]fforts to respond to the kinds of public problems that I'm talking about cannot be sought only in developing the knowledge for policy solutions. . . . [also needed is] a strengthening of individual virtues, ethical virtues, civic virtues on the part of individuals—especially the kinds of influential individuals who flow through our colleges and universities.[9]

Clearly, if they are to catalyze good work, leaders need ethics as well as knowledge, information, and IQ points.

In a publication dedicated to leadership, it is important to acknowledge that leaders and leadership are rarely properly located in a single, authoritative individual. As John Gardner puts it, "I think of leaders as running down through all levels and segments of the system."[10] He cites problems with leadership in the United States, in part, because of a breakdown in this system of leadership: "We need a much healthier substratum of leaders down the line before we can get great leadership at the top."[11] Such a substratum is most unlikely to arise in the absence of role models that are convincing and worthy of emulation.

It is possible that practical interventions in our schools may encourage the development of ethical, excellent, and engaged leaders. We have developed one such intervention, the GoodWork Toolkit. This instrument provides a framework for individuals to consider the kind of workers they are now and the kinds of professionals they want to become. Designed originally for high school students, it has been piloted in middle schools, high schools, and university settings, and also used as a professional development tool. The Toolkit encourages excellent and meaningful work while at the same time evoking reflections about the consequences of one's work on others.

It is important to stress that exemplary leaders do exist. Because of the pathographical bias of current media, that is, their tendency to accentuate the flaws of leaders, exemplary leaders are simply not garnering the attention they deserve. (Magazines devoted to the presentation of good work do not survive, while many of those that focus on the foibles of the great and the not-so-great sell in the millions). John Gardner spoke to this issue:

> [Y]ou've probably heard me talk about the number of Jeffersons and Washingtons and the like around today. Six world-class leaders when we had a population of three million. We now have eighty times that many, we ought to have eighty times six—four hundred and eighty

Jeffersons, Madisons, Franklins, Washingtons. And I'm convinced they're out there. I don't throw up my hands and say, "Where are they?" They're out there, not fully aware of their capacity to lead because it isn't a big crisis. Not conscious of what they have to give the world.

If Gardner is correct in his belief, another solution would be to find and inspire these potential leaders. Preferably, this process of identification and nurturance will occur before the eruption of a major crisis.

Up to this point we have cited leaders who are personally known to us, but numerous other exemplary models could be mentioned. To cite a particularly vivid example, Anita Roddick, founder of the Body Shop chain of stores, continually examines her work and her values, and does so *keeping in mind that she is an example* to young people:

> I . . . travel with the vagabond for two or three weeks, just going through the black belt of America. Living in shacks. Seeing crack . . . being made, living outside, in prison communities. It is incredibly important that I continue to do that, whether it's [the] Appalachian trip or whether it's the Albanian trip. It's so important because that's a role of leadership. A leader in my eyes is not someone who sits on top of an ivory tower, lots of dosh, lots of money, and proclaims it. It is moral leadership. It's doing things that the young girls or young people that work with me can say, "God, she did that. Now what does that make me?" And how do I—my job is, how do you keep them away from a value system of endless increasing wealth to one where humanity, community, is part of the value system?

Roddick holds her business accountable to high standards of both excellence and ethics. At the time of our interview (in 1999), she struck us as fully engaged with her network of enterprises. Asked how she balances work with family, she replied, "I don't. One bloody big creative stew. Because what is work to me isn't work." Roddick has achieved a fair amount of attention in the media. But our study on Good Work confirms that there are many other exemplary leaders—or potential exemplary leaders—who are either unnoticed or are unaware of their abilities to lead.

Conclusion

Threats to effective leadership today are very real, as real as the power of markets, the dystopic flavor of the press, and the rapid and unpredictable emergence of new technologies. Prescient leaders have already discerned methods to transform these threats into opportunities.

Frustrated by the lack of funding for the socially minded leaders of the future, William Drayton founded an organization designed to alleviate the problem. He has become a leader among social entrepreneurs, a group that by definition acts with innovation and on behalf of others, and a group that is almost universally engaged in meaningful work. As a result of her business success, Anita Roddick found herself in a position of power. She used her position self-consciously, to model the behavior of a good leader, trying to combat less positive examples. It is as important to know of these exemplary leaders as it is to know about the sins and peccadilloes of whoever the poster boy or girl for corporate bad behavior is at the moment. The individuals portrayed here illustrate that good leaders are able to turn potential threats into strategies that can help others—leaders or followers—to execute good work.

Endnotes

1. Howard Gardner, Mihaly Csikszentmihalyi, and William Damon, *Good Work: When Excellence and Ethics Meet* (New York: Basic Books, 2001).

2. Unless otherwise indicated, all quotations come from interviews granted to the GoodWork Project.

3. Rushworth M. Kidder, *Shared Values for a Troubled World: Conversations with Men and Women of Conscience* (San Francisco: Jossey-Bass, 1994), 135.

4. Kidder, *Shared Values for a Troubled World*, 136.

5. Kidder, *Shared Values for a Troubled World*, 137.

6. Kidder, *Shared Values for a Troubled World*, 151.

7. Derek Bok, *Universities in the Marketplace: The Commercialization of Higher Education* (Princeton, NJ: Princeton University Press, 2003), 15.

8. See Wendy Fischman, Becca Solomon, Deborah Greenspan, and Howard Gardner, *Making Good: How Young People Cope with Moral Dilemmas at Work* (Cambridge: Harvard University Press, 2004).

9. Kidder, *Shared Values for a Troubled World*, 100.

10. Kidder, *Shared Values for a Troubled World*, 199.

11. Kidder, *Shared Values for a Troubled World*, 199.

25

Distinctive Characteristics of Successful Leaders of Voluntary Organizations

Past, Present, and Future

Brian O'Connell

Brian O'Connell is founding president of INDEPENDENT SECTOR, *the national umbrella organization for philanthropy and voluntary action, and professor of public service at the University College of Citizenship and Public Service at Tufts University. He served as president of the National Council of Philanthropy and executive director of the Coalition of National Voluntary Organizations. For twelve years he was national director of the Mental Health Association. He was also with the American Heart Association and finished as director of its California affiliate. O'Connell served as chairman of the organizing committee for CIVICUS: World Alliance for Citizen Participation, and as its first chairman. Among his current assignments are the boards of The Bridgespan Group and the Cape Cod Foundation.*

Much has been made in recent years about the lessons that leaders in the independent sector can (and some say, should) learn from their counterparts in the for-profit sector. And while it is certainly true that leaders of voluntary organizations can learn a great deal about leadership from successful business executives, success in voluntary organizations depends also on some leadership characteristics that are unique—or at least different—from those most commonly encountered in business. Consider these examples.

Peter Drucker was once asked by a business reporter, "What's the most effective organization with which you've ever worked?" The inquirer assumed that Drucker's response would be a business corporation such as General Electric, Xerox, or Hewlett-Packard. Drucker thought a moment and replied, "the Girl Scouts," whereupon the reporter laughed and said he hoped Drucker would give a serious answer. Drucker responded that he was absolutely serious in believing that the Girl Scouts are the most effective group with which he has worked. He elaborated that if you took that many dedicated volunteers, with a professional staff oriented and trained to increase the impact of the volunteers, and you pointed all of that energy, commitment, and talent toward an important social purpose such as the development of women and girls, the ingredients for effectiveness and excellence were clearly in place.

On another occasion Drucker was asked where one is most likely to locate the best leaders. Again, there was an expectation he would point to business or maybe to the military, but again he surprised. He said that in just about every American city, the very best leaders were most likely to be found heading the major religious congregations. He explained that such ministers, priests, and rabbis demonstrate a staggering array of talents, including recruiting, retaining, inspiring, unifying, counseling, communicating, fundraising, and networking—all on top of instilling and building faith. Those who can do all of that and more, Drucker said, are extraordinary leaders but are somehow almost always overlooked when we think and write about leadership.

A special edition of *Across the Board*, a publication of the Conference Board, profiled a number of successful business leaders who had transferred to the social sector. There were two key reactions these leaders had to changing sectors, one before their change of work and the other afterward. Just about everyone acknowledged that in advance of their switch they thought the new roles would be a piece of cake, contrasted with the demands of running large business enterprises. However, before long all of them had retreated to the corporate ranks, bewildered and bedeviled by the independence of the professionals working in the social sector such as faculty, musicians, curators, medical boards, women's auxiliaries, and so on.

Again, I want to repeat that a great many qualities of the best leaders are the same in all types of human enterprises. Those qualities are reflected in many of the other chapters of this volume and are the basis of the best book I've read on the subject, John W. Gardner's *On Leadership*. In this chapter I emphasize the far less understood characteristics of the best social or independent sector leaders.

In a *Harvard Business Review* (HBR) article titled "Better Performance of Nonprofits," Cecily Cannan Selby, former national director of the Girl Scouts, examined the similarities and differences between profit and nonprofit organizations. Her findings help to remove the "excuses proffered by nonprofit organizations when they are not performing in a 'businesslike' way," but she also helps us "to understand the areas where comparisons are not practical or fair." In the article, Selby names three "key differences" between nonprofit and profit organizations: "(1) 'the bottom line'; (2) the confusion in direct-line accountability [for example, she asks, 'In a board appointed program committee on which volunteers serve, is it the committee or the staff that is accountable for the function, and can staff members be held accountable for what volunteers fail to do?']; and (3) the mixed allegiance of many professionals in voluntary organizations who do not see themselves as part of the organization's hierarchy, at least in terms of accountability." (For example, "the university professor and other intellectuals and artists who have their own sense of creative integrity—an accountability that can override all others.") She concludes by calling for nonprofit organizations "to be more effective but not always with the business model in mind."

In another HBR issue headed "Management Control in Nonprofit Organizations," Robert A. Anthony and Regina Herzlinger highlighted the quintessential difference of that "bottom line": "In a profit-oriented organization the amount of profit provides an overall measure of both effectiveness and efficiency. In many nonprofit organizations, however, outputs cannot be measured to quantitative terms. . . . The absence of a satisfactory, single, overall measure of performance that is comparable to the profit measure is the most serious management control problem in a nonprofit organization."

There is also confusion of roles between the chief volunteer officer and the chief staff officer in a great many of our social sector organizations. Some chairpersons come from business backgrounds and tend to leave too much to the staff, weakening the chair and the board. The next time around, the new chairperson might come from an organization that does not have a staff and therefore the volunteer leader tries to do it all, inadvertently taking over the role of executive director. The problem is compounded today by the use of the term *chief executive officer* to describe either of the two positions, usually the staff director, but this title and the corporate model it represents rarely fit a vibrant voluntary organization.

I personally don't use the title "chief executive officer." It just doesn't describe the unique roles and relationships of the chief volunteer officer and the chief staff officer in a voluntary organization. The former must be active and effective in building the volunteer side of the organization. Committee heads, project chairpersons, and other officers are the chief volunteer officer's subordinates. I'm afraid the title "president and CEO" has become so established that we can't change it, but we can at least add to the chairperson's title "and chief volunteer officer" and make clear that this is the senior position.

Several years ago, a nominating committee I staffed recognized that a particular individual was the most deserving for selection as chairman and chief volunteer officer, but they were not going to select him because he was an absolute tiger in the way he approached responsibilities. The retiring chairperson felt that if the deserving individual could learn to understand the difference between being an aggressive board member and being the chairperson, the situation would change. He therefore agreed to provide orientation and mentoring for the individual if nominated. I never saw such a difference in performance in one human being. Instead of having a strong opinion and plan for everything—and pushing it stridently—the individual became a builder of confidence and of people and turned out to be an absolutely first-rate leader. He acknowledged later that the difference was that he had never really thought about the job description, and once he did, he realized that he would have to behave very differently to succeed at it.

A different, but equally serious challenge to future volunteer leadership is the drift toward the "principle of least number" and away from the long-term concept of "maximum feasible involvement." Increasingly, management consultants are convincing nonprofits to follow the business model of devoting the fewest possible number of people necessary to a project, board, or committee, including the fewest possible number of meetings. This approach is pursued in the name of efficiency, but it leaves out the advantages of maximum feasible involvement so important to shared decision making, followership, and implementation—especially for organizations that need to build and sustain community or continentwide causes. It's been a hallmark of the best of our leadership in the past that such leaders could be counted on to rally, motivate, and coordinate the largest possible force on behalf of their urgent missions. With fewer volunteers at the table or in the loop, the void is filled by staff members who, however able and dedicated, are no substitute for the legions.

Some of the most important learnings of my fifty years in leadership roles in public causes grew out of hiring the wrong people. For a long time, I hired a lot of individuals who looked just right and referenced well, but who just didn't work out. Finally, when I was executive director of the American Heart Association in California, I realized that the people most likely to succeed in leadership roles in voluntary organizations fit a profile that is different than in business. Working closely with volunteer and staff leaders whom I considered to be people builders helped me develop the following profile of successful staff leaders:

They're committed to public service. This is more than a generalization. People who succeed will face many rocky times. They'll be underpaid for their ability, and they'll put up with a great deal of conflict. For these reasons and many more, they must have a dedication to public service that will get them over these obstacles and through the rough times.

They like people and get along well with them. Liking people is often used as the only criterion for selection and therefore can be exaggerated. In carrying responsible positions in voluntary agencies, however, most staff people deal with a wide variety of individuals and must be able to get along with them.

They have a great deal of patience and tolerance. Staff members work with a wide variety of volunteers who are often at their most excitable pitch. The more vibrant and active an agency or institution, the more this holds true. A staff person must be a stable and patient human being, otherwise the emotional aspects of working together for significant goals will get out of hand.

They are mature. Psychologists define maturity as the ability to forego short-term satisfactions in favor of long-term goals. This applies to organizations as well as individuals, and particularly to successful staff persons. Most goals are long range and require persistent, dogged pursuit through all kinds of difficulties. The satisfactions are rarely found on a weekly or even monthly basis. It's only as the organization looks back from a fuller perspective that the attainments are visible and the satisfactions apparent.

They are willing to work hard. Successful people usually work hard, and this is particularly true in the nonprofit field. There is so very much to be done, the dedication of volunteers is so high, and the number of forces to be dealt with is so great that the only way to achieve success is by working awfully hard.

Selecting the right staff leaders was so important that I developed a fund that allowed us to sweeten the pot if we had a good candidate for an available position but the local chapter's search committee or board felt our candidate was too expensive. We would offer to carry the full salary for the first year, one half the second, and one quarter the third. In almost every case, chapters large and small accepted the offer. It was expensive, but on balance a tiny investment with early payoff and a long-term bonanza.

The problems of contemporary society are more complex, the solutions more involved, and the satisfactions more obscure, but the basic ingredients are still the caring and the resolve to make things better. From the simplicity of these have come today's exciting efforts on behalf of humanitarian causes ranging from equality to environment and from health to peace.

Whether your interest is wildflowers or civil rights, arthritis or clean air, oriental art or literacy, the dying or the unborn, organizations are already at work, and if what's available doesn't suit your passion, it is still a special part of America that you can take the lead and start your own.

In the course of these efforts, there is at work a silent cycle of cause and effect that I call the "genius of fulfillment"; that is, the harder people work to help others and for the fulfillment of important social goals, the more fulfilled they are themselves. Confucius expressed it by saying, "Goodness is God," meaning that the more good we do, the happier we are, and the totality of it all is a supreme state of being. Thus, he said, God is not only a Supreme Being apart from us, but a supreme state of being within us.

A simpler way of looking at the meaning of service is a quotation from an epitaph:

> What I spent is gone
> What I kept is lost
> But what I gave to charity
> Will be mine forever.

How we express the meaning of service doesn't really matter. It can be charity or enlightened self-interest or simply humanity to other people. These are all ways of describing why we serve, why service provides some of our happiest moments, and why the good that we do lives after us.

That's the dream our best leaders engender and nurture.

26

The Leader in Midlife

Richard J. Leider

*A pioneer in the field of career coaching, Richard Leider is an internationally respected author and speaker, and a noted spokesman for the power of purpose. He has written or cowritten five books—*The Inventurers, Life Skills, Repacking Your Bags, The Power of Purpose, *and* Whistle While You Work—*and he has contributed to* Coaching for Leadership *as well as the first* Leader of the Future. Repacking Your Bags *is an international best-seller published in fourteen languages.*

Richard is a Certified Master Career Counselor and a contributing columnist to Fast Company's Website. An avid hiker and backpacker, Richard leads yearly Inventure Expedition walking safaris in Tanzania, East Africa, where he helped found the Dorobo Fund for youth leadership and village conservation.

For most of my working life I have thought, written, and spoken about callings. Calling has been central to my own vocation and is essential to people who become wise leaders. Wise leaders heed their own callings and enable others to do the same. It is a critical characteristic of the new leader of the future to find and lead from his or her callings.

Heeding our callings, of course, doesn't guarantee that we will become great leaders. Another necessary condition is that we possess the *gifts* for leading. There are simply too many people today who occupy leadership positions yet have neither the calling nor the gifts of leadership. They were chosen for a leadership role, but their selection was not embraced in the hearts and minds of those who work for them or with them.

Leadership is a calling. Its purpose is service to others. Leo Tolstoy captured the true nature of it: "The vocation of men and women is to serve others."

What Is Calling Me?

The essential leadership question today is, What is calling me? As we live with this question in mind, we not only uncover the meaning that we seek in our lives, we also affirm our life's work. Whether we ask this question during adolescence, during midlife, or in elderhood, it is *the* big question, and it is *the* question we must continue to ask and answer even in retirement. Because what shapes and directs our lives more than anything else are the questions we ask, fail to ask, or never dream of asking ourselves. It is our questions that create the lives we lead.

After three decades of coaching leaders, I can say with absolute certainty that most of the leaders I have coached discover their callings through ordinary living, not through special things they do for personal growth or spiritual development. Calling speaks not from some religious fringe but from deep within their lives. Heeding their calling is a core thread of living a life, not a process with a life of its own. By following the inner voice that calls them to lead, they discover the path that they recognize, in hindsight, as their calling.

Heeding Our Call

The greatest and wisest leaders are those who discover their calling. People tend to follow those leaders who have a core framework about leading, and who are willing to stand up for their beliefs. Calling is hard to define but easy to see when it is present in the lives of others. Leaders who heed their calling share three common characteristics: *service, passion,* and *fit.*

Service

Wise leaders exhibit a strong sense of servant-leadership. They are authentic servants to their work and through their work to larger and more important purposes than themselves. They like the money they are paid (and some do become wealthy), but they are not in it for the money. They do not work, first, for financial gain. They work, first, to serve.

Passion

Wise leaders are most noticeable for the genuine passion they exhibit in their work. Work, for them, is a genuine source of joy. This joy is supported by practices—daily disciplines that put their passion to work and get results. Midlife is frequently characterized by the awareness of new levels of passion, and the struggle to discover how best to channel it in our work. One of the major questions that arises is what to do with one's life: the issue of calling, of vocation, of "fit."

Fit

Wise leaders exhibit gifts—*passion* and *values*—that align with the needs and requirements of their role. They appear to have found the work they love to do. They seem to do what comes naturally— their hand seems to turn to the work naturally. They also bring out this natural productivity in their followers. They may use the term *fit* in explaining their work or some aspect of it. There appears to be no gap between *what* they do and *who* they are.

Answering Our Call

How does our work fulfill who we are, and what do we do with it? One way of answering our call is to observe others who appear to have found their calling. What characteristics do they have in common, if any? Think of people whom you know, have read about, or have seen publicly whom you consider to be heeding their calling. There appears to be a good fit—no gap between *who* they are and *what* they do. You can hardly imagine a better role fit. Try to identify at least three such people. What are the characteristics that these people have in common? Then, ask yourself these three essential questions:

- Do you observe a sense of *service* in their work?

- Would you use the term *passionate* to describe them or the way they go about their work?

- Do you observe the natural *fit* between their gifts, the connection between their passion and values and their role?

The voice that leads to calling is open to us all. It is not restricted to a limited number of people nor to special leaders, teachers, musicians, artists, priests, ministers, and rabbis. They are merely clear examples of a universal phenomenon. In varying degrees all of us have and need a calling worthy of our commitments.

Wise leaders enable others to heed their callings. They help them uncover their gifts and natural talents. They help people see beyond whom they are today to whom they can become tomorrow. "Always the beautiful answer. Who asks a more beautiful question?" asked the poet, e. e. cummings. Wise leaders know how to ask the more beautiful question to open their colleagues' minds and spirits to their larger potential. The wisest can intuitively sense people's potential and help them tap into it.

Meaning in Midlife

Heeding our calling means giving our gifts, naturally, to make deep contributions to our organizations, communities, families, and the world. *Heeding* comes from listening to and accepting our true self, our natural gifts and private yearnings. Heeding means asking uneasy questions. It means not resting easy with easy answers. Carl Jung pointed out that a person in his or her middle years without a larger purpose was destined to be neurotic. The question, What is calling me? awakens us, eventually, beyond the missing answers of our upbringing and first half of life. We find that old answers make us restless. They bind us to lives of repeated or secondhand experience. We feel like we're dying from the inside out.

It is important to understand that calling is not only a leadership issue, it is a vitality issue. To experience vital aging in midlife and beyond, we need to feel whole from the inside out. The path of vital aging is an inner one as well as an outer one. An inability to integrate our inner life with our outer life can be a source of considerable pain, anxiety, and boredom. Vital aging requires being integrated from the inside out. It means, for example, that our leadership is a true expression in the outer world of who we are in the inner world. When our leadership voice is constricted, we become dis-eased. When the gap is closed between who we are and what we do, blood flows and energy is released. We feel like we are answering our call.

There are millions of vocationally joyless people in the world, who are deaf to the voice that is trying to call them. They think they want easy answers. But in truth, they want the liberation that comes from meaningful work.

The Ultimate Leadership Challenge

There has been a lot of media attention lately on why so many people at midlife are searching for meaning in their work. The searchers are labeled "cultural creatives" or "early adaptors" in societal trends. But I'm convinced that the media are wrong. The search for meaning is not a trend. It is something much deeper. It is in our DNA. And it drives all of us eventually. If it needs a label, it is "servant-leader."

The most meaningful roles in life are ones in which we serve others or create solutions that make life better for others. Leadership has meaning if it serves others. Calling joins self and service. As Aristotle said, "Where our talents and the needs of the world cross, there lies our vocation."

One of the essential questions to ask ourselves in midlife is, When have I been willing to fully commit myself to something beyond my career or my own self-interest? Our true callings are revealed in our willingness to go the extra mile, to serve others in spirit well beyond the work itself; to do what needs to be done, not just what we need to do.

Robert K. Greenleaf coined the term *servant-leader*. In his worldview, the first and foremost choice a leader makes is the choice to serve. In his powerful essay *The Servant as Leader*, Greenleaf takes a stand and sets forth a framework that connects calling to leadership.

The essence of leadership, Greenleaf claims, is the desire to serve one another and to serve something beyond ourselves—a higher purpose. The ultimate leadership challenge is selfleadership—mastery of the inner wisdom and courage to serve others. The potential of power to corrupt would diminish, according to Greenleaf, if leaders chose to serve those they led.

Greenleaf wrote in *The Servant as Leader*, "The best test is: Do those served grow as persons? Do they, while being served, become healthier, wiser, freer, more autonomous, more likely themselves to become servants? And, what is the effect on the least privileged in society: Will they benefit, or at least not be further deprived?"[1]

The Leader in Midlife

The midlife leader today faces an identity search. Behind the midlife leader's role lies a big question: Is leading still my calling?

By asking this question, we remind ourselves that leadership work is both a gift and a mystery. We must continually remember that our lives are not problems to be solved. They are callings to be answered, mysteries to be lived. Whether we feel called to lead by God, by economic necessity, or by circumstance, the key to answering the call is to address the question of *who* before the question of *what*. This requires identifying with the deepest, most core parts of ourselves. The development task of midlife leaders calls for *generativity*—the urge to serve.

Calling is an inner urge—the urge to give our gifts and talents to something that we passionately believe in. Nothing is more important in leadership than directing it toward its true purpose. George Bernard Shaw summed it up:

> This is the true joy in life, the being used for a purpose recognized by yourself as a mighty one; the being thoroughly worn out before you are thrown on the scrap heap; the being a force of Nature instead of a feverish selfish little clod of ailments and grievances complaining that the world will not devote itself to making you happy.

Endnote

1. "What is Servant-Leadership," Greenleaf Center for Servant-Leadership. Available at www.greenleaf.org/leadership/servant-leadership/What-is-Servant-Leadership.html.

27

Leading from the Spirit

Darlyne Bailey

In fall 2006, Darlyne Bailey became the founding dean of the newly transformed College of Education and Human Development at the University of Minnesota. In addition, she is serving as assistant to the president in the oversight of two universitywide consortia, focusing on postsecondary education for children, youth, and families in the Twin Cities. With an M.S. degree in psychiatric social work from Columbia University and a Ph.D. degree in organizational behavior from Case University, she most recently served as vice president for academic affairs and dean of Teachers College at Columbia University. In spring 2003, Bailey was acting president of the College. Bailey's passion for instigating collaborative practice is reflected in her research, teaching, and national and international presentations. In addition to numerous articles and book chapters, Bailey's recent books include Strategic Alliances Among Health and Human Services Organizations *and* Managing Human Resources in the Human Services. *She is currently working with nine women from across the country on her long-held dream to cocreate a book and documentary on the role of spirituality in the lives of women leaders.*

> **Spirit** (spir'it) n. The vital principal or animating force within living beings. The essential nature of a person or group. Latin, *spiritus*, breath.

Leadership is always in the process of becoming—as they perform in the present, leaders by nature are informed by the past as they look ahead to the future. Conscious appreciation of the nexus between past legacy and future dreams emerged in the middle of the twentieth century, when leaders realized that their effectiveness and that of their organizations required a confrontation with three central questions: What needed to change? What needed to be maintained? and How could all of this be sustained?

The typical approach to change almost always led to this series of questions because, however defined, true leadership had become synonymous with a departure from the current state to a "bettering" through the introduction of a new way of thinking, being, and acting. Issues of maintenance therefore were left to managers—those men and women distinct from leaders who focused on the "how" through the efficient use of resources.

Yet fortunately, over the past decade, leadership thinkers and doers have recognized the need for leaders to remember—to discern elements of the past that are critical to the health of the present and the viability of the future. As a result, attention to the latter two questions—the concerns of maintaining and sustaining—has resurfaced in the world of leadership. Today's leaders still operate within a paradigm different from that of their organizational partners in management but now more fully value the nuances of maintaining and sustaining within their organizations, rather than simply making wholesale change.

A product of these times, my own journey has been no different. Over the past decade, my appreciation of the requisite components of effective leadership has broadened to embrace elements of maintenance and sustenance that have long endured, elements that can be readily seen but which have been rarely acknowledged—a cluster of attributes unique to each of us yet, paradoxically, common to all. Sometimes referred to as "values," "beliefs," or "dispositions," these attributes can be taught and learned. Only when internalized, however, are they recognized as the very essence of life itself—the spirit. Having nothing to do with political or even religious doctrine, it is spirit that forms the invisible web that connects us all. And it is through this life-giving force that our organizations of the future will be best led.

What follows is a lesson plan for leading from the spirit, comprising seven core lessons drawn from the essence of spiritual leaders, their lives, and their writings. These lessons offer a framework within which to address all three of the central leadership questions while, concurrently and more important, providing opportunities to directly confront many of the tragedies of today's realities that can be the undoing of tomorrow. By inspiring deeper sensitivity toward all of humanity, the "lessons of the spirit" encourage leaders to understand their organizations as living systems within an interconnected world, rather than as independent mechanical apparatuses, and aid them in collectively creating systems designed to enhance the human condition and co-construct cultures of inclusion. These lessons collectively outline many of the core characteristics, areas of knowledge, skills, and values for our leaders of the future, purposely connecting humanistic intentions with effects.

The First Lesson: The Wisdom of Authenticity. Leading from the spirit begins with self-discovery—taking the time and mental space to be aware, to gain an understanding of who we really are, and assessing our talents and our weaknesses. It has been said that if you know others, you are intelligent, but if you know yourself, you are wise. Central to this wisdom is having the courage to honor the gift of life by being all of who we are, to live with integrity, and to live what we believe—knowing that our lives are the sum reflection of the hundreds of small choices we make every day.

The Second Lesson: The Power of Humility. Derived from the word *humus*, or earth, humility speaks to a way of being in the world that is most stable, centered, and grounded; to know where we stand and what we stand for; to transcend our egos and resist the love of the trappings of authority. Positions of power are just that—positions. True leaders know that who they are is much more than what they do. Being grounded means being secure enough to appreciate that each one of us is unique, yet all of us are required. When we transcend ego, we build character, which takes us beyond the need for approval from others at any cost. Ironically, true humility allows us to have room to take in the ideas and feelings of others and even see criticism as part of our collective search for truth. This strength of character reminds us that negativity from others and even their applause are both fleeting, and best held lightly.

The Third Lesson: The Self-Knowledge of Empathy. The third leadership lesson is articulated by many yet best lived by those who are authentic and humble. It is the self-knowledge that comes from being able to "hold" the perceptions and the emotions of another. Being empathic requires that we stay centered and stay true to ourselves, while opening our hearts and minds to really know each other. As leaders we have learned that our ability to drop our guard and open ourselves up to others is only limited by our desire to do so.

The Fourth Lesson: The Balance of Courage and Compassion. I combine these two attributes into one because they work best together. In concert, courage and compassion call for the ability to act decisively and strategically, while maintaining a reverence for life. The union of courage and compassion enables us to bravely see problems as opportunities, to hear complaints as different (and potentially valuable) ideas and perspectives, to understand resistance as possibilities, and to boldly recognize that most people in our lives are doing the best they can with who they are and what they know. The balance of courage and compassion reminds us to not "get stuck" in the small conflicts of the moment, but to risk seeing all of what really is—the good and the bad. Doing so enables us to see the larger patterns of potential harmony and strength.

The Fifth Lesson: The Understanding of Faith. This fifth leadership lesson is best known by what it is not: it is not the opposite of reason; it is not blind to people and situations that are dishonest or dangerous; and, like spirit, it is not about religion. The faith of leadership is about living with uncertainty, walking forward and knowing that the ground will meet your feet, trusting that all that happens serves a higher good; that there is a lesson to be learned in every pleasure and every pain. Faith can indeed be a "leap." As both a source of initial inspiration and sustenance for continuing efforts, a "leap of faith" does require us to stretch beyond what we know and dare to see the yet unknown opportunities. In fact, the best "vision" statements are based on this type of faith. A vision articulates an open invitation—it goes beyond the here and now to speak to what can be. While most organizations speak about vision statements rather easily, for organizations and individuals, faith is one of the most difficult qualities to hold onto. Why? Because fear gets in the way. There's an old adage that says, "Faith knocked on the door. Fear answered. There was no one there." In other words, faith and fear have a very hard time coexisting.

Yet as we all know, we will always have some fear—but we must not lead from that place. We must work hard to avoid creating a world in which fear is multiplied. Our challenge is to stand on the ground of faith and to encourage others to join us.

The Sixth Lesson: The Reflection of Patience. Patience is the ability to be steadfast in our attending to ourselves, and it is the willingness to engage in deep listening, knowing that timing is critical. To know when and what to hold onto, and of what and when to let go. To be able to step back, give up the urge to control, and wholeheartedly trust in the process. To benefit from the wisdom of nature, remembering that one "season" (even one like today, of global uncertainty and unpredictability) leads to another in its own time and way.

The Seventh Lesson: The Transcendence of Love. In the realm of leadership, we're talking about a very special kind of Love. One that is even greater than the love one shares with a partner or spouse. A love that is even deeper than the love a parent has for a child. A real leader's love is the kind that was evidenced in the lives of people that many of us saw as heroes—Mahatma Gandhi, Mother Teresa, Martin Luther King Jr., Abraham Joshua Heschel, Grace Longwell Coyle, and Paulo Freire—just to name a few. The type of love that leaders must cultivate and share is *agape*. Agape is a love for *all* simply because they exist. Not because of who they are, what they have done, or whom or what they know. Agape transcends all of that and, obviously, all of the "isms"—all our learned prejudices. In fact, this type of love is the collective blossoming of *all* of the leadership challenges we have just explored. Agape love requires that we have planted the seeds to be authentic, humble, empathic, courageous, compassionate, faithful, and patient. My late friend and colleague, Paulo Freire, the Brazilian educator who was kicked out of his country for teaching peasants how to read, has said that this type of love always generates acts of freedom. So as leaders, we must remember that when our actions generate freedom for ourselves and others, our actions are true gestures of agape love.

These seven lessons are not new, yet most have been forgotten, misunderstood, or misused. They remind us that true leadership is a messy process. It is not just about connecting the "dots," nor is it just about pushing forward change to achieve results. Effective leadership of today and tomorrow is about a commitment to tap into the essential nature of oneself and others to engage in the exchange of deep thoughts, honest feelings, and purposeful action. This type of leadership is more than a noun—it is an authentically dynamic, interconnected, and highly interactive relationship. The lessons for leading from the spirit enable us to bridge past history with future goals, fostering wisdom to provide those of us who have the responsibility to envision, inspire, evoke needed change, and support maintenance and sustenance with the means to join with others so that we all can fulfill our highest potential. And that is, to me, the real work of the leader of the future.

The Editors

Frances Hesselbein is the founding president and chairman of the board of governors of the Leader to Leader Institute, formerly the Peter F. Drucker Foundation for Nonprofit Management. She served as CEO of the Girl Scouts of the U.S.A. from 1976 to 1990. Among her many honors, Mrs. Hesselbein was awarded the Presidential Medal of Freedom, the United States of America's highest civilian honor, in 1998 by President Clinton for her role as "a pioneer for women, diversity and inclusion." In 2002 Mrs. Hesselbein was the first recipient of the Dwight D. Eisenhower National Security Series Award for her service "to national security and the nation." Most recently she authored *Hesselbein on Leadership*, published in August of 2002, and with General Eric K. Shinseki (USA Ret.) introduced *Be, Know, Do: Leadership the Army Way*, published in February of 2004. She is the coeditor of twenty books in twenty-eight languages and is editor-in-chief of *Leader to Leader*.

Marshall Goldsmith been recognized by the American Management Association as one of fifty great thinkers who have influenced the field of management and by *Business Week* as one of the most influential practitioners in the history of leadership development. He was ranked in *The Wall Street Journal* as one of the top ten executive educators, listed in *Forbes* as one of five most-respected executive coaches, and described by *The Economist* as one of the most credible thought leaders in the new era of business. Along with *The Leader of the Future 2*, Goldsmith is the author or coeditor of twenty-two books, including the upcoming *What Got You Here, Won't Get You There*. In 2006, Alliant International University named their school of management and organizational psychology the Marshall Goldsmith School of Management.

Index